Building and Breaking Families
in the American West

A Volume in the Calvin P. Horn
Lectures in Western History and Culture

Building and Breaking Families

in the American West

GLENDA RILEY

A Volume in the Calvin P. Horn
Lectures in Western History and Culture

University of New Mexico Press
Albuquerque

© 1996 BY THE UNIVERSITY OF NEW MEXICO PRESS
ALL RIGHTS RESERVED.   FIRST EDITION

LIBRARY OF CONGRESS CATALOGING-IN-PUBLICATION DATA
RILEY, GLENDA, 1938-
BUILDING AND BREAKING FAMILIES IN THE AMERICAN WEST
GLENDA RILEY. — 1ST ED.
       P. CM.
CALVIN P. HORN LECTURES IN WESTERN HISTORY AND CULTURE
INCLUDES BIBLIOGRAPHICAL REFERENCES AND INDEX.
     ISBN 0-8263-1719-7 (CLOTH)   ISBN 0-8263-1720-0 (PAPER)
1. FAMILY—WEST (U.S.)—HISTORY.
2. MARRIAGE—WEST (U.S.)-HISTORY.
3. FRONTIER AND PIONEER LIFE—WEST (U.S.)—HISTORY.
I. TITLE. II. SERIES.
HQ535.R55 1996
     306.85'0978—DC20   95-41743
     CIP

Permission has been granted by Oxford University Press to use, in altered form,
material from *Divorce: An American Tradition* (1991), pp. 85–107, 130–33, 135–57, 161–64;
and from Harlan Davidson, Inc., to use, in altered form, material from
A Place to Grow: Women in the American West (1992), pp. 164–75.

DESIGNED BY SUE NIEWIAROWSKI

For Anne Butler and Dick Etulain
Friends to cherish and scholars to emulate

Contents

Illustrations

Acknowledgments

The insightful suggestions of Anne M. Butler, Richard W. Etulain, and Sharon Hannum Seager have enhanced the grace and readability of these essays. I am also thankful for Ball State University's willingness to provide financial support and writing time and to underwrite the herculean efforts of research assistants Cameron M. (Mike) Sears and David J. Ulbrich.

I owe a further debt to the students in my 1994 Summer Institute course on "Women in the American West" at the Buffalo Bill Historical Center in Cody, Wyoming, for their enthusiastic and helpful responses, and to BBHC conservator Terry Schindle for her telling metaphors. I am also grateful to Robert J. Chandler, a member of the Wells Fargo Company's history department in San Francisco, for sharing his research.

I could not have asked for more enthusiastic support from the director of the University of New Mexico Press, Elizabeth Hadas, associate director David V. Holtby, and editor Durwood Ball. From acting as a cheering section to offering technical advice, they were a splendid team.

Ultimately, however, I am responsible for any missteps or glaring omissions.

Introduction

These essays, which examine the building and breaking of western families, result from the University of New Mexico's Calvin Horn Lecture Series in October and November 1994. I owe thanks to Richard W. Etulain and his colleagues for inviting me to present the lectures and for their gracious reception of me and my ideas. As always when visiting UNM, I came away refreshed and inspired.

The original invitation to give the Calvin Horn lectures included a request that I speak on some aspect of women and family in the American West. The occasion presented an opportunity to return to issues I had raised in a chapter on the American West in *Divorce: An American Tradition* (1991)—especially the question of why the American West had, and still has, the highest divorce rate in the world—and to put into practice my oft-asserted opinion that it is time to experiment with, and move toward, a new kind of multicultural history by examining parallel institutions across a range of cultures in a specific region.

In my view western families lend themselves to this approach, because they represent numerous cultures. In addition every society in the American West developed comparable institutions. Every group encouraged its members to go through courtship, enter marriage, and establish a family unit. Moreover all western cultures provided forms of separation or dissolution in cases of destructive or unworkable unions.[1]

In this approach to western family history, I owe a great debt to the growing number of family historians for the rich concepts and methods they have developed. Generally these historians first focused on "*the family*," meaning the family as a societal institution. Next they established

1

such subcategories as "the premodern family," "the British family," "the American family," and "the black family."

To study these family types, researchers concentrated on statistical and demographic information. From these data, they established family profiles and identified changes over time. Then many shifted to studying the family cycle, or stages of family evolution, ranging from early marriage to postparental marriage. Today many scholars utilize the life-course method, which follows an individual member of a family through the family's phases. This latter technique concentrates not on the whole family, as does the family-cycle approach, but centers instead on experiences of specific members of families.[2]

Because historians demonstrate great sensitivity to the effect of economic transformations on the family, an abundant literature exists regarding preindustrial, modern, and postmodern families.[3] Furthermore scholars stress class awareness, so that family types now include working-, middle-, and upper-strata families. Ethnicity is also an important topic, particularly in discussions of "the immigrant family." Even more recently, feminist scholarly perspectives encourage study of the roles and power of women in families.[4]

Despite its apparent variety and acumen, however, family history still contains notable limitations. For one, generalized notions of "the family," or even "the black family" and "the Native American family,"[5] engage inexact categories and thus supply misleading and inaccurate classifications.[6] Such broad typologies obscure important western variations, including Creek, slave, free black, Issei, and intermarried families.

Other western variants are often overlooked as well. As a case in point, western states established and still hold their individual conceptions of and legal rules for marriage and family within their boundaries. As recently as 1990, a compilation of marriage regulations revealed that most western states defined marriage as a civil contract between people at least seventeen or eighteen years of age, but differed on other qualifications. For instance some western states presumed that a marriage contract involved the use of a married couple's common name, but others, notably Iowa, required a couple to request in writing a "surname mutually agreed upon by the parties." Others, such as Minnesota, North Dakota, and Wyoming, specified that only two people, one female and one male, could be joined in wedlock, whereas Texas declared that "a license may not be issued for the marriage of persons of the same sex."[7]

Additional differences abounded. Idaho specifically outlawed plural marriages; Montana proclaimed children of a prohibited marriage illegitimate; and Nevada refused to acknowledge common-law marriages. Utah recognized interracial marriages. Meanwhile South Dakota released from a commitment anyone who learned of the lack of sexual "purity" in the other: "neither party . . . is bound by a promise made in ignorance of the other's want of personal chastity, and either is released therefrom by unchaste conduct on the part of the other, unless both parties participate therein."[8]

Waiting periods between obtaining a license and marrying also deviated throughout the West. Moreover more western states than southern or northeastern states had no waiting period, perhaps a residue from an era when people could obtain such rights as voting, holding office, marrying, and divorcing by doing little more than moving into town.[9]

Given these numerous deviations in western marriages and families, it is clearly impossible to study *the* American family in the West. One must reject scholars' claims that *the* American family not only existed in the West, but followed a similar pattern of development there as in the rest of the United States.[10] Likewise assertions that this American family originated in Europe is inapplicable to the West, where the "American" family was only one type among many, and such families as Native American and African American came from areas other than Europe.[11]

Similar problems occur with the periodization that family historians usually employ. These typically fall into three periods: the era before 1815, the years between 1815 and 1930, and the period since 1930. The first is based on the American colonial period and preindustrialization; the second on nineteenth-century industrialization; and the third on twentieth-century postindustrialization.[12] But to understand families in the American West, one must begin long before the first Europeans settled in New Mexico in 1598. Note, too, that industrialization seldom occurred uniformly across a region, especially one as large and disparate as the West. In fact it cannot even be argued with certainty that industrialization exerted the primary influence on "periods" of western family development.

Nor do the accepted definitions of family and kinship apply to the American West. Historians generally define family as a kinship and legal unit based on marriage or on parent-child linkage and kinship by descent, either patrilineal through the father or matrilineal through the mother. Yet some western peoples structured family and kin very differently, especially Native American groups, who established kin lines without direct reference to biological relationship and Spanish-speaking peoples who included such individuals as godparents and compadres among family and kinship networks.[13]

A more subtle difficulty in applying family-history models to the West concerns the notion that "the family" has achieved increased autonomy, including more mobility, a wider choice of occupations, and numerous means of dissolution.[14] This assertion lacks validity for such western families as Native American, African American, Spanish-background, and Asian-heritage families. Although these families may have gained some characteristics of autonomy, in other ways they shifted to dependence. Specifically, western families of color frequently lost the freedom to adhere to their own laws and rituals; rather, they moved to the often destructive, unhappy position of adjusting to Anglo ways.

This inapplicability of the common terminology, assumptions, and periodization of family history to the American West results in a lack of texture and accurate historical context for western families. Moreover even though several scholars argue for culture as a key concept in determining marriage and family practices, most historians continue to use industrialization as an explanation for family change and evolution.[15] In addition historians of family usually study the inner dynamics of families, thus slighting such "outside" influences as regional factors.[16] As a result, few scholars have looked across many cultures in a particular region for valuable comparisons.[17]

This inquiry, by contrast, focuses on disparate cultures within one region of the United States. This strategy might be termed "cultural layering," in that it explores the consequences for families as group customs overlay one another. The region under consideration is located west of the Mississippi River, including Alaska and Hawaii. The primary time period under consideration is the high immigration and culture-contact years of the nineteenth and early-to-mid-twentieth centuries, when cultures overlapped according to the vagaries of migration patterns. Exceptions occur when it is helpful to supply antecedents or subsequent developments.

In looking at families across cultural lines, these essays demonstrate that interaction among western familial units often led to conflict. Families frequently developed disorientation from having one foot in their world and the other forcibly in another, as well as from having to live with laws and policies incompatible with their needs and desires.

Yet at the same time, western families played active rather than passive roles in the historical drama. Although such factors as the market economy, changing class structures, and gender roles indeed affected westerners, family members also initiated strategies—and sometimes purposeful schemes—to hold on to what they desired to retain.[18] Families also influenced each other, for example, by merging courtship, marriage, and divorce rituals, laws, and policies. Rather than passively accepting Anglo ways, families of color resisted, rebelled, and occasionally reshaped Anglo practices.

Many illustrations of the latter dynamic exist, both old and new. During the late nineteenth century, the Bureau of Indian Affairs, for example, recognized as valid marriages Indian traditional ceremonies and Anglo civil or religious services. A late twentieth-century instance of such cultural merging is the acceptance of Indian marriages in Nevada, where "marriages between Indians heretofore or hereafter consummated in accordance with tribal custom shall be of the same validity as marriages performed in any other manner."[19]

Combining, then, the framework of cultural layering with region and incorporating the idea of family agency, this inquiry offers glimpses into four aspects of building and breaking families in the American West: courtship, the fusing and rending factors influencing marriage, difficulties of intermarriage, and the dissolution of marriage through separation, desertion, and divorce. Rather than an exhaustive synthesis or a comprehensive model of marital change, what follows is an exploration of how regional circumstances affected families and helped generate the West's unusually high divorce rate. As these first divorce figures collected by the United State Census Bureau indicate, the West's rate already outdistanced those of other regions during the nineteenth and early twentieth centuries, well before the emergence of extreme ease of divorce in such states as Nevada and California:

Divorces Per 100,000 People				
North Atlantic Division	South Atlantic Division	North Central Division	South Central Division	Western Division
1870	26	8	43	18	56
1880	29	13	56	37	83
1890	29	21	73	63	106
1900	39	33	95	97	131[20]

The following pages also include an overview of many cultures' families, sometimes engaged in conflict, but on other occasions blending their practices and beliefs. The epilogue suggests reasons why the American West has produced the highest divorce rate in the world, reasserts the usefulness of the technique of cultural layering, and offers suggestions for easing the problems of western families.

1
Courting and
Committing

According to *Webster's New Universal Unabridged Dictionary* (1983), courting means endeavoring to gain favor, win the affections of, or solicit for marriage. Sociologists add more functions to their definition of courtship: to provide recreation, achieve status, effect socialization, and, of course, identify potential spouses and select a single best mate. Neither Webster nor sociologists point out, however, that in the United States courtship practices have varied by region. In what is today the American West, courtship possessed a distinctive history, one which remains largely unexplored by western historians.

Using the perspective of cultural layering(defined here as studying a wide range of cultural practices as they overlay each other)it becomes obvious that in the American West numerous groups contributed myriad courtship beliefs and practices to emerging western society. Rather than resulting in cultural synthesis, this complicated process led to a *lack* of courtship norms and standards of judgment. Although western courtship appeared effective on the surface, for people continued to select mates and marry, the selection of compatible spouses proved imperfect. If nineteenth and early-twentieth-century western divorce rates, the highest in the world, give any indication, western courtship constituted a flawed selection system. A growing number of women and men were neither satisfied with their choices nor willing to remain with the spouses they had chosen.

A closer look at the five major stages of courtship—motivation for courting, meeting potential mates, following courtship rituals, dealing with opinions of parents and others, and bringing courtship to resolution— during the high migration periods of the nineteenth and early twentieth centuries reveals the tensions among groups that thwarted an effective

fusion of courtship customs. Although it cannot be statistically demonstrated that ineffectual courtship contributed to divorce, it is reasonable
to believe that poorly matched spouses were more vulnerable to marital
strain, and thus more likely to divorce, than companionable mates.

Motivations for Courting

Given the diversity of human nature, reasons for initiating courtship
differed from western individual to individual, depending upon age, religious beliefs, gender, and other similar factors. Beyond these personal influences, western societies also established norms, or sometimes hard-and-fast
rules, that thrust people into courtship whether they wished it or not.

During much of the nineteenth century, for example, Pima Indians
staged a puberty ceremony as soon as a young woman began menstruating.
After the woman had remained in isolation for seven days, an elaborate
community feast and all-night celebration followed. In the opening dance,
often the Middle Run, the initiate lagged behind the others, while young
men studied her and decided whether to ask her father for her hand. Later,
while the father deliberated, the woman received ceremonial tattoos around
her eyelids and lower lip.[1]

As other peoples, including French, Spanish-speaking, and Anglo explorers, trappers, traders, settlers, and entrepreneurs, entered the region,
they brought with them less fixed reasons for courting. Rather than culture and tradition impelling young men and women to marry, economics
often provided the primary motivation during the early years of an area's
settlement.

Anecdotal evidence indicates that, much like Pima Indians, many settlers made such decisions around the age of puberty. Women who needed
financial providers and men who required skilled domestic artisans to produce finished goods and bear children often married during their teen
years.[2] In fact the image of teenaged spouses has become synonymous with
settlers in the nineteenth-century West.

In truth, however, a significant number of early settlers waited until a
later age to marry. In some cases a woman's birth family could afford to
support her until the "right" mate appeared. For instance Spanish-speaking California settler María Encarnación was twenty-three years old when
she married widower José Dávila.[3] In other cases daughters and sons remained with their birth families to help them achieve economic stability.
Members of the 1850s Peters Colony in Texas generally stayed with their

families as workers well into their twenties.[4] Unlike Pima women, Peters Colony women could delay courtship without dishonor and even become more attractive as they gained in skills and property. Peters Colony men expressed decided partiality either to attractive women slightly younger than themselves or to landed widows. A Missouri newspaper of the 1850s indicated that these desires were hardly unique to Texas settlers. Its editor remarked, "Give us a rich widow or pretty young girl all the time."[5]

Alongside economic needs, such cultural dictates as youth and beauty increasingly propelled western settlers into courtship.[6] In addition romantic love assumed growing importance in an Anglo culture that idealized romance and eroticism. Certainly the changing nature of Anglo breach-of-promise suits revealed many peoples' growing belief that love might even outclass property in importance. Before the 1820s, property damage or loss constituted the primary legal ground in such suits, but beginning during the 1820s and continuing throughout the nineteenth century, grounds included emotional damage or deprivation.[7]

Besides economics and affection, social pressure convinced other Anglo settlers to begin courting. Although such pressure often remained unspoken and thus unmeasurable, some westerners articulated their thoughts regarding courtship. One married Nebraska woman of the 1880s told a single, female teacher "it's kind-a-queer you been running around this country all this time and have not found a man." When the startled teacher revealed that she had not been looking for a husband, the married woman reinforced her point: "it's about time you were." The teacher reassessed her attitude, bowed to social convention, and soon married.[8]

By the end of the nineteenth century, even though migrants' motivations for courtship had multiplied, men and women still considered economic factors. One young Oklahoma woman who drew a land claim in a turn-of-the-century lottery expressed astonishment at the number of suitors who soon appeared: "a young fellow brought his outfit, got down in front of me and with many flourishes started to shine my shoes." Next "the letters began pouring in—men wanting to marry me, men all the way from twenty-one to seventy-five."[9]

During the nineteenth and early twentieth centuries, African American people added yet another cultural layer to western courtship. By necessity western blacks generated a slightly different set of rationales for courting and marrying. Of course western slave women and men married for companionship and a desire to establish families, the primary institution in most slaves' lives. But western slaves also had to take into account critical concerns: who was likely to stay on the plantation or in the area for a while and seemed suitable enough to gain an owner's permission.[10]

The question of permission was especially crucial. Although a slave suitor might out of courtesy ask the parents of a slave woman for their permission, real power of consent lay with a woman's owner. One Texas slave who married around 1860 at age fifteen explained that slave men usually initiated the permission process. Slave men "asked marse" and, "iffen he 'grees," they married. But if the master disapproved, the man had "to find heself 'nother gal."[11]

In cases of "broad marriage," which involved slaves from two planta- tions, both owners had to assent. One would have to issue Saturday-night passes to the husband, while the other would have to insure that the wife's family's cabin could accommodate him. Other owners had to consider dis- tances between plantations in agreeing to matches. When, because of dis- tance, Emma Taylor only got to see her husband, Rube Taylor, every two weeks, her master found himself with an unhappy slave. Fortunately Emma's owner willingly remedied the situation by buying Rube and bringing him to live with Emma.[12]

Throughout the West, free blacks experienced fewer restrictions than slaves, yet those who desired to marry other African Americans had a limited pool from which to select a mate. Although African Americans early entered the upper Louisiana country with exploring expeditions and the military, settling as far north as present-day Minnesota, their numbers stayed small. By the 1820s only an estimated two to three thousand slaves and free African Americans lived in upper Louisiana; among these, free black women especially remained relatively scarce.[13] After the Civil War, this short- age of black women eased somewhat, as Exodusters left the South to migrate to Kansas and Colorado. Other African Americans, including mine owner and philanthropist Clara Brown, homesteader John W. Dobbs, and miner John Frazier, migrated westward as part of Colorado's postwar mining boom.[14]

Beginning during the 1850s, Asian immigrants also added to the stew their particular motivations for courting. On the one hand, Asian men living in the U.S. experienced biting loneliness and thus yearned for spouses. In 1902 one Chinese man who felt forlorn in a strange land thou- sands of miles from home returned to China, where he followed the custom of using a matchmaker to find a wife, whom he subsequently brought back to the United States.[15]

On the other hand, Asian women living in their homelands entered relationships with such immigrants for a variety of reasons: their parents ordered them to do so; they hoped to escape a life of poverty and arduous labor; or they were attempting to avoid a social embarrassment, such as their own pregnancy. One Korean woman of the early twentieth century lamented her indigence and the adversities she faced as a Christian in a Buddhist society. She explained that stories concerning Hawaii especially enticed her: "Hawaii's a free place, everybody living well . . . If you like talk, you can talk, you like work, you can work." In hopes of launching a courtship that would eventually lead to marriage and migration, she sent her photograph and personal information to Hawaii.[16]

Unfortunately some Asian women faced disillusionment when they finally reached U.S. shores. A few disliked their new husbands, but others found they had entered forced prostitution rather than marriage. In turn this discovery created yet another reason to seek courtship—as a potential escape hatch from prostitution. In 1862 a California woman, Ah Soo, convinced Ah Cut to rescue her from prostitution by purchasing her for $400. Ah Cut subsequently persuaded a judge to uphold the purchase and to marry him and Ah Soo, thus saving her from a life she found repugnant.[17]

Disparate reasons thrust western women and men into courtship. Consequently during the late nineteenth and early twentieth centuries, a chasm grew between groups who held dissimilar beliefs regarding acceptable motivations for courting. For instance the emphasis that many Anglos placed on romantic love had little meaning for Native Americans, who viewed courtship as a natural part of the life cycle, nor for Asian parents, who wanted their daughters and sons to court other Asians. Instead of westerners blending their ideas and reaching a modicum of agreement regarding suitable reasons for inaugurating courtship, they not only disagreed, but sometimes denigrated each others' ideas.[18]

Meeting Potential Mates

The second stage of courtship, identifying and meeting potential mates, also began simply in the American West. Residential and occupational propinquity set the stage for mate identification among early western groups.[19] For Native Americans, the village typically provided the locus for courtships.

For nineteenth-century Paiutes, in particular, the village hub and tepee offered opportunities for meeting future spouses. Usually a Paiute man utilized the village center to attract a woman's attention by displaying his horsemanship and other skills. If she reacted favorably, he entered her family tepee during the night and seated himself, fully dressed, at her feet. The woman's grandmother, who slept at her side as chaperon, awakened her. Neither the man nor the woman spoke; when the woman wished her suitor to leave she lay down by her mother. According to Paiute leader Sarah Winnemucca, this process went on "sometimes for a year or longer, if the young woman had not made up her mind." When the woman finally decided, her father summoned the man, offered a feast in celebration, and erected a tepee to hold the presents that poured in "from both sides."[20]

To expedite the procedure of mate identification, some Native American groups marked those women available for wooing. Mourning Dove, a Salishan woman born in 1885 in eastern Washington, recalled that at puberty a Salishan girl's mother placed a "virgin cape" around her shoulders to signify her unmarried state. After that the unmarried woman never removed the cape in public and took off her undergarment of heavy buckskin only with the consent of, and in the presence of, her mother or chaperon.[21]

Like such native peoples, Spanish-speaking groups also believed that mate identification should proceed in a formal manner. As they settled in the region they called El Norte during the 1600s and 1700s, Spanish peoples too allowed propinquity to exercise significant influence in mate identification. Women and men spied potential spouses at fandangos, fiestas, weddings, and other social events.[22] Afterwards men advanced their suits by visiting women's homes or serenading outside their windows.[23]

Despite cultural change over time, such restrained wooing even continued into the twentieth century. During the early 1900s, one Chicana helped friends pursue their courtship by carrying notes between them, for in her words, "it wasn't proper . . . in those days, to speak to your beau directly."[24] As late as the 1920s, a Chicana who lived near Tucson, Arizona, explained that she "first met" her husband when he and a friend came to serenade her with guitars. In another case a woman recalled that she met her husband-to-be after a close friend selected him for her.[25]

Numerous Anglo settlers followed a prescribed manner of meeting mates as well, usually through family members, church, and matchmakers. Increasingly, however, many western Anglos produced a free-market theory of mate identification: both male and female consumers exercised individual choice among as many prospects as possible. But during the early years of settlement, the open-market concept of courtship proved difficult to implement, especially for men. Although Anglo men seldom outnumbered women by as high a ratio as often thought, numbers of men usually outdistanced those of women.[26] These population imbalances, combined with geographical isolation and physical distance, often made men frantic to find wives from among the few single Anglo women living in their area of the West.

Anglo men who faced a shortage of marriageable women explored a range of solutions. Especially during the early nineteenth century, some chose women of color, who were readily accessible throughout most of the West (see chapter 3). But for others, their own racist attitudes, as well as emerging nineteenth-century antimiscegenation laws prohibiting intermarriage, discouraged them from thinking about women of color as potential mates. Still other men preferred to marry women similar to themselves.

To meet the needs of these unmarried western men, a number of innovative people shipped women west, much like market goods. In 1849 Eliza W. Farnham organized the California Association of American Women. Because she had to travel to San Francisco to settle her deceased husband's affairs, Farnham issued a broadside inviting "intelligent, virtuous and efficient women" to accompany her. Farnham believed that "the presence of women would be one of the surest checks upon many of the evils" in California and that women, "with all [their] kindly cares and powers," would tame western men.[27] During the 1860s, Bostonian Asa Mercer took twelve potential wives to Seattle. On his second journey, he took approximately one hundred women, one of whom he married. When he reached Seattle, residents gave Mercer a hero's reception and welcomed the women they hoped would "refine" their corner of the West.[28]

Because such shipments of women could not begin to answer western men's demand for wives, individuals advertised for mates. Eastern women especially learned of the West's wife shortage and placed notices in western newspapers and magazines. In 1860 a revealing announcement appeared in a Waterloo, Iowa, newspaper:

> A young lady residing in one of the small towns in Central New York is desirous of opening a correspondence with some young man in the West, with a view to a matrimonial engagement . . . . She is about 24 years of age, possesses a good moral character, is not what would be called handsome, has a good disposition, enjoys good health, is tolerably well-educated, and thoroughly versed in the mysteries of housekeeping.

On the editorial page, the editor recognized the importance of women to the development of the West. He wrote that this notice presented "a rare chance for a young man to obtain that useful and essential article of household furniture—a wife."[29]

Mail-order brides also helped fill the gap. Writer Mari Sandoz, daughter of a Nebraska homesteader, recalled that her neighbors obtained many items, including wives, through catalogs. According to Sandoz, such advertisements described "the offerings rather fully but with, perhaps, a little less honesty than Montgomery Ward or Sears Roebuck." Still, Sandoz recalled homesteaders carrying what she called heart-and-hand publications around until "they wore the pictures off the pages." Sandoz also remembered that once prospective grooms sent railroad or steamer tickets to their intended, they felt committed, but some women did not; they sold the tickets and never arrived in Nebraska.[30]

Sandoz added that other men pursued sweethearts they had left back home "or someone who began to look a little like a sweetheart from the distance of a government claim that got more and more lonesome as the holes in the socks got bigger."[31] In fact thousands of men returned home to marry someone they already knew, or a woman suggested by a family member, friend, or former neighbor. Emery Bartlett, who settled in Poweshiek County, Iowa, in 1854, first lived above a store with several other bachelors, but soon returned to New Hampshire to marry a woman he had begun to court before he left for the West.[32] In the following years, literally thousands of farmers, miners, army officers, and other types of men replicated Bartlett's strategy and journeyed home to marry proverbial girls-next-door.

For those men who found the distance and expense too great to travel to their former homes, letters carried by friends, stagecoaches, steamboats, and the U.S. Postal Service proved instrumental in the process of locating a potential mate. Such letters, largely written by men living alone or with other bachelors, enjoined friends, family members, and even casual acquaintances to assist in the search for potential wives. Other men simply initiated correspondence with a woman they had known previously.

During the California gold rush, Frank Rumrill began writing to Henrietta Stewart, a woman he had known in Ohio. Eager in 1851 to make his fortune, Frank Rumrill established first a hotel, then a restaurant, and finally became an agent for Gregory's Express. After delaying his return to Ohio several times, Rumrill received protests from Stewart, who wrote: "I wish you were not so much in love with California." Rumrill, by then aware of the lack of single Anglo women in California, responded, "it grieves me to disappoint my friends so often in my return home." He also promised Henrietta that he would return to Ohio in "the state of single blessedness." Apparently Stewart decided to gamble, because the correspondence continued. In 1855, learning of a financial panic in California, Henrietta nudged Frank: "You need not be afraid of writing too often or coming home too soon." Frank, finally unable to find either fortune or matrimony in California, returned to Ohio and married Henrietta.[33]

Other correspondence courtships ended a similar way. In one case, a young man started corresponding without the benefit of prior acquaintance. After seeing a young woman's picture in her uncle's home, he obtained her address in Scotland and began to writing to her. In 1881, when the man asked his correspondent to join him in Aurora County, Dakota Territory, to help him settle the claim he had filed, she readily assented.[34] Similarly, when Emma Odegaard migrated to her uncle's home in Northfield, Minnesota, in 1884, she entered a correspondence courtship with a Dakota man she had known in Norway. In 1889, he proposed and asked her to join him; again the answer was yes.[35]

Obviously such women benefited from the lack of single Anglo females in the West. Either they convinced men to relocate to where they lived, like Henrietta Stewart, or, like Emma Odegaard, they joined their fiancés in the West. Gradually, however, the gap between the numbers of marriageable Anglo men and women eased in most of the West, especially by the early twentieth century.[36]

Increasingly, then, the problem became one of locating and identifying mates already living in the West. As among other types of western peoples, propinquity exercised great influence, but an expanded variety of social events insured that single people would meet. Traveling through the U.S. during the 1860s, French author and social commentator Auguste Carlier described what he called "reunions," parties at which single people conducted flirtations "whose intended aim is always marriage."[37] Other courting opportunities occurred at husking and work bees, sleighing parties, lectures, literary clubs, dances and parties, candy pulls, socials, clubs, and church services. In 1912, for example, one young Montana woman "attended church at Grace." Later she recalled that "Mrs. Bangs introduced her son, William. He held the hymn book for me and I thought him a very gentlemanly man."[38]

During the late nineteenth and early twentieth centuries, box suppers supplied an especially popular venue in which to meet mates. For such affairs women prepared meals, which men bid for at auction. The couple then ate together and got to know each other. But couples sometimes conspired so a would-be swain purchased the "right" package. A Wayne, Oklahoma woman of the early 1900s explained that as she and a friend "spent hours decorating the boxes with crepe paper," she added ruffles and a rose to her box to alert her beau. In the meantime, he had convinced the auctioneer to pull his ear when her supper came up for sale. When the auctioneer unconsciously pulled his ear at the wrong moment he "nearly caused Mr. Berry to get the wrong box." But all turned out well: Mr. Berry bid on the right box, the couple ate together, and in 1903 they married.[39]

In the aftermath of such courting events, social etiquette decreed that a man with an interest in a young woman pay her and her family several formal calls. Many western women made clear, however, that they, rather than their parents, would pass judgment on a suitor's acceptability. This independence of spirit struck some observers as odd. Coming from a European background, where arranged marriage was commonplace, Auguste Carlier found it strange that young women had to "depend upon *themselves* to find a husband."[40]

Of course whether a western Anglo woman found her own mate often hinged to a great degree upon her social class. While middle- to upper-class women utilized chaperoned garden parties, school events, and church services to locate potential spouses, working-class women more often fended for themselves. During the 1890s Emily Butcher of Kansas interspersed farm work, including plowing, with a rich social life of parties and dances. In July 1896 Butcher noted that she plowed on Friday; on Saturday she attended a celebration where she "got acquainted" with a number of eligible young men and returned home at 2 A.M. On other occasions, Butcher hunted rabbits, prairie chickens, and plovers, then enjoyed picnics and dances, on one occasion returning home at "half past 4" A.M.[41]

Besides social class, race could also influence the manner of mate identification one employed. Although western free blacks and slaves, much like Anglos, met at parties, dances, church services, weddings, wakes, and work, these opportunities had certain constraints. For slaves social events occurred on their home plantations or might include such cross-plantation socials as weddings, dances, and wakes, in which they participated as servants, valets, and nursemaids. In addition slaves met eligible mates in slave "quarters" where they lived, at slave-family celebrations and wakes, and in fields and other workplaces. Often a slave man interested in courting a woman initiated his suit with a call to her family.[42]

Because of the small number of African American women in the West, free blacks occasionally courted slave women as well. A Missouri free black man, George Kibby, courted and married a twenty-three-year-old slave woman named Susan, then bought her out of slavery. According to an 1853 emancipation contract, George agreed to pay his wife's owners $800 plus annual interest and to maintain a life-insurance policy on Susan, thus guaranteeing her owner's financial return should she die in childbirth. In return, Susan's owners promised George that, upon full payment, he could have his wife "and such child or children as she may then have." To fulfill his part of the bargain, Kibby paid a total of $567.40 and a mule worth $65. Although this did not quite total $800, Susan's owners released her in December 1855.[43]

For reasons different from those of African Americans, Asian men also found their choice of mates limited. On the West Coast, Asian men (largely agricultural, manufacturing, and railroad laborers) soon discovered that the entry of single women was restricted by U.S. immigration law. At the same time, antimiscegenation ordinances prevented Asian men from marrying non-Asian women. As a result Asian men relied upon others to find mates for them. Chinese men sent home for wives, whom they married by proxy, and after the 1882 Chinese Exclusion Act, some men, swearing the women were their own wives, brought women for other men.[44]

Japanese men also frequently turned to matchmakers. These matchmakers, central to Japanese courting procedures, gave information concerning prospective mates to family members and brought them together to discuss terms.[45] The American practice of picture brides, or Japanese men finding a wife through an exchange of photographs, genealogies, health information, and financial data, grew logically out of this tradition. As the numbers of Japanese men rose in the American West, the picture-bride practice intensified. Between 1910 and 1920, when San Francisco's Japanese daily newspaper, *Nichibei Shimbun*, especially urged Japanese men living in the U.S. to find wives, numerous men sought "picture brides."[46] Although the actual numbers are unknown, scholars believe they were significant before the U.S. Customs Service ended the practice in 1920, by issuing passports only to women already married to Japanese men living in the U.S.[47]

Typically numerous stories attest to the ineffectiveness of the picture-bride practice in locating suitable mates. In fact Japanese newspapers reported the ways in which Nisei associations tried to limit *kekeochi*, or desertions, which occurred when men sent women false information and outdated photographs of themselves. But men were sometimes disenchanted as well, in at least one instance because, according to one observer, a new wife was "short and squat—a real country hick."[48]

Numerous Koreans also identified mates through the use of photographs and family information. Between 1910, when the Korean government approved the emigration of young women who agreed to marry in this fashion, and 1924, when a U.S. exclusion act ended the immigration of such women, almost one thousand women came to Hawaii alone.[49] Koreans' use of the picture-bride process proved no more flawless than that of other Asians. One Korean woman wrote, "I saw him for the first time at the immigration station . . . . He was really . . . old-looking. So my heart stuck." She cried for eight days, but gradually decided that marriage to him was better than returning to Korea. Although the woman married her fiancé on the ninth day, she refused to speak to her new husband for three months.[50]

How effectively, then, did mate identification work in the West? Fairly well when allowed to follow its own course. But as cultural contact and friction grew in the West, so did one group's imposition of its own customs on other groups increase. In spite of the grace and civility of Native American methods of identifying mates, incoming Spanish and Anglo settlers interfered.

As Spanish-speaking settlers spread across the frontier they called El Norte, many of these migrants thrust their own middle- and upper-class customs upon Indians. An obvious case in point was the Catholic mission, where priests, matrons, and teachers routinely separated unmarried men and women, regulating their contact according to Spanish tradition. At the nineteenth-century mission at San Diego in southern California, supervisors locked Indian men and women in separate quarters at night, with an older Indian woman supervising the unmarried women constantly, even taking them to their baths.[51]

During the nineteenth century, Indians living at the Mission San José, also in California, could court only through upper windows facing the street. Women sat behind iron-barred windows set in thick adobe walls, waiting for Indian men to visit the windows, and women, of their choice.

When a woman accepted a proposal, she informed the priest, who, if he agreed with her decision, married the couple.[52]

This is not meant to suggest that Indians passively accepted such impositions. Although Native Americans often went through the form, they resisted the substance. Thus an Indian woman might follow the prescribed procedure, but might also "arrange" which man would appear at her window. As a consequence of such quiet resistance throughout the Southwest, one Anglo settler noted in 1848 that "there is a curious blending of the ceremonies of the Roman Catholic Church with the Indian customs of the natives."[53]

Anglo settlers also imposed their ideas regarding mate identification upon other peoples, with mixed results. From Indian schools to missionary homes, teachers and missionaries separated Native American, Spanish-heritage, and Asian charges by gender to regulate the onset of courtship. Teachers at the Phoenix Indian School kept male and female pupils separate, allowing them to talk to each other only at supervised social functions. Predictably students found ways to evade such restrictions. In 1912 the Pima Ross Shaw sent notes to a fourteen-year-old Pima girl, Anna Moore. Shaw would also "sneak over" to the girl's side of the campus to play croquet with Moore, until a matron shooed him back. The couple found additional ways to elude their chaperons and eventually decided to marry.[54]

Because Anglos increasingly constituted the "dominant" culture in the nineteenth-century West, they also attempted to inflict their ways upon Spanish-heritage and Asian peoples. For example, nineteenth-century antimiscegenation laws gradually prohibited marriages between Anglos and people of Spanish background. In addition nineteenth-century and early-twentieth-century Anglo law and policy makers first restricted immigration of potential Asian wives, then ended picture brides. Most Anglos branded this matchmaking practice as immoral and impersonal, even though numerous Anglos found mates in a similar way. In 1907 for example, one eastern European, rural woman not only agreed to a marriage her family arranged for her, but anticipating improved financial prospects, happily migrated with her new husband to Montana.[55]

In response to such cultural intrusions in their ways of courting, some western societies clung even more strongly to traditional rituals. As a result fewer changes occurred over time among such groups than one might expect. Even as recently as the 1980s, a number of Native American groups utilized the "courting walk" at powwows. In this rite young women and men stroll around outside the ring of spectators, greeting and meeting each other. Under the watchful eye of parents and family members, they identify those they would like to know better. A Native American college student said she preferred this method because, unlike college social events, the courting walk left little room for artifice and posturing.[56]

Moreover little cultural synthesis occurred among groups of westerners regarding ways of meeting and courting potential mates. How, for example, did one effectively meet potential mates in the American West? What did each party expect in such an encounter? The answers varied widely according to race, ethnicity, social class, and era; in fact, no general pattern existed at all.

Courtship Rituals

Because local folkways determined the customs and rites that courting couples followed, western courtship rituals also developed tremendous complexity and controversy.[57] For instance Native American suitors of the nineteenth and early twentieth centuries frequently offered gifts to potential mates or their parents. Many Anglos, however, misinterpreted this custom to mean that Indian men purchased women with "bride prices." In truth, the Blackfoot Beverly Hungry Wolf explained, many Indian societies expected a courting man to show his generosity to a potential bride's family by sending horses and other gifts. Moreover because a woman's parents were about to lose a valuable domestic worker, the groom tendered compensation to family members who had raised and supported her.[58]

Numerous other Indian courtship rituals appeared strange to generations of Anglos and other westerners, who viewed them from their own perspectives. In some tribes for example, engaged couples exchanged tokens. Although this practice resembled the Anglo habit of exchanging rings, Indian symbols were very different. During the 1870s a Chickasaw man followed the customary way of his people; he gave his intended bride venison, while she gave him an ear of corn, indicating their promise to provide for each other.[59]

Spanish-speaking peoples also contributed their own courtship etiquette. Especially among the middle and upper classes during most of the nineteenth century, supervision by parents and chaperons usually limited courting couples' public opportunities to express affection. Yet in certain circumstances, such as social events and weddings, single people could divulge romantic affiliations in a prescribed manner. Among Californios, a young man could drop his hat over the head of a woman for whom he felt affection. In turn she could publicly admit her feelings for him by wearing his hat during the dance, or she could repudiate him by tossing the hat aside. On at least one occasion, Anglo men misinterpreted the degree of fondness expressed and interfered, setting off a brawl.[60]

Anglo settlers, of course, introduced their own folkways, especially during the 1800s and early 1900s, when the numbers of Anglo migrants grew rapidly throughout the West; their customs varied according to ethnic background and religion. Anglos who were Roman Catholic, but who had originated in such countries as Ireland and France, diverged widely in their practices. Moreover, many Anglo couples in the West retained European practices, while others modified them.[61]

Some couples, especially those from wealthier families, preserved the European habit of bringing property or a dowry to marriage. In time, the dowry largely disappeared among most western courting couples. Because women were often in short supply, men usually felt fortunate to find a wife, whether or not she had a dowry. Thus although most self-respecting women foresaw owning several quilts, bed linens, and dishes, they felt little need for anything else in the way of material goods.[62] Typical was Emma Odegaard's limited trousseau; for her 1889 wedding in Northfield, Minnesota, her aunt made Emma a wedding dress of rust-colored velvet and a selection of quilts, pillows, and other bedding. As it turned out, Emma wore the dress but left the bedding behind, because it was so bulky to transport.[63]

During the nineteenth century, Anglo courting couples also rejected European notions of privacy and modesty, accepting instead public displays of affection. In general among Anglos, an unmarried couple could publicly kiss at corn huskings. Acceptance of public kissing might vary by area of the West, however. On the boisterous Nevada frontier, editor Alf Doten reported that kissing frequently occurred at miners' parties: "surprise party—Jolly girls—Jolly time—Ever so much kissing—most I ever saw."[64]

Another public demonstration involved exchanging rings. An engaged man not only gave his intended a ring, but she often reciprocated. Montanan Mary Ronan accepted a diamond engagement ring from her beau, giving him in return a ring made from the gold of Montana's Alder Gulch diggings.[65] Unlike the gifts of Native Americans, which were pledges to succor each other, rings indicated promises of unending love.

As a further manifestation of affection, courting couples, especially of the middle and upper classes, increasingly believed that they should share their innermost thoughts with each other. It became a matter of ritual to bare one's soul, usually in flowery, Victorian language. When Florence Crawford, daughter of a former Kansas governor, discovered that her fiancé, journalist Arthur Capper, had to travel for eight months, she proposed that they keep journals. Her 1891 entries illustrated the influence of Victorian sentiment on such middle- and upper-class couples.

Shortly after Arthur's departure, Florence wrote, "He—Arthur—is gone, gone—and the feeling of desolation and loss that now and then comes over me is almost unbearable, and far, *far* worse than I even thought it would be, although I knew I had a hard battle to fight." In spite of numerous friends, social activities, and exciting trips, Florence continued to lament, knowing that Arthur would eventually read her emotional outpourings. Although Arthur's journal entries proved shorter, he similarly wrote, "I am heart broken and feel as though all my courage has deserted me. But I must brace up. I know it is all for the best."[66]

The letters that flowed back and forth between such western couples also became effusively romantic by the end of the nineteenth century. Anglo men proved to be as emotional and tender as women, while both men and women created tests for the other. For instance one person might make jealous charges regarding another woman or man their beloved had mentioned, hoping in turn for a protestation of undying love. Other tests comprised eliciting promises to quit smoking or drinking. In 1911 a traveling road worker responded to his love's complaints with this reassurance: "dear girlie . . . don't be afraid I smoke to [sic] much. For I always think of you every time I smoke. And I always think of you when there is another thing [alcohol] offered me. Sweet Heart I love you too much to let such a thing as that ruin me."[67]

The more educated the writers, the more high-toned and romantic their letters. Undoubtedly they borrowed from the numerous examples in writing manuals and etiquette books, which recommended such phrases as "without you no place can be home to me." In 1888 a traveling attorney wrote his intended that he wanted to take her to the "western wilds" of Kansas, but "would not wish to gain your consent to such a rash procedure without suggesting to you all the inconveniences and hardships to which you would come." When she assured him of her willingness to move to Kansas, he replied "we will roam the wild west o'er, and canvass the world for the sweetest, nicest spot for our little home . . . . the bliss of a pure, holy home is the grandest ideal I ever contemplated. It shall be ours in all its purity, love and holiness."[68]

Only in the case of second courtships did letter-writers lean more toward the utilitarian. In one set of letters written in 1892, a forty-four-year-old widowed farmer with eight children courted a twenty-seven-year-old women, either widowed or divorced, who worked as an itinerant dressmaker. When she, Jessie Bledsoe, chastised him with the accusation that "matrimony is a matter of business with you is it not?" David Fain duly attempted to include a sprinkling of syrupy sentiments in his letters. Still, most of David's and Jessie's correspondence concerned itself with domestic arrangements, should they decide to marry.[69]

The result of such candid correspondence is debatable. Perhaps it led to genuine emotion between couples, as well as to an examination of themselves and each other.[70] At the very least, it indicates that many Anglo women knew their worth and negotiated the best deal possible. They not only exacted pledges regarding such habits as smoking, drinking, and gambling, but they also converted men to active Christianity and defined their own decision-making powers in future relationships.[71]

Had westerners of color been given an opportunity to comment, they might have found Anglo courtship correspondence as odd as Anglos found some of their customs. Of all the courtship rituals, however, the most difficult for one group to comprehend about another concerned sexual relations.

That premarital sex indeed occurred in the nineteenth- and early-twentieth-century West was indicated in national pregnancy rates.[72] In the West, each culture and era viewed premarital sex differently and established a wide variety of sexual mores, social pressures, laws, and policies. In general cultures that defined intergenerational relationships, had institutions reinforcing family values, and integrated its members into a central value system appear to have experienced lower premarital pregnancy rates than groups lacking these features.

Yet it is impossible to assess any one group's success in maintaining chastity. In part nineteenth- and early-twentieth-century observers frequently disagreed concerning another societies's sexual standards. Anglo observers of Californios judged some Spanish-speaking women to be highly moral and others less so, but failed to take into account social-class differences.[73] Further inaccuracies occurred when Anglo observers in New Mexico assumed, and then reported, that local women became immoral when they entered marriages forced on them by parents. They apparently believed that men and women who had little choice of mates could not love each other and sought sexual satisfaction outside their marriages.[74]

In addition to such skewed observers' reports, western records are inaccurate and contradictory. On the one hand, most Spanish-speaking peoples were Catholic, subject to numerous sermons and edicts regarding the importance of waiting for marriage to establish sexual relations. On the other hand, church marriage documents demonstrate that during the 1800s a significant number of couples used a premarital pregnancy to force priests to perform marriages they might have otherwise opposed.[75]

Similar problems interfere with understanding premarital sexuality among other western groups. Like slaves in other parts of the U.S., western slaves observed sexual mores based upon the realities of their lives. More specifically, although other groups may have desired to preserve female purity in order to establish heirs to land and other property, slaves owned no property. Indeed slaves were themselves property, often denied the right to enter formal or legal marriage, and seldom aware of when they might be separated from a partner by sale. Thus in most western slave communities, sexual mores were more flexible than among some other groups. Before marriage a woman could bear what were termed "outside" children without scorn, as long as she refrained from "loose" behavior. Often these women married the father of one of their children and established long-term marriages.[76]

The prevalence of premarital sexual relationships among Anglo westerners also remains clouded. By the 1860s Victorian couples wrote openly of sex in their diaries and letters and probed eroticism in their allusions, yet most seemed to flirt with danger more than participating in premarital sex. A number commented that premarital sex was to be regretted, especially in women. According to this double standard, a man could break an engagement without censure, if he discovered that his betrothed was unchaste.[77]

During the last third of the nineteenth century, a sexual rebellion occurred among Anglos, especially urban dwellers, members of liberal denominations, and single, employed men and women. Premarital intercourse increased in incidence, although most women and some men intended to marry their sexual partners. Given the lack of reliable birth control, premarital sexual relations led to a significant number of white women entering marriage already pregnant.[78]

The need to marry to "cover" a "sin" existed especially among more conservative Anglo groups. These included European immigrants who "fell by the way," as a German woman of the 1870s termed the problem. In her neighborhood, one young farm woman participated in a "rush marriage," followed five months later by the birth of a robust baby boy.[79] Unfortunately in such circumstances lower-class European women who worked as domestics and farm laborers seldom had families capable of championing them or men who would agree to marry them. Thus they sometimes resorted to self-induced abortion, migration, or suicide instead.[80]

Premarital sex among western Anglos became even more complicated during the early twentieth century. In the first decades, and certainly by the 1920s, a man's "call" to a woman's home and family had given way to the "date." Rather than courting with the woman's family present, an unescorted couple left the woman's home to attend a social event. Attracted by dance halls, amusement parks, and motion picture theaters, couples joined their peers in a growing array of public venues.

Consequently family members often had only a brief acquaintance with a daughter's or sister's date. In addition the privacy provided by automobiles allowed a couple to engage in whatever behavior they wished. For a significant number of Anglos, sex became a kind of currency for women, who lost the power and control they had held during the days of the home-based call. A young man now entertained a woman and expected in return compensation; increasingly that compensation involved some form of sex, ranging from petting to intercourse.[81]

Such transformations in courtship ritual often left adherents to traditional cultures confused. Some Native American peoples simply ignored the growing visibility of sex in western society. During the late nineteenth century, Southern Cheyenne parents continued to teach their daughters to avoid smiling and glancing at men, who would judge them "too easy and immoral." Although sexual information became more pervasive during the twentieth century, many Indian parents continued to shield their daughters from it. And as recently as the 1970s, for example, Blackfeet women learned little about sex and childbirth, ostensibly for their protection. But "with the modern lack of discipline," one said, "this has created many problems."[82]

Not surprisingly, given this diverse situation, traditional courtship rituals frequently disappeared in the West. More typically than not, established rituals clashed, then diffused. Consequently no clear protocol guided a couple toward marriage. Rather, westerners increasingly, to paraphrase the old saying, married in haste, repented in haste, and divorced at will.

The Role of Parents and Others in Courtship

Another significant casualty in the breakdown of western courtship was the declining influence of parents, clergy, and neighbors. Throughout world history, parents have preferred to perform mate selection, because such choices link kinship lines, a process which in turn affects social status, economic resources, or political power. Thus parents and others channeled biological needs in the direction they desired.[83]

In the nineteenth-century American West, Native American societies achieved these ends by utilizing a range of controls, including kinship rules designating eligible spouses and prohibiting others, child betrothal or marriage, social and/or physical isolation of young people, and close supervision by parents or chaperons.[84]

Kinship rules performed this function among nineteenth-century Pimas. Common aphorisms preached that young people should "not steal your brother's or friend's wife." Also Pimas were admonished to marry within their own group: "Evil spirits will take away your strength if you marry a girl from an enemy camp. You will become a weakling."[85] Because the Osage saw the matter differently, their rules allowed a woman to marry only *outside* her clan group.[86]

Child marriage is demonstrated by a Crow woman's recollection that her parents promised her, Pretty Shield, to Goes-Ahead when she was thirteen-years-old. Goes-Ahead, who had already married Pretty Shield's older sister and would eventually marry her younger sister as well, claimed Pretty Shield when she reached the age of sixteen. Pretty Shield explained that among the Crow of Montana during the late nineteenth century, "Young women did not then fall in love, and get married to please themselves." Instead they listened to "their fathers," which she believed to be "the best way."[87]

Virtual isolation was also widespread among nineteenth-century Indian societies. Mourning Dove remembered that her people kept their daughters away from men, even those of the immediate family. A Salishan suitor made a social call on a young woman's parents, returning several times if they encouraged him. He also presented a woman's father with gifts, including robes and ponies, followed by yet other gifts to her grandparents and other near relatives. Finally a suitor sent his mother or another close female relative to ask for the woman as his wife. Women usually had the final right to approve or reject suitors, but given women's lifetime seclusion from men, most willingly concurred with their parents' judgment.[88]

Close supervision was slightly less restrictive, in that women could interact with men, but they were closely watched by everyone from personal chaperons to general members of the community. Nineteenth-century Osage, for example, adhered to strong taboos that protected older women who guarded female charges. In addition community members also participated in parents' decisions regarding suitors.[89]

Spanish-speaking peoples in the Southwest followed comparable patterns and instituted similar courtship controls. Parents frequently arranged marriages, betrothing girls as young as age thirteen.[90] To avoid marriages repugnant to the bride, a *madrina,* or godmother, often served as intermediary in negotiations and gave the woman an opportunity to accept or refuse. In other cases, parish priests insured that brides knew grooms and wished to marry them.[91] Further community involvement occurred when a local church published notices of betrothals, or banns of marriage, which allowed neighbors to bring charges of deficient character, unstable financial condition, or consanguinity.

Such charges sometimes led to countercharges and legal complexities, vindicating or maligning the character of the people involved. As early as 1697, two sisters in Santa Fe accused the widowed mother of a bride-to-be, Juana Argüelo, of being "una puta alcahuete" (a bawdy whore). When the engagement disintegrated, Juana's mother sued for defamation of character, saying she was an honest widow. The court not only found for her, but fined and banished her accusers.[92] Other similar cases punctuate Spanish court records through the late nineteenth century.

As Anglos entered the West, they brought with them a range of ideas regarding the degree of authority parents or others should exercise in mate selection. Some middle- and upper-class parents tried to protect daughters by negotiating prenuptial agreements. Among all classes, Anglo parents tried to oversee courtship, involve all members of an extended family unit, include clergy and neighbors in the decision, and express their opinion of a match.[93] In addition some Anglo groups (notably East European immigrants, Jews, and Catholics) retained tight control over their children's marital choices.

At the same time, many Anglo women and men resisted parental authority in the matter of mate selection. By the 1830s throughout the country, many women were restless, often expressing dissatisfaction with the restrictions on their lives, as well as indicating an expanding awareness of women's rights. In the West such regional factors as distance from birth families, fluid communities, emphasis on individual choice, and desire to maximize one's opportunities further eroded the willingness of women, and men, to solicit or accept advice.

During the early nineteenth century, a growing media emphasis on romantic love likewise exacerbated the situation: love became the criteria for making marital decisions. Such thinking fit well with the western ethic, which, more than that of other regions, emphasized ideals of unregulated private competition, individualism, personal satisfaction, and a never-ending quest for "happiness."[94] As a result young women, customarily more dependent financially and psychologically than young men upon their parents, rebelled against parental control.[95] One young woman explained that "the Civil War broke out when I was eighteen. My lover since childhood answered President Lincoln's first call for volunteers. I married him before he left and without my mother's knowledge."[96]

Understandably parents resisted this trend toward young people choosing their own mates. In gold-rush California, for example, middle- and upper-class parents feared their daughters would chose unwisely. Such families in the town of Chico tried to skirt the danger by enrolling their daughters in the Chico Academy, hoping they would become women of considerable sense and thus avoid men of little substance. Chico parents also held parties, dances, and picnics, always inviting young men from the area's best families so their daughters would "meet well." Even so middle- and upper-class Chico women married gold miners, ranch hands, and in one case, a traveling sewing-machine salesman from Sacramento.[97]

Two key problems resulted from this growing tendency to eliminate parents, as well as neighbors and church officials, from courtship decisions. First, the want of judicious advice left courting men and women on their own in making critical decisions. Second, the lack of parental and other involvement could adversely affect the course of a marriage; parents and others who had played little part in such decisions sometimes refused to assist a couple when their marriage soured.[98]

Sometimes western media tried to bridge the growing gap between parents and their courting children. On the one hand, nineteenth-century journalists and editors counseled courting men to look for industry, economy, intelligence, morality, and honesty in women.[99] On the other hand, such writers sometimes urged women to accept a marriage proposal, as another might never be tendered. More often, however, writers cautioned women to give their love slowly and observe men's leisure habits, shunning those who indulged in "gaming" and other amusements.[100]

Because Anglo ideas and policies soon dominated most parts of the West, peoples of other societies also had to live with them, however uneasily. For instance Anglo laws usually decreed that an engagement ring, as a personal gift, belonged to a woman in case of a breakup, but they said nothing about ponies or other forms of bridal gifts. Such omissions created disorder for native groups who clung to their own customs yet lived under Anglo folkways and law.[101]

In addition by the early twentieth century, most western states had substituted marriage licenses for marriage banns. Under the bann system, interested parties and family members could raise objections, but under the licensing system, officials made decisions based on such considerations as age, consent of the parties involved, lunacy, and preexisting marriages.[102] Thus licensing reinforced the shift from community involvement to state control, as well as from personal interest to impersonal regulations.

Another western group forced to adjust their ways were Mormons, or members of the Church of Jesus Christ of Latter-day Saints. The practice of some nineteenth-century Mormon men marrying several wives led to atypical courtship patterns, but ones meaningful to many Mormons. For instance Mary Ann Stucki Reber Hafen of Utah explained that John Reber, an uncle married to her father's sister and already the father of four children, courted her around 1860. His wife minded the children while John escorted Mary Ann to dances and other social events. John's wife also assessed Mary Ann's potential as a wife and even made her wedding dress.[103]

Some Mormons in other parts of the West followed similar practices. In Arizona during the early 1880s, Mary Coleman Pomeroy's husband, Lide, courted his second wife while Mary stayed home, pregnant with Lide's son, Elijah.[104] Such courtship practices ended or went underground during the mid-1880s, with the passage of antipolygamy legislation, and especially in 1887, when the Edmunds-Tucker Act made earlier laws against plural marriage enforceable.[105]

From Native Americans to Mormons, then, the role of parents and others in courtship lessened. Rather than being guided and supervised by parents, clergy, and community, courting couples now "fell" in love and, often despite advice to the contrary, acted on that heady emotion.

Resolution of Courtship

The final stage of courtship brought closure, either through the couple parting or through establishing a form of pseudomarital or formal-marital relationship. In the West a significant number of couples ended their courtship with cohabitation. These relationships often became long-term and, in some jurisdictions, achieved the legal status of common-law marriage.[106]

All societies in the American West, however, encouraged formal marriage as the preferred conclusion of courtship. In addition virtually all honored the ideal of long-term marriage but provided some form of dissolution. More than forty years ago, anthropologist Margaret Mead first revealed this apparent conundrum: "no matter how free divorce" or "how frequently marriages broke up," most groups presumed marriages would last. Mead explained that "no known society has ever invented a form of marriage strong enough to stick that did not contain the 'till-death-us-do-part' assumption," yet most also recognized that some marriages were incapable of enduring for the long-term.[107]

Paradoxically then, even though the courtship process might itself be ineffective, most groups in the American West expected it to result in strong and solid relationships. The underlying and alarming contradiction was that while courtship came to depend on romance, marriage continued to rely on the development of conjugal love. Little evidence indicated that the first automatically led to the second. Nor did western courtship any longer involve parents and others who could provide the couple with the necessary support to make the transition from romantic to conjugal love. It appeared highly unlikely that western courtship would result in successful, lifetime marriages.

※

No evidence indicates that Anglo settlers in the West intended to throw other cultures into disarray with their courtship practices, policies, and laws. Rather, most Anglos simply assumed that other cultures' ways were strange, primitive, and outmoded, while their own usages were proper, progressive, and modern. Of course in actual practice, Anglos' enforcement of their ideas frequently upset other groups, as well as creating a general cultural disorder that affected Anglos themselves. During the nineteenth century, western courtship proved itself increasingly chaotic. In turn the nineteenth century passed on a less than solid base to twentieth-century generations. Thus by the late twentieth century, western courtship as a formal institution was so diverse as to hardly exist.

As the turn of the twenty-first century approaches, perhaps no form of courtship can lead to long-term marriage. The forces battering marriage may simply be too overwhelming. Or possibly the idea of lifetime marriage has become too daunting; because of longevity and early ages of first marriages, people who marry for a lifetime will spend a greater proportion of their lives in wedlock than has any previous generation.[108]

Aside from such general considerations, however, western courtship appears to have broken down, at least in part, as a result of such regional phenomenon as cultural layering, cultural conflict, and the expression of will by members of beleaguered groups. Rather than benefiting from the West's great cultural diversity, western courtship experienced considerable strife and friction, becoming so eclectic that it was no longer of much help in selecting compatible, long-term mates. As a consequence many matches made in such a situation were vulnerable to all the forces that produced the world's highest divorce rate.[109]

1

The popular mid-nineteenth century stereotype of the wife
was especially inapplicable in the culturally diverse American West.
(From an 1831 issue of Godey's Lady's Book)

2

Above: Scholars tend to focus on Anglo marriages in the West, but it must be remembered that because members of all cultures married, a spouse could just as easily be a person of color, such as this Chippewa woman. (Courtesy Museum of New Mexico, negative no. 90554)

3

Opposite: Other marriages and spouses who deserve more study include Chicanos/Chicanas, such as these New Mexican women. (Courtesy Museum of New Mexico, negative no. 31501)

4

Western cultures prescribed various ages for courtship.
Like these Native Americans in about 1880, most Indian
women were considered marriageable at puberty.
(Courtesy Museum of New Mexico, negative no. 102081)

5

*As in this Niwok camp in California, the village usually provided
the locus of courtship for Native American men and women.
(Courtesy Museum of New Mexico, negative no. 89917)*

6

Such special events as fandangos gave couples the opportunity to meet and court.
(*From* New Mexico in the Nineteenth Century: A Pictorial History)

7

*Typically men outnumbered women in early settlements like
this one in South Dakota. Thus, men sent home for wives, sought
wives through correspondence, or married "picture brides."
(Courtesy South Dakota State Historical Society)*

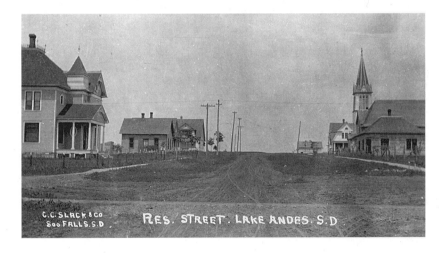

8

*As towns like Lake Andes in South Dakota became more settled,
churches and social clubs provided venues for courting.
(Courtesy Glenda Riley, private collection)*

9

*Picnics and Fourth-of-July celebrations like this one near Sioux City, Iowa,
gave women and men a chance to look each other over.
(Courtesy Glenda Riley, private collection)*

10

*As with this courting couple near Sioux City, Iowa, men of every culture
were expected to make formal calls to women's homes.
(Courtesy Glenda Riley, private collection)*

A variety of wedding ceremonies reflected the cultural traditions of couples.
Pictured here are William and Anna Belle Steintemp, February 20, 1881.
(Courtesy Minnesota Historical Society)

12

Married couples often combined cultures in their dress and customs.
Pictured here are doctors Tai Heong Keng (Li) and Kai Fai Li.
(Courtesy Bishop Museum, Hawaii)

Marrying:
For Better or Worse?

Courtship did not stand alone as a catalyst of marital breakdown in the West. Marriage also passed on muddled traditions. Because marital stressors abounded in the nineteenth- and early-twentieth-century West, western marriages developed a wide range of responses to such regional tensions and thus provided conflicting models to people about to enter marriage. At the same time, the western ethos, which preached individual satisfaction and happiness, increasingly supported experimentation and change in marriage.

Whether a marriage survived and gained some degree of effectiveness in this complex setting depended on its response to positive stimuli (the "better") or to negative influences (the "worse"). Oddly enough, the fusing and rending factors were the same. In the West in the nineteenth and early twentieth centuries, these forces consisted of laws and mores, ritual, love, community and milieu, gender roles, children, religion, plural marriage, and marriage within one's own group, all of which had both "up" and "down" features.

Fusing Factors in Western Families

What kept people together in the American West or elsewhere? Only recently have experts and researchers studied cases of success to see what works, rather than analyzing cases of failure to see what does not. A 1984 study reported that six factors bond marriages in the United States: family members expressing appreciation for each other, sharing time, utilizing good communication, displaying commitment to the family, practicing religious beliefs, and effectively negotiating family crises.[1]

These elements, however, function internally in family dynamics. Even though such inner forces are fundamental to marital success or failure,

43

external pressures also played an important role. In the American West, outside conditions formed the historical context in which families lived, worked, and developed, and they presented families with a unique set of regional circumstances.

Laws and Mores

Whether legislated and written down or acted out in social standards, law served as a powerful force holding western families together. In the American West, every society established and enforced principles designed to bind marriages. For instance numerous Native American societies governed marriage by mores and proscriptions. Among nineteenth-century Mohave Indians, such rules included an elaborate set of incest taboos, ranging from the Mohave creation myth to Coyote tales and marriage customs.[2]

Spanish law also regulated marriage and attempted to insure compatibility. Statutes provided negative sanctions against adulterers, concubines, and men and women leading "the bad life," meaning those engaging in cohabitation or other illegal sexual relationships. Moreover local magistrates hauled in husbands for slandering wives, chastised women for physically assaulting husbands, and acted as agents of reconciliation. Such legal intervention had a long history in the West. As early as 1763, Juana Martín sued her husband for keeping a mistress, thus depriving her and their children of adequate support. When the court banished the mistress, Juana reconciled with her husband. Similar cases continued to appear well into the nineteenth century. For example in 1836 Rafaela Sánchez persuaded a court to order her abusive husband to post a bond to insure her satisfaction with his future conduct.[3]

Spanish law especially protected wives and tried to keep them content in marriage. Courts punished such acts as molestation and wife abuse and regarded such violence as grounds for divorces of bed and board. Courts also provided a forum for settling women's domestic grievances. In New Mexico tense family situations revealed themselves in 1843, when Francisca Romero sued her husband for gambling away her burro and, in 1844, when Grogira Quintana sued her husband, Jesús Martínez, for selling her grain mill without her consent.[4]

In other cases of distressed marriages, some Spanish courts allowed married women to live independently of their husbands and to conduct their own business affairs. In Los Angeles, California, in March 1872, Dolores Romero de Correa petitioned a county court for permission to sell real estate she held within the city. After proving that she was "living separate and apart from her husband" and describing her land as extending from a road to "a certain fence" to a brewery, she received permission to dispose of her holdings.[5]

French-based law in the Louisiana Territory also tried to encourage marital satisfaction. French statutes allowed individuals to attempt to insure marital success through prenuptial contracts. These began as early as the 1600s and continued to exist among many classes of people throughout the nineteenth century. In 1839, for example, Thomas Alexandre Morgan and Azelie Brosset, both free people of color residing in New Orleans, agreed that they would hold as community property the land, money, and slaves they brought to the marriage, but would have no liability for any premarital debts.[6]

In addition French law strove to make marriage gratifying to wives. During the early to mid-nineteenth century, it recognized a married woman's existence apart from that of her husband by including her birth-family name in her married name, authorizing her to act as a joint partner in marital community property, allowing her to own and manage property, permitting her to make a separate will, and stipulating that she owned one-half of the community property after her husband's death. In case of irreconcilable marital strife, a married woman could petition for and receive, especially in cases of physical cruelty, a separation of bed and board. In this limited divorce, spouses lived separately, but the husband, if the guilty party, continued to honor his pledge to support his wife. A divorce of bed and board usually assigned a woman *feme sole* status, meaning she could conduct her own business affairs.[7]

As Anglo-American settlers entered the West, especially during the nineteenth century, they introduced their own traditions supporting marriage. They not only carried a belief in the importance of formal marriage with them, but they also tried to impose their ideas on native peoples. The U.S. territorial and state governments that formed in areas beyond the Mississippi River institutionalized white American perspectives, pushing aside those of such groups as Native Americans and Spanish-speaking settlers. Marriage became monogamous and contractual. It might also involve a religious sacrament, but this was not a legal requirement. In addition government comprised a third party in every marriage; it established and enforced requirements for licensing, terms of the marital contract, the legal and social status of each party, and the general obligations of matrimony.[8]

Unlike earlier Native American standards or French and Spanish codes, Anglo rules tried to solidify the family unit by making women dependent on men. Thus Anglo marriage generally deprived women of civil rights and declared husbands sovereign heads of families.[9] During the late 1880s, individual western states also tried to prevent the occurrence of unsatisfactory unions by raising the age of marriage for minors, prohibiting marriages between people of different races, and restricting marriages involving those with mental defects, venereal disease, alcoholism, or a previous marriage ending in divorce.[10] Clearly the intent of each of these policies was to shore up marriage. Whatever form these rules of conduct assumed, law regularized and regulated a marriage, provided community acceptance, and established provisions for its continuance.

Ritual

Rituals also held western families together. Wedding rites proved especially important as public recognition of a couple's new status, but additionally they allowed an opportunity for family, friends, and neighbors to demonstrate support and involvement. Wedding gifts usually formed an important part of this marriage protocol. A practicality in all cultures to help a couple get started, gifts also stood as symbols of a new marriage and household.

Native American groups developed variations on such themes. During a nineteenth-century Paiute wedding feast, for example, a bride fed the groom food of her own making, thus pledging to succor him. Afterwards her father pronounced them husband and wife, and the guests enjoyed a wedding banquet.[11] But, according to Mourning Dove, wedding rituals among the Salishans of eastern Washington varied according to a couple's social class. For commoners Salishans conducted private ceremonies, usually held in a tepee with only family members present, but a chief's daughter married in public with villagers as witnesses. The chief and his wife also presided at other important weddings, where he gave an oration, after which the groom removed his bride's virgin cape from her shoulders and everyone enjoyed a sumptuous meal.[12]

Spanish-speaking settlers took a different tack, usually solemnizing marriages in a Catholic church, followed by such events as feasts and dancing. In 1852, when fifteen-year-old Juana Machado Alipáz married her soldier husband in San Diego, the wedding party emerged from the church at 10 A.M. Family, friends, and the entire San Diego military company attended a wedding breakfast, followed by a dance, a 2 P.M. dinner, and another dance that continued all night. According to Juana, "all the weddings in those times were generally celebrated in the same way."[13]

Of course, diversity existed among Spanish-heritage peoples throughout the West, depending on social class and locale. Throughout the nineteenth and early twentieth centuries, those of lesser means scaled down wedding celebrations to fit family economies, whereas the more well-off living in rural Colorado and New Mexico during the late nineteenth and early twentieth centuries expected a groom to provide the wedding, trousseau, and reception. After the wedding, families exchanged gifts, thus forming a new network based upon mutual commitments.[14]

When permitted to do so, nineteenth-century western slaves also married in formal Christian wedding services, performed either by white or black ministers. If a slave marriage originated with a couple's owners or met with owner approval, a meal and presents might follow. Most owners, however, refused slaves the legal right to contract white-style marriages. Thus slaves devised their own ceremonies, often jumping over a broomstick to seal their commitment to each other.[15]

Naturally Anglo westerners also held specific ideas regarding appropriate wedding ceremonies. At first Anglo settlers usually married simply, perhaps in the bride's home, the office of a judge or justice of the peace, or a newly constructed church. After all, ritual had to bend to circumstance. In 1853 when Alfred A. Plummer, the founder of Port Townsend, Washington Territory, married Irish immigrant Anna Hill, he recorded his own marriage after a neighboring justice of the peace performed a brief ceremony.[16]

As in other cultures, Anglos often followed wedding services with a meal and perhaps dancing. In the Plummers' case, a roasted pig served as the dinner's focal point, while neighboring fiddlers provided music for dancing. Anglo guests also believed in offering gifts to the newly wed pair. In 1863 A. O. Cowles gave his daughter, Gertie, a cow when she married Will Valentine in Rochester, Minnesota. At a 1913 home wedding in Iowa, however, the presents ran to household goods, covering two tables and a chiffonnier.[17]

Regional manners also influenced such customs as gift giving. More than one westward-bound couple departed from their wedding in the South with gifts of slave women and men in tow. During the 1850s a newly married Oklahoma couple received the present of a slave couple. In 1862 newly wed Ellen Bell and Thomas Tootle set off for Colorado, accompanied by an African American house slave, a wedding gift from her family.[18]

Local and ethnic customs further shaped Anglo celebrations, which, especially during the nineteenth century, sometimes lasted for several days. A serenade by town youth might be followed by a shivaree (charivari). Derived from an old world custom and especially popular in rural areas of the U.S., a shivaree was an informal, often raucous party, usually outside the bedroom of a newly wed pair. According to a neighbor, at an Iowa shivaree during the 1840s, "cow-bells, whistles, horse-fiddles, drumming on tin pans enlivened the neighborhood until morning."[19] Most westerners regarded such escapades as good fun, but in Oklahoma City during the 1880s, one shivaree created so much noise that some neighbors concluded someone was raiding and killing townspeople.[20]

Of course as Anglo civilization spread and the white middle and upper classes prospered, weddings frequently became larger and more lavish. A wedding supper, or "feast" as some called it, might feature several meats and as many as five kinds of cake. In addition Anglo culture imparted both the concept of, and the desire for, white-style weddings among other peoples who wanted to appear firmly married in the eyes of their own group and of whites. One late-nineteenth-century woman of Indian and French heritage wore her traditional dress and moccasins, yet married in a Catholic ceremony.[21] And when an early-twentieth-century Aleut bride and Norwegian groom in a remote part of Alaska called in the marriage commissioner to marry them but did not have the book containing the ceremony's words, they seemed content to listen to the official read local bear-hunting regulations.[22]

Early twentieth-century Chinese living in Los Angeles also came to prefer elements of Anglo wedding ceremonies. Through missionaries who provided them with a window on the Anglo world, Chinese and Chinese Americans learned about Anglo wedding styles and rituals. Although first-generation mothers often preferred traditional Chinese weddings, one observer remarked that their daughters' weddings "took on increasingly Western aspects." Soon many Chinese referred to such events as "Wen Ming," or "civilized" weddings. Still most Chinese held on to at least some aspects of their culture, so that women of a wedding party might wear Chinese dress, while the men donned American tuxedos or suits, or a ceremony in a western church might be followed by a Chinese banquet and an American honeymoon.[23]

Evidently such people hoped to cover all possibilities in the matter of marriage ritual. If rites helped solidify a marriage, then couples wanted to incorporate customary ways with newer ideas, especially those held by Anglo culture, which was rapidly becoming the most visible and influential one in the West.

Love

No matter how a marriage might come into being, love frequently evolved and held a family together. Whether through an arranged match or a romantic one, wives and husbands in all cultures developed true affection for each other. Only recently, however, have scholars and other commentators recognized that arranged marriages could indeed lead to conjugal love.

Because nineteenth-century Anglos esteemed romantic love as a primary criterion for marriage, they usually assumed, and widely reported, that arranged marriage led to distaste and even loathing. When Anglo migrants first encountered arranged marriages among Spanish-speaking peoples, and later among Asians, they again fell victim to such assumptions. Consequently, not until the 1930s did anthropologists reject such biases, acknowledging instead that arranged marriages among Native Americans often resulted in devotion. Combining the guidance of parents with a suitor who esteemed his potential wife enough to offer valuable gifts to her family created an atmosphere in which affection could bloom.[24]

Anglos meanwhile assumed that romantic love automatically translated into conjugal love. Especially during the nineteenth and early twentieth centuries, Victorian thinking glorified and idealized such love, which supposedly comprised life's highest experience, sustained faith, and turned one's life toward higher aspirations. For many Victorians, love, mystical rather than logical, also gave meaning to life, eradicated loneliness, and made one selfless.[25]

The intensity of this love ethos permeated Anglo relationships, often keeping spouses together. In 1849 Mary Jane Hayden, bound to home by an ailing six-week-old baby, learned that her husband wished to go to California. "I was very fond of my husband," Hayden explained, "and was nearly broken-hearted at the thought of the separation." Hayden told her spouse that they had married to live together and that she was willing to go with him "to any part of God's Foot Stool." She added that if he went without her, he had no need to return, for she would look upon him as dead. Mary Jane's husband gracefully capitulated and remained at home until she could accompany him. In similar situations, other wives packed up and followed their husbands to remote places, including Arizona and California.[26]

Western women soon came to believe that love had the power to offset the rigors of migration and settlement. Faye Cashett Lewis attributed her mother's adaptation to the South Dakota frontier near the turn of the twentieth century to the presence of marital love. She maintained that her mother "had such complete trust" in her husband that "she thought of him as an indestructible anchor to which she was firmly tethered."[27] Women also called upon love to help their marriages through other troubled times. In 1884 when her marriage encountered personal difficulties, Californian Dorothea Lummis plead (ultimately unsuccessfully) with her husband Charles Fletcher Lummis: "do you not know how deep, how broad, how lasting is my love for you. O! let us try & cherish and hold fast to one another for truly I do believe that 'love is all.'"[28]

Besides western women's faith in love, western men also expressed love and relied upon its potency to safeguard their marriages. In 1865, writing to his wife Mary from Dakota Territory, an army surgeon at the Crow Creek Agency poured out his loneliness and fondness for her. Dr. Noah Glatfelter repeatedly begged his wife Mary to come live with him, urged her to write more frequently, and even imprinted some of his letters with kisses.[29]

Other married men forced temporarily to leave their families behind similarly relied upon love to bridge the distance. In fact as men moved farther West, their affection for their wives seemed to grow in ratio to miles covered. Gold-seeker Samuel McCoy claimed that by the time he had reached Independence, Missouri, his love for his wife had "doubled, trebled . . . and run over." Another argonaut stood with his arms out-stretched eastward from the Continental Divide, wishing for his wife's "answering look of affection." Still another lamented "no one can appreciate a companion & family until deprived of their society."[30]

Nor were these simply letter-book sentiments dutifully transferred from a manual to an epistle intended for a loved one. Numerous women and men revealed similar feelings in other types of documents as well. In 1860 Mollie Dorsey Sanford confided to her journal that she spent her first wedding anniversary keeping "the Kettle singing on the stove," while peering "out into the midnight darkness" awaiting her husband's return from a trip. When her husband finally appeared, Mollie noted with satisfaction that he "had walked 10 miles over that lonely road just to be with me on our first anniversary, and if *anyone*, or if *I* myself, ever thought him devoid of sentiment, *that* decides that he is not."[31]

Apparently numerous Anglos extolled romantic love and carried its idealization to a new height, but other western peoples also drew on it to make their marriages effective. Alice Jackson of Minnesota remembered that her father, a former slave and later a barber, was a "kind and loving man," who never quarrelled with her mother.[32] Another Minnesota African American woman, Eva Bell Neal, who grew up in a similar warm family environment around the turn of the twentieth century, came to define love, much like the Bible, as "very Patient, Very Kind, Love knows no jealousy, Never rude, Never selfish, Never Irritated, Never Resentful, Love is never glad when others go wrong, Love is gladdened by goodness, Always slow to expose, Always eager to believe the best, Always hopeful, Love never disappears."[33]

Unfortunately the significant question of how such professions of love translated into sexual relationships remains unclear. Whether such loving couples also relished the marriage bed is usually absent from nineteenth- and early-twentieth-century documents; modest people of all cultures seldom talked about satisfactory sex lives. Indeed women of many cultures distanced themselves from the personal side of marriage even further by referring to their husbands as "Mr." When such letter-writers as Noah Glatfelter mentioned his and his wife's "sweet relations towards each other" one can only conjecture that marital love spilled over into sex as well.[34]

Community and Milieu

Along with the growth of love, western marriages also benefited from community support. During the spring of 1869, for example, William Tracy of Bozeman, Montana, left for Illinois to marry Sarah Jane Bessey, thus triggering a chain of preparations in Bozeman. Upon Tracy's return with his bride, local women sponsored a welcoming dinner and taught Sarah to cook. According to Sarah, "in all there were just fourteen women in the town in 1869, but they all vied with each other to help us and to make us welcome."[35] After such a start it would have been difficult for William and Sarah Jane Tracy to admit any marital dissatisfaction they might have felt: they needed at least to make a good try at their marriage.

At the same time, elements of the nineteenth- and early-twentieth-century western circumstances drove family members together. Shortages of women's paid employment in some areas kept wives economically dependent on husbands or encouraged wives, who may have preferred to labor elsewhere, to form economic partnerships with their spouses. Meanwhile mobility created moves away from kin and neighbors that forced individuals to rely more on spouses than did those who had stable support networks around them.

Another element of the western milieu, popular culture, sent additional unifying messages. During the nineteenth and early twentieth centuries, Spanish-speaking couples listened to ballads and poems emphasizing family unity and demonstrating spouses' satisfaction with marital roles. During the same era, Anglo art and film depicted western families as based on marital bliss and unanimity.[36]

Even the existence of racial prejudice in the western environment caused mates to cleave to one another in the face of onslaughts from the Ku Klux Klan or neighborhood associations that enforced restrictive housing covenants. Chicanos in Los Angeles *barrios*, African Americans in Los Angeles ghettos, and Asian Americans in Los Angeles's Chinatown and Little Tokyo may have wished for different conditions, but spouses learned to rely upon each other.[37]

Gender Roles

In the nineteenth- and early-twentieth-century West, gender roles often proved flexible enough to supply additional glue to marriages. Rather than finding themselves rigidly locked into one set of functions, spouses could vary their roles and enlarge their rights.

Native American women especially wielded wide influence and savored their freedom. When a French settler in South Dakota during the late 1890s observed an Indian woman give two horses to a friend in her husband's absence, the French woman felt it necessary to chastise the Indian woman by remarking that "in my country a woman would consult her husband before giving such expensive presents." The native woman responded haughtily, "I would not be a white woman!"[38]

Other married Native American women expanded their roles by fighting alongside men. A Gros Ventre woman in the 1820s, Woman Chief, organized war parties and became such an important warrior and hunter that she obtained "ceremonial" wives to perform domestic work.[39] Even as late as the 1880s, women of the Plains tribes also accompanied their warrior husbands in a rapidly disappearing tradition—attacks and raids on enemy camps. When a member of the Blackfeet Indians called Hate Woman insisted on accompanying her husband, Weasel Tail, into battle, he explained that "my wife said she loved me, and if I was to be killed on a war party she wanted to be killed too." Rather than requiring her to cook and perform other domestic duties, Weasel Tail equipped Hate Woman with a six-shooter and applauded her exploits in stealing enemy horses.[40]

In a similar way, gender roles proved adaptable among Spanish-speaking peoples. Because wives could manage their own property, sign mortgages and business notes, and participate in land-grant and other litigation, they gained influence in other decisions as well. In addition, especially in rural settings, community members monitored patriarchal behavior while mandating that women learn numerous skills. Around 1900 Coloradan Patricia Luna recalled that she had worked on a farm, "in the fields, whatever," alongside men.[11] At the same time, Chicanas in Arizona worked as *vaqueras* and in the fields, soon developing into effective labor organizers in their own right.[42]

Even among Anglos, who during the nineteenth and early twentieth centuries tended to deify separate spheres for women and men, frontier conditions tempered customary gender prescriptions. Although Anglo women often rationalized their involvement by saying they were "helping" their men, they earned cash income, held paid employment outside the home, kept family farms and other enterprises afloat during hard times, and participated in decision-making. As a case in point, a recent study of Colorado homesteading women and men during the late 1800s indicated that they shared workloads as well as decisions.[43]

Mormon women also stretched the boundaries of Anglo gender expectations. Beginning in the 1850s, Mormon women engaged in "home industry," producing necessary goods rather than purchasing them from gentile (non-Mormon) merchants. These women also proved themselves strong and influential in temple activities and relief organizations.[44]

Some prostitutes who continued to work after marriage comprised another example of women who rejected traditional gender roles. Apparently such women were able to divide work and love in their minds, as well in their husbands' thinking. In more than one such case, married prostitutes earned cash income and sometimes purchased land or made other investments benefiting their families.[45]

Not only were gender roles frequently elastic in the nineteenth- and early-twentieth-century West, but even in their most rigid form they often provided satisfaction to wives and husbands.[46] Separation of women's and men's spheres had its own reward. Nineteenth-century Ojibway women and men worked at different duties, yet extended mutual respect to each other and their work. Similarly Mourning Dove explained that Salishan people judged a wife's status by her skill in cooking, weaving, tanning, and caring for children, but in return eventually elevated her to a position of respect and reverence.[47]

Moreover such distinct gender roles had a utilitarian side. When Spanish-speaking families immigrated to such places as El Paso during the late 1800s, they resisted outside employment for women, preferring instead that wives remain at home. Wives provided critical services by guarding cultural traditions within the family and helping men and children adjust to the new conditions. Even when wives left their homes, especially after 1900, to take employment as domestics, seamstresses, and washwomen in commercial laundries, they continued to maintain strong kin networks and family ties.[48]

By prescribing separate work, gender roles also kept wives and husbands from bothering each other with details. As Susan Magoffin of New Mexico wrote in 1847, she need not trouble her merchant husband with her domestic problem—an inebriated cook: "I can manage my own domestic concerns without worrying his already perplexed mind with my little difficulties."[49]

In addition there was usually only one career; wives generally assumed they would assist in whatever work their husbands undertook. When Mary Ronan's husband started mining in Montana during the 1870s, she learned skills useful to a miner's wife; when he took assignment as an Indian agent in 1877, she duly mastered the knowledge and faculties necessary to an Indian agent's wife. During the same era, a Nebraska woman who married a doctor spent her married life running her household and serving as cashier, bookkeeper, office cleaner, laundress of surgical linens, and member of the local Women's Auxiliary of the American Medical Association.[50]

Furthermore, then as now, some women enjoyed and appreciated strictly domestic roles. An Arizona Chicana who married in 1924 expressed delight that her husband wanted her to stay home, because she herself preferred to spend her time raising their children.[51] And when an Arizona Anglo woman married a park ranger in 1938, she moved into Sunset Crater National Monument's Wupatki Ruin with him, where she happily cleaned, cooked, and entertained. When in 1949 he took a job as superintendent of a new national monument in Puerto Rico, she not only accompanied him but was thrilled, "for he's so enthusiastic about the possibilities."[52]

Numerous husbands exercised patriarchal power in a congenial way. One Kansas woman remembered that although "Grandfather Little was the real head of the Little family," his "quiet manner" was "undisturbing in any company." Even his reasons for migrating to Kansas in 1859 appeared benign; he hoped to better his wife's health and asked the hired man to spade the kitchen garden, cut wood for the cookstove, and perform other domestic jobs.[53] Men further softened patriarchy's sting by crossing gender lines to help with "women's work." During the 1860s Sarah Tracy repeatedly jotted in her diary such notations as: "Will and I have out [sic] a big washing today. Will scrubbed the two floors. We worked very hard and are both tired tonight."[54]

Women, too, could modify gender expectations by working toward partnerships with their husbands. Certainly many nineteenth-century farm women did so. During the early 1900s, Korean women made themselves indispensable in homes, fields, businesses, and such community activities as relief and religious activities, thus gradually moving from subordination to something resembling partnership.[55]

Similarly Japanese American women parlayed their responsibilities into increased power within the family. Notably in World War II internment camps, Japanese American men lost their functions as breadwinners and family heads. Although Japanese families showed their strength and usually survived internment, gender expectations changed in that women left the camps with enhanced influence and men with less.[56]

Thus gender roles bonded families in many different ways. Although mention of the concept of separate spheres might evoke a negative response today, at one time distinct gender expectations provided positive benefits for numerous westerners, both female and male.

Children

Children also united families, especially if birth occurred with great regularity. During the frontier stage, the expectation existed that marriages would produce large numbers of children. Supposedly a wife's duty, indeed her joy, centered upon bearing future laborers and citizens—all for the greater glory and expansion of the American West. At the same time, a husband's responsibility, and happiness, involved supporting these future westerners during their dependent years.

Moreover among Catholic peoples, the church prohibited birth control and urged couples to bear and raise numerous children. Californian

Dorotea Valdez recalled that during the 1810s and 1820s the local "population" increased very rapidly. According to her the average number of children raised by one mother "was rather above than below the number of eleven."[57]

Families also grew through the inclusion of children from previous marriages. During the 1870s, when Jesús Moreno married Antonia J. Soza near Tucson, she accepted four children from his earlier marriage, then bore several of her own. Other couples took in relatives' children or adopted children. During the early 1900s, Belle Chigley, a part-Chickasaw woman living in Davis, Oklahoma, adopted and subsequently raised two orphan Indian girls.[58]

Some Anglo women held different attitudes, however. According to Valdez, family size declined after the arrival of Anglos, "because the American women" were "too fond of visiting doctors and swallowing medicines." Although Anglo family size indeed decreased during the nineteenth century, occasional instances occurred of Anglo women bearing as many as eighteen or twenty children. Anecdotal evidence also indicates that in some families childbirth took place every two to three years and that families of ten, twelve, and even fourteen children were not unknown.[59]

Besides keeping couples together for the practical reasons of rearing a large brood, children could also weld marriages by providing certain benefits. Native Americans believed in raising strong, resilient children to carry on their family, kin, and tribe, whereas Anglos increasingly saw children as special and important gifts from God. Between the 1830s and 1850s, Mormons, for example, rejected the Puritan-inspired theory that children came into the world soulless and depraved. Instead the Book of Mormon proclaimed that "little children are whole, for they are not capable of committing sin" (Moroni 8:8). This statement encouraged an emphasis on child nurture and a corresponding belief that children played an important part in the Mormon celestial family. Mormon parents who lived in a righteous manner and fulfilled their parental duties could expect the reward of unending family life, both on earth and in the hereafter.[60] Such beliefs could also impart to Mormon parents a sense of great and important responsibility that might keep them together when other factors failed to bind them.

Religion

Religious commitments further cemented families. This influence operated in every culture, but Anglo examples are widely available. The marriage of Narcissa Prentiss and Marcus Whitman constituted an early and well-known case. Prentiss and Whitman wed in 1836 for religious reasons, that is, to meet the requirements of the American Board of Commissioners for Foreign Missions that missionaries be married. After marriage they entered mission work among Cayuse Indians in the Oregon Territory, and their religious faithfulness held them together through subsequent difficult periods.[61]

Religion also helped the marriages of less well-known couples survive. Kansan Julia Lovejoy repeatedly invoked God's grace during the 1850s and 1860s, to help her and her husband survive illness, want, a daughter's death, and attacks by Indians and border raiders. Lovejoy said "the Lord was indeed a present help" through all, and that during twenty-five years of marriage she and her husband had enjoyed "the smiles" of the "Savior." Similarly a Montana couple of the 1880s believed their marriage endured because of their Irish Catholic faith.[62]

Plural Marriage

A couple's agreement regarding plural marriage could also help stabilize their marriage. Many Native American societies continued to practice polygyny during the nineteenth century, for despite Anglo proscriptions to the contrary, Indians perceived benefits in plural marriage for both men and women. Plural marriage provided men with more children and relatives, which led to increased wealth and standing in the community, while plural wives bore fewer children than monogamous women and could share residences, work, and childcare with co-wives, often their sisters. As a Northern Cheyenne named Wooden Leg, born around 1858, explained, marrying sisters could prevent "jealous quarreling likely to occur were they from different families."[63]

In the 1880 census, Cheyenne Indians frankly admitted practicing polygyny. In a society still based largely on the pursuit of game, a number of men ran large extended family households, in which women worked in close cooperation as stretchers, scrapers, tanners, and decorators of hides and even buffalo robes. Such men tended to be traders, chiefs, and other prominent figures, who could support multiple wives. Economic cohesion combined with the sorority of wives cemented such polygynous marriages.[64]

Mormons also adopted the practice of plural marriage. After a group of Mormons migrated to Nauvoo, Illinois, during the 1840s, Mormon leaders declared plural marriage a policy that would yield religious and spiritual benefits. Not only could spouses in plural marriages wield increased influence in their local communities through their saintliness, but they could also expect an insured place in eternity. As one Mormon leader explained, "we believe that such experience fits us for our after-life, as we are only preparing for life beyond while here."[65] After additional migrations to Utah beginning in the 1850s, and later to Arizona and Nevada, a significant number of Mormons established harmonious plural marriages. Wives stated that they had "sister" wives to share work, childcare, and other household responsibilities. One even maintained that "children of polygamy are healthier."[66]

Intramarriage

Far more prevalent than plural marriage as a binding force was intramarriage, or endogamy, in which individuals married people of their own group. Study after study indicates that marital satisfaction rises sharply depending on similarity of mates, whether the similitude might stem from race, ethnicity, religion, social class, or challenging physical conditions.[67] Accordingly numerous groups used endogamy to strengthen family ties, kin networks, or social-class power.[68]

Most societies in the American West also believed that a marriage would fare better if one spouse knew what to expect of the other, or if the union was easily accepted by kin or other social group.[69] The principle of ease of adjustment between like mates was proven by Asian peoples living in the American West. Studies of Chinese Americans in San Francisco indicated that such endogamous spouses not only experienced a high rate of marital satisfaction, but credited for their success spousal agreement on such matters as daily behavior, life aims, and moral standards.[70] Such consistency between mates not only underwrote compatible relationships, but provided a common identity that melded family members into an abiding unit.

Stress Factors in Western Families

So far this analysis has painted a rosy picture of western family life, but the story has an underside as well. Although one might think that divorce statistics would readily reveal the causes of divorce among western couples, divorce figures are fickle and often inexact. In addition divorce-seekers chose from among legal grounds available to them at the time. They usually selected the charge that approximated their situations, might prove the least damaging to everyone involved, or would persuade a judge to grant a divorce and a favorable settlement.

Thus divorce statistics and even case records supply less than complete stories about causes of marital breakdown. To understand pressures on western marriages, it is necessary to dig deeper and to sift anecdotal evidence as well. An examination of the other side of the positive catalysts discussed above reveals that the same influences could also handicap western families.

Law

In many ways laws protected marriages, but codes and statutes also limited spouses' rights, especially those of wives. Even in the early and mid-nineteenth century, French law required that a wife accept and adopt a husband's dwelling place as her marital domicile, obtain a husband's permission in managing her property and signing contracts, and abstain from marrying for ten months after his death (presumably to determine whether she was pregnant, so his child would remain his heir).[71]

Nineteenth- and early-twentieth-century legal restrictions further burdened marriages by forcing mates to stay together when they preferred to part. In virtually all societies, men, and sometimes women, coped with this situation by taking lovers. Another survival strategy involved one spouse or the other adopting a suffering martyr stance, which may have kept a marriage in force but contributed little to its effectiveness.[72]

In other instances during this era, legal provisions allowed people to leave marriages too fast and easily. Separation and divorce codes supplied escape routes, which some people utilized rather than confronting problems or resolving differences. Throughout the West, abandonment of spouses also occurred with great regularity and provided deserted mates with assured grounds for divorce.

Legal constraints also kept spouses apart physically. Especially during the 1880s and 1890s, Chinese exclusion laws created split families, by allowing husbands to migrate to the United States as workers, but prohibiting their wives from following. It might take years to reunite a married couple. One Chinese husband, Sam Chang, invested nine years in petitioning and waiting before bringing his wife and eldest daughter to join him in 1923 in the United States.[73]

In addition the mixing and layering of different cultures' laws often muddled family codes and practices. Despite Anglo pronouncements that everyone must marry according to Anglo law, throughout the nineteenth century many Native Americans continued to marry by their own customs. They resisted white-style marriage, because it forced them to adopt the principle of indissoluble monogamous marriage, accept legal limits on wives, and perhaps undergo a Christian ceremony. By the late nineteenth century, the Bureau of Indian Affairs responded by classifying such marriages as Indian "custom" marriages, or cohabitation without force of Anglo law or religious ceremony. These native couples thus had a foot in each culture, married in their own but unwed in Anglo society. According to one anthropologist, such pressure proved "considerable in weakening the stability of Indian marital and family life as a whole."[74]

In New Mexico a complicated situation also developed, at least in part because people of Spanish heritage and Anglos tried to follow separate legal principles. Under long-standing Spanish law, a wife could not give her property to her husband or receive some of his, unless he was squandering hers. A wife also inherited a portion of her parents' estate, which she controlled and could will to any heirs.[75] But these tenets proved incompatible with Anglo law, which entered the area in the mid-1840s and mandated no property rights for married women. Adherence to conflicting legal beliefs frequently led to judicial tangles concerning such matters as heirs, inheritance rights, and the responsibility of surviving spouses for debts of deceased mates. Frequently in these complex situations, individuals found their legal assumptions unfounded and, consequently, forfeited rights, property, or money.

Ritual

Negative rituals also undermined western marriages. In most nineteenth-century western cultures, for example, family members had a right to participate in a couple's relationship, especially in times of distress, and to make a couple's problems a matter of public debate. For instance, if a Kiowa wife left her husband and rejoined her family, the man had to give her family considerable gifts to gain her return, while an abandoned Cheyenne husband had to endure a public airing of his wife's grievances, defend himself, and often beg pardon of his wife and her family.[76]

Marital strife also seemed to give license to family members, close friends, and others to advise one spouse regarding the other's conduct, tell one the "truth" regarding the other, and encourage separations or divorces. Also, especially during the nineteenth century, families, friends, convents, and Catholic missions regularly harbored fugitive spouses.[77]

Such widespread western rituals as excessive drinking created other family problems. Although alcoholism did not constitute a marriage ritual, it underwrote certain destructive practices, including neglect, spousal abuse, and inadequate support. Throughout much of the West, a double sexual standard also prevailed, so that barrooms, hurdy-gurdy girls, and prostitutes constituted an important part of the male ritual world.[78] Female temperance leaders and other reformers, who especially linked alcohol to wife abuse, might not provide the most unbiased viewpoint, but other evidence also connects alcoholism and spousal abuse.[79]

For instance women's writings indicate that alcoholism and subsequent spouse abuse occurred from one end of the West to the other.[80] In letters from the 1830s originating in Louisiana, a French wife described her husband as "dissipated," meaning alcoholic. On one occasion he fell over the bannister at the top of the stairs, to land at the bottom without serious injury. On others he physically molested her. During one of these episodes, in spite of restraint by family friends, the drunken husband stabbed his wife. Fortunately for her, a corset bone stopped the knife and saved her life.[81]

Farther north the memoirs of Cleora Cassady, whose family settled in Fairbanks, Alaska, in 1906, reveal that when her six-foot, red-haired, Irish father "became too liquor-laden to sing and his disposition soured, the saloon-keeper sent him home to us, usually late in the night." Cassady added that when her mother heard him coming, she hid the children under the bed. The next day Cleora's mother bravely bore her bruises, trying to "pretend it never happened." On more than one occasion the drunkard left his wife and children to fend for themselves; the wife earned a few dollars by taking in sewing or nursing the sick, while the children performed the chores in their crude cabin.[82]

Of course mistreatment of spouses was not always linked to alcohol. Some episodes stemmed from widespread acceptance of a man's right to treat his wife and children as lesser beings than himself. For example in customary Anglo wedding ceremonies, officials emphasized the imbalance between bride and groom. When the president of Luther College in Decorah, Iowa, performed an 1883 wedding, he told the bride that her husband's calling must be paramount, thus she could never be "first" with him.[83]

Congregations and other public bodies supported and defended such thinking regarding wives. When a Minnesota pastor of the same period proved stingy with his wife, she appealed to the members of his church, taking, in her words, "a stand against the Synod's teaching of a wife's blind and absolute obedience and subjection." Despite her protests the congregation voted overwhelmingly in favor of her husband.[84]

Throughout the nineteenth century, then, neglect and persecution re-sulted from widespread adherence to the idea of women's inferiority. Every-thing from nineteenth-century novels, newspaper accounts, U.S. Commissioner of Agriculture reports, and women's own writings indicate that spouse abuse occurred throughout the West.[85]

In 1935, when Nebraskan settler Mari Sandoz published her autobio-graphical *Old Jules*, she looked back on her father's settlement in north-western Nebraska beginning in 1884. Sandoz especially revealed the physical and emotional battering that many nineteenth-century frontierswomen tolerated. Not only was Sandoz's father, Jules, abusive, but another man kicked his wife until "she almost bled to death." In addi-tion Polish husbands forced their wives to walk three steps behind them, "peasant fashion," and treated them in other demeaning ways.[86]

These beliefs and behaviors continued into the early twentieth cen-tury. In 1909 a German-from-Russia wife in South Dakota regularly endured torment at the hands of her husband, yet never thought of leaving him. Similarly a Japanese immigrant to California, Akemi Kikumara, excused her husband's cruel treatment during the early 1900s, saying he had wanted to marry his brother-in-law's daughter, a beauti-ful geisha, instead of her. When Akemi's husband humiliated her or disappeared for weeks at a time, Akemi considered this his right and did not contemplate divorce.[87]

Yet another destructive ritual in the nineteenth- and early-twentieth-century American West involved public mockery, which deprived certain types of families of self-esteem and the will to persevere. Some of Mark Twain's work, such as *A Connecticut Yankee in King Arthur's Court* (1889) and *Pudd'nhead Wilson* (1894) made the splintered family, or the family in the throes of resolving internecine strife, appear normal and even amus-ing. At the same time, other people made fun of specific family categories in jokes, vaudeville sketches, songs, and stories, as well as on radio and in early motion pictures. Families of color, when they appeared at all, emerged as dysfunctional, exceptional, victimized, or threatening.[88]

Such imputations of inferiority offered a rationale for abuse and thus more pressure on families. For instance Antonia de Soza of Tucson re-membered that during the 1880s, men she identified as Texans would drink heavily at a saloon near her family's ranch, don masks to hide their iden-tity, and attack Spanish-speaking ranch families. De Soza remembered that on other occasions, local people, both Hispanic and Anglo, harassed

Apache and Chinese families living in Tucson, even forcing them out of public parks and off dance platforms on *fiesta* days.[89]

Love

Surprisingly romantic love also had its dark side. Expectations of companionship in marriage often led to disillusionment with marital realities. In the nineteenth-century West, expectations rose especially rapidly due to assertions emphasizing the right of every person to obtain satisfaction and happiness.[90]

At the same time, marital discontent seemed to erupt everywhere. Many disenchanted spouses simply ran away. In Louisiana Territory newspaper advertisements indicated that a significant number of desertions occurred. Husbands especially placed notices warning merchants to refuse credit to runaway wives. Later in the nineteenth century, police "wanted" posters from Oklahoma Territory indicated that women deserted their marriages in as large, or perhaps even larger proportion than men.[91]

Other unhappy spouses remained in their marriages but exhibited their disenchantment by complaining vociferously about sex. Although mates displayed reticence to discuss satisfying sexual relations, Victorian modesty evaporated among angry couples. Growing numbers of women protested in letters, journals, and divorce petitions that their husbands demanded sex far too frequently, a claim that often sounded a responsive chord in some Victorian-era judges, ministers, and other officials. Men's protests regarding unresponsive wives, however, elicited far less concern.[92]

To make up for the lack of romance in their marriages, numerous mates took lovers. Because many societies viewed men's affairs with more tolerance than women's, wives' complaints abounded. During the second decade of the 1900s, Californian Anita M. Baldwin protested that her husband was not only adulterous, but pursued his affairs at her expense: "He spent everything I saved on other women for lunches, dinner, etc. in French Restaurants—upstairs!!!"[93]

In some cultures women could also take lovers, escaping retribution as long as they chose from their same race and class. Women taking lovers proved especially acceptable among such groups as upper-class French- and Spanish-heritage peoples, whose families had forced them to marry against their wills for reasons of property, family alliances, or social class. Although it is difficult to prove the existence of lovers, documents sometimes reveal more than intended. Early nineteenth-century church and family records indicate, for instance, that while Marianne Decoux of Louisiana Territory married three times in the Catholic church and had no children with her husbands, when she died she left her plantation to her natural daughter.[94]

Among most groups, however, spouses tried to keep the existence of lovers a secret from mates. They seldom succeeded, and adultery frequently became public knowledge. During the mid-nineteenth century, California particularly gained notoriety for families riddled with adultery. In 1853 Daniel Dustin wrote to a relative in Quincy, Massachusetts, that it would astonish him "to notice the frequency of family difficulties resulting from the infidelity of husband or wife or both." Dustin explained that even upright women fell victim; in his view, "a woman's virtue cannot stand the test of California and *flattery* and *fine presents* are poured upon them in such profusion that they soon forget themselves."[95]

Often onlookers not only observed such adulterous relationships but also informed spouses of them. During the early 1860s, an Oklahoma slave woman, embittered by her mistress's beatings, told her master that his wife was "fiddling round with a neighbor man" while he was "out fighting the Yanks."[96]

In any event it is clear that some spouses who were disappointed with romantic love in their marriages sought it, or at least sexual satisfaction, elsewhere.

Community and Milieu

Community support for families often disappeared. During the nineteenth and early twentieth centuries, western families regularly relinquished much-needed community support to undertake migration. Pulling up their roots, Spanish-speaking people traveled northward, Anglos and African Americans westward, and Asians eastward, all toward what became the American West.

Besides leaving community networks behind, migrating families entered a hostile milieu. In 1849 one newspaper reporter warned potential migrants of the journey's perils, including dangerous routes, high prices, and a need for mothers to return home to find adequate schools when their children reached school age. Few people heeded such messages, however. In 1855 a woman traveled across the Isthmus of Panama, sailed to San Francisco, buried a son at sea, yet persevered until she reached Olympia in Washington Territory. She was less than cheerful by the time she reunited with her husband.[97]

The West also bristled with psychological hardships. For example despite repeated migrations, Mormons failed to escape bigotry in the West. As a consequence by the late nineteenth century, young Mormons tended to leave their family homes early, a high proportion initiating their own quests in search of a promised land.[98]

As a result of travails, sometimes one spouse refused to follow the other to the West or returned to his or her former home, leaving the other behind. In numerous instances both mates experienced dissatisfaction with the West, so they moved back to their previous home or forged their way even deeper into the West.[99] Extended separations afflicted numerous other marriages, with husbands especially leaving wives behind for long stretches of time to seek employment, travel on business, serve in the military, or work as itinerant preachers. Moreover Mormon men regularly pursued religious missions far from home or, after the 1887 prohibition of polygamy, "skipped" about the West or sought exile in England to escape detection and arrest. Such separated mates frequently wrote to each other of their loneliness, isolation, discouragement, and money problems.[100]

Other settlers, ranging from homesteaders to military families, lived with isolation, dirt, boredom, and perpetual fear of Native Americans.[101] On the nineteenth-century frontier that Hispanics called El Norte, scattered ranch families faced Indian resistance that involved revolts, attacks, arson, and death.[102] As Anglos increasingly entered this area, which they called the Southwest, they too found themselves fighting everything from loneliness to Indians.

Lack of money also caused anxiety for western families. Hard times turned even more dismal when such misfortunes as blizzards, drought, tornadoes, grasshopper plagues, illness, and accidents occurred. One Nevada woman wrote in 1907 that it broke her heart to see her miner husband, ill with consumption, seek jobs that "he had neither the health nor the strength to hold." This mother of five took up a homestead to keep her family together.[103]

Ironically surplus wealth and property plagued others. Western slave owners engaged in marital spats over disciplining slaves and the use of slave women as husbands' concubines.[104] Westerners interested in real estate rather than slaves also created family imbroglios. In an 1834 dispute concerning a young wife's property, one well-known Louisiana settler shot his daughter-in-law and, believing her dead, killed himself. Although she recovered, her marriage ended in a legal separation.[105]

Moreover westward migration disrupted families of color. African American westerners, relatively few in number in the West, lacked community support and were especially vulnerable to stress. In addition western slavery institutionalized widespread acceptance of abuse of black women and men, as well as sexual exploitation of black women, which slave and free-black husbands found themselves powerless to halt.[106] Like Anglos, Native Americans also journeyed to new areas west of the Mississippi River or, by the late nineteenth century, to western reservations. Their migrations put tremendous pressures on Indian families, including injury and death, poverty, and loss of property.[107]

To counter such intolerance, families tried to adapt to the expectations of the increasingly widespread and powerful Anglo culture in the West. As coping strategies, Chinese settlers of the early twentieth century learned English, adopted Anglo clothing styles, sought American education, and even embraced Christianity. Chinese parents also loosened their control of children, encouraging them, even daughters, to obtain education and choose careers.[108] All this required that Chinese families make numerous adjustments, even though family networks and other support institutions were thousands of miles away.

As the West developed during the early twentieth century, conditions for families usually failed to improve. Prejudice led to segregated housing and schools, while the vicissitudes of growing western cities placed more strain on marriages than did rural living. Consuelo Rocha of Laramie, Wyoming, remembered that local shopkeepers refused to serve her father during the 1920s. When attending movies the family had to sit in the upper balcony, and at school Anglo children verbally and physically attacked the Rocha children.[109]

Popular culture, moreover, increasingly suggested alternate ways of living without benefit of family. These images include such hardy types as single *soldaderas* (female soldiers) in Spanish literature or female Anglo literary characters who survived and even prospered in occupations ranging from madams to outlaws.[110]

Gender Roles

Traditional gender roles also disrupted family life. Gender functions, for example, often included onerous domestic labor for spouses, especially wives. Mourning Dove maintained that a nineteenth-century Salishan woman's work made "her old long before her time." According to Salishan custom, "if a husband needed anything, it was his wife who got it for him." Yet a Salishan woman "did not complain," because such work "was expected of her."[111]

Early twentieth-century Asian-heritage women often found their workloads overwhelming as well. A significant number of Japanese "picture brides" discovered that their husbands assumed they would labor not only in homes, but in fields, family businesses, or fishing enterprises as well. Similarly Korean wives who worked on Hawaiian sugar plantations spent ten hours a day in fields, then cared for their families and several boarders far into the night. Chinese men also expected wives, even those who worked outside their homes, to undertake domestic chores and participate in family businesses. According to one woman, the rare Chinese man who helped with housework was criticized as falling outside "the true Chinese tradition."[112]

Another destructive influence was the patriarchal family structure, which gave a husband the right to control and coerce his wife. As patriarchy spread over the nineteenth-century West, it often threw matrilineal and matriarchal cultures into disarray. In particular, Native American women lost domestic and public influence. Oglala women watched their power dissipate as a result of the establishment of reservation schools based on gender separation and concepts of gender inferiority, a division of labor that promoted dominant/subordinate gender roles, and family law favoring husbands.[113]

Chicanos also gradually adopted Anglo interpretations of patriarchy. When Spanish-speakers moved to Arizona during the nineteenth century, they carried with them a strong sense of tradition, family, and community, including expectations of cooperation between wives and husbands. But when others migrated to the Midwest during the 1920s, they accepted Anglo-style divisions of labor. Husbands became "breadwinners" and wives stayed home.[114]

Gradually reformers began to criticize such patriarchal principles. Nineteenth-century women and men charged that matrimonial expectations of women amounted to little more than slavery, while others called for an end to patriarchy.[115] The women's-rights movement and demands for woman suffrage, which emerged from Iowa to California, reinforced such thinking.[116] But as customary ideas regarding gender roles altered, change itself upset families. New questions confronted spouses: should wives seek paid employment outside their homes? Should mates make decisions together, or should some matters remain the prerogative of the husband? These and other vexing issues tore at the very fiber of those western families who could not satisfactorily resolve them.

Children

Children also provided their share of family duress. Thus some societies limited numbers of children to those that they could adequately support and raise. During the nineteenth century, Native American women used roots and herbs to prevent conception or induce abortion. Also many Indian groups encouraged wives to place limits on sexual intercourse and to avoid it entirely while nursing a baby. Delay of intercourse might last as long as three or four years, but among the Cheyenne some women nursed until their children reached nine or ten years of age.[117]

Among western settlers a different philosophy prevailed. Roman Catholics and other pronatal groups such as Mormons often opposed birth control and abortion, at least in public statements if not in private practices. Even non-Catholics and non-Mormons believed they had a responsibility to populate the frontier. Still migrants must have employed patent medicines and birth-control devices to some degree, for falling western fertility rates during the nineteenth century paralleled rates in the Northeast, where birth control was used.[118]

Newspaper advertisements also indicate that Anglo wives, distressed at the thought of yet another pregnancy, turned to patent medicines subtly advertised as abortants. In an 1859 advertisement, James Clarke's Celebrated Female Pills claimed to provide a "Remedy for Female Obstructions and difficulties from any cause whatsoever." This medication was said to have special appeal to "Married Ladies," for whom it would "bring on the monthly period with regularity."[119] Thousands of women spent hard-earned money on such tablets, in hopes of purchasing salvation from further childbearing.

Nor did husbands always want more children. Some used condoms or coitus interruptus to avoid conception or expected their wives to take precautions. When in 1890 Cynthia Pringle told her husband she was pregnant with their third child, he blamed her for negligence and demanded a separation. Although she begged him to reconsider, Pringle had the necessary papers drawn up, bought train tickets, and sent Cynthia and their children to her parents' home in Wisconsin.[120]

Despite attempts to control fertility and a resultant drop in the birth rate, western family size remained substantial, even by contemporary standards. One study of the Dakotas during the 1880s indicated that only 10 percent of families did not have children. The median length of time between date of marriage and a first birth was a mere twelve months. Variations in family size depended upon such factors as ethnicity, social class, and religious affiliation. More specifically, German-from-Russia women in North Dakota bore a median of 7.5 children, Norwegian-born women a median of 6.6 children, and American-born women a median of 3.9 children. Among Anglo western women, for example, German-from-Russia women had one of the greatest birth rates, with families ranging to between ten and eighteen children.[121]

In addition childbirth tended to be more difficult in the West, especially during migration, in rural areas, and in urban ghettoes and barrios. With doctors scarce and midwives frequently unavailable, childbirth constituted a high-risk affair for mother and child.[122] As one North Dakota woman described another who gave birth in 1881, "childbirth was without an attending doctor. Nature was allowed to take its course." As a result some women chose to return to their families back home to await the birth of their babies, thus depriving husbands of seeing their newborns.[123]

Child death created yet another dilemma. Women and men wrote poignant accounts of making coffins for dead infants, enduring wrenching grief after a child's death, or burying a child in one place and then moving on to another.[124] When asked how many children they had, women typically enumerated both living and dead. One Montana woman who married in 1874 recounted her family in such terms: "after six years, a baby girl came to our home, who died in July, 1893, at the age of 13 1/2 years. Another baby girl lived only one month. Then a baby boy, who still lives."[125]

If children survived infancy, they might pose other difficulties for families. Large numbers of children were physically, mentally, and economically taxing to wives and husbands. As a South Dakota woman of the late 1890s said of one sizable family: "while the mother was kept busy finding employment for six pairs of hands and feet and six very active brains, the father was kept equally busy getting the bacon for six hungry mouths."[126]

Ineffective socialization of children and resulting misconduct also troubled many western families. Early in the twentieth century, Nez Perces of Idaho, for example, experienced such culture chaos as a result of contact with Anglos that communal discipline declined and juvenile delinquency increased. At the same time, delinquency contributed to a rise in marital instability, which in turn aggravated the problem of delinquency.[127]

Religion

Religion also troubled some western families. When one group of people forced its religious beliefs upon another, unsettled family life sometimes resulted. As a case in point, nineteenth-century Oglala people divided among themselves when members embraced a variety of Christian denominations. Similarly at Pine Ridge, South Dakota, a once-unified Sioux people often brought disparate Christian beliefs and values to marriage.[128]

Throughout the nineteenth and early twentieth centuries, differences of religious opinion plagued other westerners as well. Catholics who married other Catholics, Jews who married Jews, Mennonites who married Mennonites, and Buddhists who married Buddhists experienced more marital satisfaction than those who wed outside their faith. Also Mormon same-faith marriages in Utah and the mountain states enjoyed a high success rate, while Mormon-gentile unions proved far less enduring.[129]

Religious beliefs also upset western families who tried unsuccessfully to adapt their faith to the West. Roman Catholics needed a church hierarchy and substantial buildings, while Jews needed synagogues and sabbath schools. South Dakotan Sophie Trupin recalled her mother agonizing about her inability to follow Jewish proscriptions, keep kosher, and send her children to a synagogue school. Sophie's mother had married a man with a similar background, and their early life together had proved compatible, yet she ultimately failed to make the transition from the Old World to the late nineteenth- and early-twentieth-century American West.[130]

Plural Marriage

Plural marriage too hurt some cultures' families more than others. While nineteenth-century Native Americans generally lived easily with plural marriage and received relatively little criticism, Mormons paid a tremendous price for plural marriage.[131] Their belief in and support of plural marriage placed Mormons in physical and social isolation from other Anglo Christians, who expected them to act in a "more civilized" fashion. Mormons' obedience to polygynous teachings also resulted in vitriolic censure. Critics freely labeled Mormons barbarians, stupid, cruel, and demoralized, while non-Mormon women publicly indicted Mormon women.[132]

Plural marriage also divided couples who held differing opinions regarding it. A number of Mormon wives who objected to their husbands taking additional wives complained regarding uncaring husbands, other wives' jealousy, and unfair treatment of children. Consequently beginning in 1847, church leaders granted divorces to unhappily wed polygynous people.[133]

Despite the availability of divorce for plural marriages, wives continued to protest. During the early 1880s, Mary Pomeroy of Mesa, Arizona, was distraught about her husband's decision to take a second wife. Although Pomeroy persevered in her marriage, she summed up many women's feelings about plural marriage when she wrote "polygamy was a great trial to me. Nobody but one who is in it knows the many heartaches which one goes through while living that order."[134]

Intramarriage

Endogamous marriages also experienced tensions, ranging from monotony to interference by relatives, other members of a congregation, or ethnic/racial organizations. Perhaps the most serious danger of endogamy, however, was marrying so closely that the union was consanguineous.

Consanguinity occurred frequently enough and created enough resulting weaknesses in children that by the late nineteenth and early twentieth centuries every western state attempted to prevent it through marriage-licensing restrictions. Idaho, for example, banned marriage between first cousins, but Kansas forbade marriages between parents and children, grandparents and grandchildren of any degree, brothers and sisters, uncles and nieces, aunts and nephews, and first cousins. Texas prohibited people from marrying an ancestor or descendant by either blood or adoption, a brother or sister, or a parent's brother or sister.[135]

Conclusion

In the American West during the nineteenth and early twentieth centuries, then, identical factors proved to have either fusing or rending consequences for western families. That being the case, why did some families achieve relative harmony, whereas a growing number buckled internally or even dissolved?

For one thing, success or failure had to do with a couple's cultural values. People who grew up in a society favoring polygyny were far more likely to accept and live contentedly with plural marriage than were men and women who came to maturity believing in monogamy.

Also crucial was the era. The Roman Catholic church, for example, gradually lost some of its influence over members. During the nineteenth century, the parish church bound families together, but by the twentieth century, Catholic families had scattered, thus becoming increasingly vulnerable to destructive forces.[136]

Individual spouses also exerted significant influence on a marriage's success or failure. Spouses' personalities, expectations, and emotional baggage directly affected the way they reacted to outside pressure.[137]

A marriage also developed its own personality. According to the contemporary "systems" approach to family dynamics, all spouses, and eventually their children, establish a distinct pattern of interaction. Thus two similar families might experience parallel situations yet respond in dissimilar ways.[138]

Finally and perhaps most crucial of all, whether stimuli proved affirming or damaging often depended upon regional factors. Marital strains and tensions flourished in the nineteenth- and early-twentieth-century West. At the same time, the tremendous diversity of western families and their responses to stress provided inconsistent models for those who would someday marry.

Moreover western values and beliefs themselves helped erode the institution of marriage. In terms of family life, the American West comprised a unique region, providing a rich medium for family experimentation, change, and transition. Individualism and the search for happiness, satisfaction, and fulfillment became a widespread and much touted ideology.

In such a situation, couples found it easier to lose patience with each other, as well as with the forces that buffeted them. Rather than encouraging mates to tolerate each other and confront their problems, western ideas regarding marriage and family increasingly allowed discontented spouses to ignore, abuse, abandon, or even divorce their mates with impunity—offering yet other unfortunate models and messages to younger generations.

3

Intermarrying:
Why So Difficult?

During the nineteenth and early twentieth centuries, western women and men generally chose to marry people similar to themselves in terms of age, religion, social class, ethnic origin, and especially race.[1] Given the diverse nature of western peoples, however, cross-cultural encounters, courtships, and marriages inevitably occurred. In spite of myriad barriers, people found each other in workplaces, schools, and social situations, and decided to marry.

Because intermarriage statistics are problematic (see discussion below), it cannot be demonstrated that more intermarriage existed in the West than in other regions. But studies do indicate that such western marriages experienced a high failure rate and thus contributed significantly to the West's spiraling divorce rate. As a western group with a striking divorce rate, then, intermarried couples and the additional pressures under which they lived deserve exploration.

In the nineteenth- and early-twentieth-century West, a paradoxical and destructive situation unfolded for intermarried spouses. Even though intermarriage regularly occurred between members of Native American groups, and later between Native Americans and incoming Europeans, intermarriage failed to gain acceptance among many westerners.[2] On the contrary, as intermarriage increased in the American West, so did negative attitudes, restrictive policies, and legal prohibitions. Like the American South, western states prohibited black/white marriages, but many also banned white/Asian and sometimes white/Indian marriages. At least in the South, discrimination against intermarriages was clear. In the West, however, such prejudice was masked by the prevalent belief, both in the United States and Europe, that the American West constituted a land of egalitarianism and opportunity.

In the matter of intermarriage, then, the American West comprised a unique situation, one that has largely escaped scholarly notice as a regional phenomenon.[3] Not only did the West offer people the chance to marry others unlike themselves and then heap dishonor on them for doing so, but the West, which symbolized freedom of choice, carried repression of intermarriage to a new high in the United States.

It is not surprising that western marriages between disparate spouses had difficulty surviving, much less flourishing. Most experts maintain that western intermarriages exhibited a higher divorce rate than intramarriages, marriages between members of the same group. Even though such factors as educational level, age, income, ethnic and cultural ties, and social class complicate the establishment of such divorce rates, it seems clear that intermarriages faced particular difficulties that often led to divorce. Thus it seems fair to contend that the harsh environment in which western intermarriages functioned and their degree of failure contributed significantly to marital instability and a climbing divorce rate in the American West.

Defining the Boundaries

Usually intermarriage refers to the union of a member of one racial, ethnic, religious, or other specific group to a person of another. As the distance and dissimilarities between such an intermarried pair increase, so do potentially destructive dynamics.[4] Thus the most troubled form of intermarriage involved spouses of different races, who often brought ethnic, religious, social-class, or other divergences to marriage as well.

Intermarriages occurred in the American West even before Europeans appeared, when members of one Indian tribal group married women or men of another indigenous nation. During the 1500s Native Americans began to marry arriving Europeans. Although we know that early westerners tended to marry across racial and other lines, accurate numbers of intermarriages cannot be determined for the West, past or present.

Information gleaned from marriage and divorce records has proved fragmentary and inaccurate. More specifically, U.S. Census Bureau statistics were collected only erratically. In 1887 the U.S. Congress directed U.S. Commissioner of Labor Carrol D. Wright to compile, for the first time, marriage and divorce statistics in all states and territories between 1867 and 1886. Even though Wright's staff inquired about race and ethnicity of people that married and divorced, local jurisdictions seldom recorded these characteristics. During a second collection period, 1887 to 1906, Wright's field-workers again attempted to ascertain race and ethnicity of spouses, but discovered that local records still omitted such information.[5]

During the twentieth century, collection of marriage and divorce data remained uneven. Census-bureau officials did not gather statistics during the World War I years or between 1933 and 1936, the height of the Great Depression. Beginning in 1941 World War II interrupted data accumulation for several more few years. In 1954 the Census Bureau established the Marriage Registration Area (MRA), a reporting scheme that included questions regarding race and ethnicity. But when the MRA began operation in 1957, not all states joined the system. Trans-Mississippi states that entered the MRA were California, Idaho, Iowa, Kansas, Montana, Oregon, South Dakota, and Wyoming. In 1958 a similar plan, known as the Divorce Registration Area (DRA) began, which included the trans-Mississippi states of Alaska, Hawaii, Idaho, Iowa, Montana, Nebraska, Oregon, South Dakota, Utah, and Wyoming.[6]

In addition to irregular data collection, it is difficult to enumerate intermarriages because people who married and divorced identified themselves in equivocal ways. Even though MRA and DRA officials inquired about such characteristics as nationality, they encountered widespread misconceptions of such classifications. In Linn County, Iowa, for example, a sample of divorce records between 1928 and 1944 revealed that most litigants gave their nationality as American. Others evidently failed to grasp the concept, for they replied that their nationality was Iowan, Kansan, Missourian, Jewish, white, Yankee, "redskin," or unknown.[7]

Complicating marriage and divorce records still further are unclear cases involving "part" Indians or "one-fourth" Asians. Did such people report themselves as Anglo, Indian, or Asian?[8] In addition other people who hoped to "pass" as members of Anglo society frequently reported inaccurately to obliterate their racial heritage. Still others rebelled against questions regarding race or ethnicity by giving false information. Finally after the civil rights movement of the 1960s, a trend developed to eliminate racial and ethnic classifications from public records or to limit availability of this information to researchers.[9]

Even if numbers of intermarriages could be ascertained, the role of racial or other differences in a marriage's success or failure remains unclear. Although the racial and ethnic affiliation of a couple might appear in the record, usually little was said regarding the role of race or ethnicity in a couple's relationship. Even in case of divorce, litigants often skipped over genuine causes of discord and cited one of a state's legal grounds. For instance because Iowa allowed intermarriage between 1928 and 1944, three interracial marriages appeared in sampled data. In two cases white wives sued black husbands for divorce. Neither wife mentioned interracial problems, which may or may not have been a causal factor, but instead tailored their petitions to fit Iowa's six legal grounds: adultery, desertion for a period of two years, conviction for a felony after marriage, habitual drunkenness after marriage, and prior pregnancy of a wife by a man other than the husband. In the third case of intermarriage and divorce, an Anglo wife sued her Native American husband for divorce, again choosing one of Iowa's six accepted grounds. She charged her husband with cruelty because he had, she testified, struck her and "damned and vilified" her.[10]

One last complicating force in defining and counting intermarriages has originated more recently. During the 1980s and early 1990s, deconstructionist scholars eschewed racial and other categories and argued that lines dividing people of different races, ethnicities, religions, and other affiliations were artificially constructed to serve society's ends.[11] Although this is a valid and significant point, racial and other classifications were certainly real to the people who lived within their constraints and hesitated to defy such boundaries.

Why Intermarry?

Given the problems surrounding intermarriage, one might well ask why some westerners chose to marry across racial and other lines. In part the answer lies in the mobility of male westerners. Men, who largely initiated such matches, migrated to western areas, where they were unable to find wives of their racial or ethnic group. Thus they sought wives among local women. Another part of the answer relates to western women, who inaugurated cross-courtships and intermarriages less actively than men. When women, who stayed home and who tolerated more parental control than men, intermarried, they did so largely because they hoped to make a step upward in social class or derive some other benefit.[12] Finally western men and women chose intermarriage because they preferred, or developed love for, people of other groups.

Generally, then, western men and women intermarried in one of three situations: when like mates were unavailable or one group was large and another small; when a marriage to a disparate spouse offered an advantage, either individually or to the person's kin group; or when the members of one group favored or loved spouses of another.

When mates in one's own group were unavailable or when one group was large and another small, intermarriage thrived. For instance, Native Americans far outnumbered Spanish men who entered the Southwest during the 1600s. Thus, Indian women and Spanish men commonly married one another. Many of these unions not only endured but changed the composition of the population by producing generations of mixed-blood offsprings termed *mestizos*.[13]

Farther north, at Fort Vancouver during the early 1800s, Native Americans also outnumbered white soldiers and officers. Anglo men thus courted native women by personally currying favor with them, or by negotiating marriage arrangements with their families. Fort Vancouver records indicate that most Anglos selected a woman, then approached her father with an offer of guns, blankets, rum, and other trade goods.[14] Such Fort Vancouver couples usually married in the "custom of the country," that is, according to Native American rituals rather than Anglo law. This included Dr. John McLoughlin, later chief factor of Fort Vancouver between 1825 and 1845, and his part-Indian wife, Marguerite McKay, when they married at Fort William sometime around 1820. Although these relationships resulted from imbalanced sex ratios, they offered mutual gain to spouses. Indian women generally achieved higher status and ownership of additional goods, while Anglo men obtained companionship, sex, affection, and ease of trade with Indian peoples.[15]

Lopsided sex ratios usually disappeared as explorers, trappers, and settlers entered any given area of the West, yet some peoples continued to experience uneven conditions. Throughout the nineteenth century, western African American men outnumbered African American women by almost two to one. By necessity, then, African American men sought mates from other racial groups.[16] Because African American intermarriage also resulted in mixed-heritage offspring, usually called mulattoes, the West's black population changed rapidly. By 1860 the female black population in California increased nearly seven times, but almost half were categorized as mulatto (740 total). And although black males living in California doubled in number, four of every ten (1,370 total) were mulattoes. Only a decade later, the figures had risen to 671 black females, 607 mulatto females, and 4 unidentified, for a total of 1,282 women; 1,776 black males, 1,137 mulatto males, and 3 unidentified totaled 2,915 black men.[17]

In early twentieth-century California, Sikhs also lived with skewed sex ratios. Because of U.S. immigration laws restricting the entry of Sikh women, Sikh men who immigrated as workers from India lacked potential spouses. Predictably they suffered from isolation and loneliness and married women from the larger population living around them, especially Spanish-heritage women.[18]

Later yet in the twentieth century, when Patti Fong arrived in Minneapolis with her family during the 1940s, she discovered that Chinese people formed a distinct minority of the population. Although Patti's parents preferred her to date Chinese men, few attended her school. When in high school Patti seriously dated an Anglo man, her parents suggested that the family consult a matchmaker on her behalf. Although she refused this offer, after graduation Patti moved to San Francisco to please her family and meet more Chinese men. After her persistent Anglo suitor followed her to San Francisco, the couple eventually married. Patti later remarked that in some ways "it probably might have been better" if she had married a Chinese man rather than a member of the dominant population in Minnesota.[19]

There are also many instances of spouses hoping to achieve some benefit from the union. Beverly Hungry Wolf, a member of the Blackfeet tribe, explained that before contact with Europeans, her people practiced intertribal marriage, largely to increase the Blackfeet population. Courtship consisted of Blackfeet men seizing women of another tribe, bringing the hostages back to the village, and appraising these women's skills. If captive women proved pliant and able to work, their Blackfeet captors married them. Frequently such intermarriages not only expanded the Blackfeet people, but increased the number of childbearing women among them.[20]

Besides native peoples, early French, British, and American government officials also foresaw potential gain in intermarriage. Accordingly they encouraged marriage between Native American women and Anglo male explorers, trappers, and settlers. French officials, who hoped to offset the shortage of marriageable French women, offered "dowries" to Frenchmen who married Native American women. French policymakers also expected such French/Indian marriages to cement political alliances, stabilize society, and produce children, called métis, who would become French citizens. Similarly, British officials favored intermarriage between native women and Englishmen, because they aspired to forge alliances that would halt conflict between natives and British migrants, and because they wanted to "civilize" and Christianize Indians.[21]

American government leaders pursued a similar line of reasoning. As early as 1784, Virginia legislator Patrick Henry introduced a bill in the Virginia House of Delegates that, if passed, would offer tax relief, free education, and ten-pound bonuses to whites who married Native Americans. Although the Virginia House rejected Henry's bill, other American officials later presented similar arguments. In 1816 Secretary of War William Crawford recommended that, if other attempts at harmony failed, the U.S. government should encourage intermarriage between Native Americans and Americans. Again numerous policymakers objected, saying that intermarriage caused more problems than it solved. In line with the latter belief, the U.S. government eventually adopted a policy restricting Indians and whites from marrying, rather than supporting such unions.[22]

Despite positive and negative government policies regarding intermarriage, some native women and their families desired intermarriage with Anglo men for the benefits that might ensue. Because many Native Americans judged Anglo men more economically stable and of higher status than native men, they frequently accepted Anglo proposals of marriage. In a representative case, Eagle Woman, a Teton Sioux in South Dakota, married first Honoré Picotte, general agent for the American Fur Company at Fort Pierre, and then in 1850 the fur trader Charles Galpin. Eagle Woman enjoyed a higher standard of living at fur posts than she would have in her own village and achieved higher status among her people. Her husbands profited from her language skills, knowledge of Indian customs, and tribal connections, which led to trade advantages.[23]

For similar reasons, some Spanish-speaking women in the Southwest (although not as many as usually reported) also married Anglo men (this phenomenon is discussed in more detail below). Like Native American women, some Spanish-speaking women viewed Anglo men as more economically mobile and of higher status than men of their own group.[24] Because a certain number of Spanish-speaking parents and family members shared their daughters' views, they sponsored parties and fiestas to create courting opportunities. During the 1850s a young Anglo soldier attended such an event in San Antonio and afterwards noted that "two or three of the bloods of Castile were present." According to him, wealthy parents of Spanish-speaking women hoped that their daughters would marry "genuine Americans."[25]

The personal preference or love of members of one group for people of another also occurred with regularity in the American West. Westerners chose partners outside their groups because they judged them more attractive, sexual, romantic, or harder-working than people of their own kind. During the 1800s observers in the Southwest reported that Spanish-speaking women viewed Anglo men as exotic and adventurous. At the same time, Anglo men appraised Spanish-speaking woman as beautiful, sensuous, and loyal. In 1841 when American George Kendall marched across New Mexico, he rhapsodized that Spanish-speaking women were not only lovely, but also "joyous, sociable, kind-hearted creatures almost universally liberal to a fault, easy and naturally graceful in their manners."[26]

Farther north, Anglo men in Alaska came to similar conclusions regarding Tlingit women. Many Anglo men deemed Tlingit women attractive, sexual, industrious, and agreeable. One man who married a Tlingit woman, and after her death married a second, explained his preference for such wives: "They were fine pardners, good workers, good fish cutters and I got used to the fish smell and loved them both very much."[27]

Alongside preference as a cause of intermarriage came romantic love. Legends regarding star-crossed Native American women and Anglo men underscore the occurrence of romantic love across cultures. Such stories derived from truth, for romantic courtships did occur between Indian women and white men. These courtships frequently led to affectional relationships that resulted in stable, long-term marriages, either by "custom of the country" or Anglo law. As proof of their attachment to Indian wives, a significant number of Anglo men chose to remain with their wives' people even after retirement, when trade advantages no longer mattered. Other so-called "squaw men" left behind the censure of their own people to live in mixed-blood settlements. As a case in point, in 1839 trader Lancaster Lupton married a Cheyenne woman named Tomasina; in 1846 they settled in the Indian-Anglo community of Hardscrabble, Colorado.[28]

Today, however, social scientists frequently credit neither positive judgments nor the presence of love as a motivating force for intermarriage. Instead most contemporary researchers maintain that preference for marriage to a member of another group resulted from complementary needs; that is, people found compensating characteristics in "unsuitable" mates.[29] Such needs might be positive, including nurturance, or coming to the aid of a weak or attacked person; recognition, or gaining praise for performing a socially constructive act such as intermarrying; or achievement, working with another person to create something against sizable odds. Complementary needs might also be negative, including abasement, or purposefully inviting shame or criticism; dominance, or controlling a weaker person; and hostility, or commanding another persons.[30]

Migration and Intermarriage

Of course before cross-courtship and intermarriage could occur, groups of people had to meet and mix. One factor that brought people together in the West was war, ranging from the intertribal conflicts such as those described by Beverly Hungry Wolf to the Civil War and world wars. Even more importantly migration caused peoples to mingle, thus making cross-cultural courtship and marriage possible. Later, as migration caused western areas to became more crowded, people increasingly met in such institutional settings as work or school.

As peoples associated in the American West, two trends emerged in cross-courtship and intermarriage. These patterns grew out of attitudes of indigenous peoples, size and demeanor of the incoming groups, and potential benefits or threats posed by migrants.

In the first pattern that emerged, a significant portion of native residents accepted and intermingled with migrants. Local people not only tolerated but even endorsed newcomers. Native residents thus facilitated courtship and marriage, especially between native daughters and migrant men. Such ease of blending, which occurred among Native Americans, Spanish-speaking peoples, and Hawaiian peoples, resulted largely from native peoples' desire to absorb newcomers into their societies, particularly through marriage. Of course native residents had no way of foretelling the huge numbers of migrants who would arrive and simply assumed that they themselves would remain numerically dominant and able to absorb migrants with ease.

At least partly as a result of such beliefs, most Native Americans welcomed and married Spaniards when they arrived in what is today Mexico and the American Southwest. Later during the 1700s and 1800s, residents of the area, including mestizos, similarly married incoming French-Canadians and Americans. Intermarriage occurred especially in New Mexico's Río Arriba area, a center of Spanish culture, which lay between the Sangre de Cristo Mountains on the east and the San Juan and Jemez Mountains on the west. Taos reportedly became something of a marriage mecca, although figures indicate that Spanish-speaking women who married migrant men comprised only a small portion of the native population. Usually closely chaperoned, Spanish-speaking women met Anglo men at parties, fiestas, and weddings. After marriage most lived in Taos or Santa Fe.[31]

In California such elite families as the Bandinis, Sepulvedas, Picos, and Yorbas reportedly also married their daughters to newly arrived Anglo men, probably in hopes of tying Anglo intruders to the Californio ruling class.[32] Soon Los Angeles became a center for intermarriage, not only between Spanish-speaking people and Anglos, but between Spanish-speakers and Indians, Asians, and occasionally African Americans.[33]

Farther west in Hawaii, migration led to intermarriage between Native Hawaiians and new residents. Because Hawaii drew migrants from Polynesia, Japan, the Philippines, and China, many Native Hawaiians believed they had little choice other than to absorb the newcomers. Chinese migrants, for example, arrived in Hawaii around 1788, pioneered the development of the sugar industry, which Polynesian settlers had started, and quickly learned to speak Hawaiian.[34] Rather than absorbing these Chinese and others, however, Hawaiians soon discovered that immigration and intermarriage altered the population composition of the area. In 1853 only 364 Chinese lived in Hawaii, but this figure rose to 18,254 by 1884. Similarly in 1866 only 1,640 part-Hawaiians existed, but in 1896 there were 8,480, or approximately five times as many. By the turn of the twentieth century, Chinese accounted for nearly a quarter of Hawaii's total population. By 1910 half of Hawaii's population was foreign-born.[35]

Such cataclysmic alterations in local populations caused the development of a second pattern of cross-courtship and intermarriage in the West. This trend, which proved more pervasive than the first, began with ease of intermarriage during early years of migration and settlement, but soon gave way to growing resistance as numbers of migrants increased. Typically this model occurred in localities where Anglos first lived in small numbers among native inhabitants; then increasing numbers of Anglos arrived; and finally Anglos became the numerical majority and dominant force.

Growing resistance to immigration and intermarriage occurred for several reasons. For one thing, the arrival of numerous migrants activated feelings of group identity, which led, in turn, to the emergence of racial prejudice and opposition. Soon gone were the days when local residents married newcomers without eliciting scorn from their own people. For instance in rural Alaska during the 1890s, the wedding of a blond Swedish man and a dark-haired Creole woman elicited congratulations from the villagers rather than disdain.[36] And when Ava Day's grandparents, a white/

black couple, homesteaded in the Sand Hills of Nebraska beginning in 1907, they lived free of discrimination from their neighbors. "Color never made a difference to Grandpa," Day explained. Although Day's grandparents may have found acceptance because a white man married a black woman, rather than the reverse, Day added that acceptance of intermarriage of any kind soon waned in Nebraska.[37]

A comparable yet more complicated pattern of tightening attitudes toward racial intermarriage occurred in Indian Territory (later Oklahoma). During the 1820s the U.S. government's relocation policy forced Native Americans and African Americans, who were often slave property of Indians, to move westward. Beginning in 1839 Cherokee regulations forbade the marriage of Indians and slaves. But after the 1863 emancipation of slaves, Native Americans and African Americans in Indian Territory occasionally intermarried. Lena Barnett was the product of one such marriage. Daughter of a former slave mother and a Cherokee Indian father, Lena attended an Indian school and, probably sometime during the 1870s, married a Creek Indian.[38] During the 1880s, however, Oklahoma Indians began to perceive marriage to African Americans as a threat to their racial "purity." For instance Choctaws and Chickasaws prohibited by legislation Indian/black marriages. In 1885 the Choctaw council passed a law making black/Choctaw intermarriage a felony, and in 1888 the Chickasaw National Party enacted a resolution opposing "the adoption of the Negro in any way, shape, or form."[39]

A second force that destroyed local peoples' initial willingness to integrate migrants derived from residents' growing recognition that natives could never incorporate all newcomers. On the contrary natives themselves faced possible absorption. Thus to maintain their cultures, local peoples had to separate themselves from migrants. Even though many native residents had once favored intermarriage and potential amalgamation of migrants, they soon opposed intermarriage to protect themselves.

For instance Spanish-speaking women in the Southwest, especially those of the upper class, grew hesitant to dilute their family lines and power. Rather than interpreting an Anglo's proposal of marriage as a compliment, Spanish-speaking women came to consider such an offer a threat. Seeing such a marriage proposal as a symbol of invasion, these women increasingly declined.

In fact statistics indicate that resistance on the part of Spanish-speaking peoples appeared as early as the 1820s. Although the Mexican government's colonization decree of 1823 offered citizenship rights, and thus trade privileges, to those who married Mexican citizens, few liaisons resulted. Between 1821 and 1846 in the Río Arriba area, then the center of Spanish civilization in the Southwest, only 122 intermarriages and co-habitations (or common-law intermarriages) occurred between Spanish-speaking women and male migrants, including French-Canadians, Americans, and a few Europeans. Moreover even though some scholars point to 1829 as a peak year for intermarriage, a total of 13 intermarriages does not appear highly significant. If Spanish-speaking women and their families accepted and appreciated Anglo suitors, surely more intermarriages would have occurred. Even when the Mexican government added land privileges to the list of perquisites, the number of intermarriages remained low and even declined.[40]

Again Indian Territory exhibited a slightly different pattern. Indians, who by the post-Civil War years regarded themselves as native to the area, at first married incoming whites with relative spontaneity, often through "Indian custom," or common-law marriages. Besides Native American women marrying Anglo men, a significant number of Indian men in Indian Territory married white women.[41] As growing numbers of Anglos arrived, Native Americans felt threatened and even feared that Indian Territory would become an American state. When in 1890 the U.S. Congress transformed Indian Territory into Oklahoma Territory and opened former Indian lands to Anglo claimants, Native Americans evidently found it impossible or perhaps detrimental to retreat from intermarriage entirely. In addition the U.S. government's offer of land allotments and other benefits to Indians encouraged Anglos to court and marry them.

Oklahoma Indians thus attempted to protect themselves legally. Although an Indian could marry another Indian simply by registering with a court clerk, during the 1890s Article XV, Section 68 of Cherokee regulations tightened earlier Cherokee restraints on intermarriage. This article required Anglos who desired to marry Indians to apply for a marriage license. An Anglo man or woman had to present a certificate of "good moral character," signed by ten "respectable Cherokee citizens by blood," swear allegiance to the Cherokee nation, and undergo a formal wedding ceremony conducted by a clerk or ordained minister. By virtue of such marriages, Anglo spouses took on Indian citizenship and became eligible for allotments and other government programs.[42]

Anti-intermarriage attitudes on the part of native populations often jibed well with the attitudes of migrants. Usually Anglo, these settlers increasingly regarded Native peoples as inferior to themselves. For instance, as Anglos became the dominant force in Oklahoma Territory, wielded growing power, and filled positions of importance, they appeared to have eschewed intermarriage with Indians. Anecdotal evidence suggests that the halcyon days of Indian/Anglo marriage were over and that growing numbers of Anglos preferred to marry other Anglos. Teacher Mabel Beavers, for example, recalled the occasion in 1907 when a father of an Indian pupil began visiting her classroom. Mabel concluded that the man was calling simply "to see that the boy had a fair deal," but when the man proposed marriage to Beavers, she, to her surprise, learned differently. Beavers recalled that "I declined with thanks."[43]

In what is today Washington state, Charles Throssell observed a comparable tendency on the part of Anglo settlers to avoid marriage to Indians. Throssell and his family arrived in Washington via wagon train in 1889. Although early Anglos in the Fort Vancouver area had married Indian women, Throssell watched children of settlers shun such intermarriage. One exception was May Dougherty, who Throssell described as leading a "western life" because she rode horseback and made friends with Native people. After May married an educated, "full blood Indian," the couple successfully farmed until May's death sometime during the 1930s or 1940s. Throssell's comments made it clear, however, that May's people regarded her as an anomaly at best and a failure at worst.[44]

Role of Family and Community

Clearly western cross-courtships and intermarriages faced a host of societal barriers, but these courtships and marriages also ran into numerous other types of opposition. Because family members typically played a key role in whether a person married within his or her group or outside it, family antagonism proved especially devastating to a couple who wished to intermarry.[45]

In spite of tales that portrayed Native families as welcoming "outside" suitors, not all proved receptive. Although Native Americans especially had the reputation of "selling" or giving their daughters to Anglo husbands, individual incidents refute this supposition. As a case in point, in Washington Territory during the 1850s, Frederick Perkins's marriage to an Indian woman drew enmity from her people, who banished her as punishment for marrying a white man.[46]

Similarly even though Spanish-speaking parents were often portrayed as amenable to their daughters marrying Anglos, this characterization was largely a stereotype. For one thing such information regarding Spanish-speaking parents usually originated with Anglo informants, who publicized fiestas and other courting opportunities beyond their actual number or importance. Migrant Josiah Gregg wrote prodigiously about New Mexican parents' willingness to arrange daughters' marriages to Anglo men, while George Ruxton depicted a similar situation in Taos. In reality Spanish-speaking parents were highly selective regarding marriage proposals. Migrant Dick Wooten learned this to his dismay, when the parents of his lover vehemently refused his suit. He persevered and planned to abduct their daughter, who crushed her parents' objections when she leapt onto Wooten's horse and rode off with him.[47]

If indeed Spanish-speaking parents were open to the intermarriage of their daughters, they were probably of the lower classes, rather than the middle and upper strata. People of modest income or less stood to gain the most in economic and social-class improvement through intermarriage. People of higher status, who stood to gain little through intermarriage, could hold themselves aloof from it.[48]

Generational change also influenced marital decision-making, with each generation typically demonstrating more or less openness to the idea of intermarriage than had their parents. In Oklahoma Mollie Beavers explained that in her family's case, the attitudes of the children were far more liberal than those of the parents. Although Mollie's father had spent a lifetime preaching to his daughters against intermarriage with Indians, after his death several Native American neighbors "were so kind" that Beavers's sister married one of them. Beavers concluded that "we have always been glad that she did."[49]

Another factor influencing parents' willingness to accept intermarriage derived from the nature of the racial or ethnic group under consideration. Some groups favored matches that demanded minimal adjustment, perhaps a German Anglo marrying an Irish Anglo, but opposed unions that would entail more adaptation, such as an Asian marrying an Anglo. In other cases some groups were less open and willing to mix than others. Asians, for example, typically encouraged their children to court and marry Asians. First-generation parents especially objected to intermarriage and attempted to prevent their children from dating non-Asians.[50]

Among Asian immigrants, Japanese families perhaps placed greatest stress on maintaining group identity, sometimes differentiating themselves from others through clothing, symbols, and public commitment to the group.[51] Historical Japanese family photographs juxtapose people to each other and emphasize group image rather than individuals. Even as recently as the 1980s and 1990s, Japanese tourists, who endure numerous jokes concerning their penchant to photograph each other, continued to care little for the photograph's background. Instead they focused on the group rather than the locale. Given such attitudes toward preserving Japanese identity and group loyalty, marriage to a non-Japanese would have presented a tremendous threat to Japanese parents' conception of what a family should be.

Besides parental opposition, cross-courtship and intermarriage also ran into community enmity. In fact just as some studies maintain that families constituted the crucial factor in a person's decision to marry outside his or her group, other investigators claim that community opinion comprised the significant force in convincing a person to intermarry or not.[52] Certainly every western community developed its own hierarchy of intermarriage preferences. These derived from economic and religious factors, similarities and differences between cultures, and one group's image of another. For instance considerably more intermarriage took place between Indians and whites than between blacks and whites, because the former two were more able to accept each other than were the latter.[53]

In such community hierarchies, race comprised the hardest category to bridge in intermarriage.[54] Like many Americans living in other regions, most westerners believed that race was immutable. Thus they developed intense interest in how much Native American or other type of "blood" flowed in a person's veins. Besides putting individuals into such classifications as "one-half" Indian or "one-fourth" Asian, western communities often attached a stigma to a person of multiple heritage. In turn, people of blended ancestry frequently reacted with feelings of shame and refusal to acknowledge their backgrounds. One Oklahoma man's "one-half Cherokee blood" so humiliated him that he not only ignored its existence, but also declined to claim the land allotments and government payments due him as a Cherokee. He thus left his "one-fourth" Cherokee daughters bereft of land and other means of support.[55]

In addition to race, religious differences created a gulf between members of one community and those of another.[56] For instance even though scholars believe that Jews found more acceptance in the West than in other regions of the country, western Jews exhibited a strong sense of special character and Jewish consciousness, which led to a desire for self-preservation. As a consequence western Jews displayed extensive pride in their wedding ceremonies, whereas they frequently opposed intermarriage with non-Jews. Western Jews also formed separate enclaves, as in Denver, which purposely used intramarriage to help the group not only survive, but also to resist absorption by others.[57] Even in the face of pressure from eastern Jewish groups to reach out to Chinese and other western immigrants, western Jews resisted and remained solicitous of their Jewishness.[58]

Compared to race and religion, national origin comprised a lesser hurdle in western intermarriage. Of all western groups, Native Americans demonstrated the greatest flexibility in overcoming ethnic differences; they simply changed a person's affiliation to fit the situation. Apache Indians, for example, who tolerated intermarriage with members of foreign bands to solidify political and economic ties, either treated captives with lesser esteem or, more often, erased the gap between themselves and prisoners. They simply transformed their captives into Apaches, through adoption and by ordering them to speak their captors' language and follow their ways.[59]

When Anglo settlers appeared on the western scene, most of them proved far less pliant than Apaches. At least among first- and second-generation migrants, Anglos even hesitated to marry other Anglos who were slightly different from themselves. Early German settlers on the Great Plains lived in separate communities, spoke German, published German-language newspapers, and resisted intermarriage with other Anglo peoples. Similarly Czechs preferred to marry other Czechs, rather than marrying outside their group. One Czech woman explained that marrying a non-Czech resulted in severing one's "ties." Subsequent generations of Czechs felt differently, however. When a young man named Tonik enlisted in the service for four years, he met and married a non-Czech woman.[60]

Community aversion to intermarriage calls into question the long-standing belief that the American West offered equality and acceptance to all. Even more contrary to the western myth is the belligerent manner in which western communities enforced their rosters of marriageable and nonmarriageable persons. For one thing communities utilized physical segregation of certain peoples, a strategy that proved an especially effective deterrent to intermarriage. Secluding Native Americans on reservations, Anglos in "better" urban areas, Latinos in urban barrios, African Americans in slave quarters or urban ghettoes, and Asian groups in Chinatowns, Little Tokyos, and Little Koreas, impeded the development of romantic attachments and insured that most marriages would remain endogamous.[61]

More specifically, spatial segregation caused members of groups to labor in disconnected locales and to use different means of transport and routes to reach their destinations. Group members also attended separate schools, shopped in different stores, and pursued recreation in disparate venues. Clearly the less physical contact members of one group had with those of another, the less chance existed of attraction occurring.

Spatial segregation led to other consequences as well. Separation often created instability and poverty among certain groups, qualities that made group members less appealing—and less noticeable—as potential mates to people on other socioeconomic levels. As a case in point, western slave and ghetto families experienced so much upheaval and were economically so disadvantaged that their members seldom met or attracted mates from other classes. Well into the 1980s, rural endogamous Indians remained poorer and less educated than any other type of married couple. In other words a self-fulfilling prophecy operated: because these Native Americans lived apart from other people, they married only each other. Thus they became even poorer, less educated, and more separate.[62]

Members of segregated communities also developed what social scientists term avoidance. People living in barrios or ghettoes identified most easily with other barrio or ghetto residents. They also felt loyalty to people within their neighborhoods and thus distrusted and avoided residents of other locales. Consequently even when people of Spanish-speaking background and Anglos came into contact at school, at work, and in other public situations, each avoided the other.[63] Moreover the former's persistent allegiance to family and kin structures inhibited socializing with Anglos, who traditionally placed less emphasis on family. Complicating matters further, this adherence to family may also have indicated their resistance to assimilation into dominant Anglo society.[64]

Ultimately spatial segregation led to a situation in which people who lived separately faced, and created, barricades between themselves and others. Moreover these barriers were renewed generation after generation. As recently as 1978, the intermarriage rate of Pecos County, Texas, remained at its 1880 level—below one percent. The Pecos County figures demonstrate the continued existence of social obstacles that separate Chicanos and Anglo Americans in the area.[65]

Besides utilizing spatial segregation, communities enforced their marital norms through assorted types of social pressure as well. For example, in the nineteenth- and early-twentieth-century West, both media and popu-

lar culture frequently inveighed against intermarriage. Blunt public statements made the epithets "squaw man" and "half-breed" common and acceptable negative terminology.[66] Novels further pontificated against mixed
marriages and sanctioned community regulation of them. One mid-nineteenth-century novel especially insulted Spanish-speaking women: an
Anglo male character warned a younger one, "I seen many a good man
marry Mexican and I ain't seen one yit that wasn't sorry. Them women
breeds like prairie dogs an' jest as careless."[67]

Soon intermarriage also captured the attention of religious and other
reformers. At Fort Vancouver, missionaries warned that intermarriage would
lead to the lowering of community standards and decline of Anglo families. At the same time, Anglo women reformers proclaimed their sympathy for Native women who, as a result of male barbarism, had supposedly
suffered degradation. Some missionaries and reformers even went so far as
to suggest that such social problems as prostitution, alcoholism, and theft
would decrease if Indian-Anglo marriages ceased.[68]

Frequently social pressure took different forms according to gender.
Communities often expected women, as part of the female "civilizer" role,
to enforce racial and other barriers. In so doing women, especially Anglos,
supposedly protected themselves from assault by men of other groups and
insured the purity of their communities. To enforce their communities'
rules, women largely utilized public disdain. As numbers of Anglo women
arrived in western areas, they especially derided the marriages and other
liaisons of Anglo men with Native American women. Anglo women
also criticized the morals of these women and imputed slovenliness
and infidelity to such wives. Furthermore Anglo women claimed that
numerous men had simply purchased Native wives with "bride prices."
Anglo women additionally lamented the existence of "uncivilized"
mixed-breed children who, in their eyes, comprised little more than a
burden to "proper" society.

At Fort Vancouver during the mid-1830s, disapproving Anglo women
soon made marriages between Native women and Anglos by "custom of
the country" appear licentious and immoral. As a result the incidence of
such marriages declined, and the climate of opinion encouraged white
men to walk away from Native spouses and children without shame. In
turn Anglo women agreed to raise mixed-blood children abandoned by
fathers who no longer felt comfortable with their families. Thus Anglo
women filled a void which they had helped create.[69]

The pattern of Anglo women deriding local women repeated itself across the West. Although such women ignored, scorned, or ostracized Anglos who cohabited, they vociferously criticized non-Anglos who did so. For instance in the Southwest a number of Anglo women belittled native Spanish-speaking women who, during the 1860s in central Arizona, cohabited with miners. In Alaska Mary Desha, a Southern woman who arrived in Sitka during the 1880s, insulted Native wives. She declared that Indian women were "obviously" from dissolute backgrounds, because they often had "the same mother but different fathers—sometimes four or five fathers [exist] in one family."[70]

At the same time, a significant number of Anglo men themselves exerted pressure against intermarriage. These men typically utilized words and phrases so raw that it is repugnant to quote them. One traveler of the early 1850s spoke disparagingly of the "confusion of races" and deprecated "half-breeds" in the coarsest of terms:

> Like the negro, the Indian belongs to a species, sub-species, or variety—
> whichever the reader pleases—that has diverged widely enough from the
> Indo-European type to cause degeneracy, physical as well as moral . . . .
> These half-breeds, are, therefore, like the mulatto, quasi-mules . . .
> The mongrels are short lived, peculiarly subject to infectious disease,
> untrustworthy, and disposed to every villainy.[71]

Similarly in 1866, army officer Randolph B. Marcy dismissed the idea of Native Americans as potential spouses. In his view Indian women were little more than commodities, bought and sold for horses and other goods. Marcy likewise damned Indian polygyny with the offhand remark that "savages" were simply "ambitious of marital fame."[72]

Men who applied coercion against intermarriage seldom stopped with words. Rather physical violence frequently accompanied male censure. During the early twentieth century, people living in California's Imperial Valley expressed vitriolic disapproval of Punjabi men who married women of Spanish heritage. Because these women were then classified as white and Asian Indians as Mongolian, in many peoples' minds marriage between them constituted vice. In 1918 a race riot occurred in the cotton fields near Heber, because Hispanic men had threatened vengeance after a Punjabi man married one of "their" women. Two years later, in 1920, an Anglo neighbor forced a Punjabi man out of a Hispanic woman's house with a shotgun and had him arrested.[73]

Role of the State

Given the intensity of sentiment against intermarriage throughout the West, it is little wonder that controls on intermarriage soon moved beyond the realm of families and communities. Especially during the early to mid-nineteenth century, western jurisdictions began to put in place an elaborate legal structure intended to deter intermarriage. Throughout most of their history, the trans-Mississippi states of Arizona, Arkansas, California, Colorado, Idaho, Montana, Nebraska, Nevada, North Dakota, Oklahoma, Oregon, Utah, and Wyoming forbade intermarriage between Anglos and African Americans. In banning such interracial unions, these states followed opposition to Anglo/African American marriage first established in the southern states, beginning with Maryland in 1661.[74] But the trans-Mississippi states of Arizona, California, Idaho, Louisiana, Montana, Nebraska, Nevada, Oregon, South Dakota, Utah, and Wyoming added additional prohibitions outlawing white/Asian and sometimes white/Indian marriages. These strictures represented a less generalized sentiment; outside the West only the states of Georgia, Mississippi, and North Carolina banned white/Asian unions.[75]

The western trend toward establishing antimiscegenation legislation occurred even in supposedly liberal jurisdictions. In 1840, for example, Iowa Territory banned marriage between blacks and whites. Although Iowa was a free territory and home to such early abolitionist centers as Grinnell, a majority of Iowans feared what they termed "inundation" by African Americans. In 1857 an Iowa editor wrote that the rise in the state's African American population "naturally" forced Iowans to fear racial "amalgamation."[76]

Farther west other states acted upon similar racial prejudices. In 1850 the newly admitted state of California banned intermarriage between blacks and whites. In 1862 Oregon prohibited intermarriage not only between Anglo and African Americans but between Anglos and "Orientals" (also called Mongolians).[77] Three years later Arizona disallowed blacks, mulattoes, Indians, and Mongolians from marrying whites.[78]

Antimiscegenation legislation continued to exist in the West well into the twentieth century. In a 1906 report the U.S. Census Bureau revealed that twelve southern states prohibited black/white marriages (Alabama, Arkansas, Florida, Georgia, Kentucky, Maryland, Mississippi, Missouri, North Carolina, Tennessee, Virginia, and West Virginia); that only two northern states forbid such marriages (Delaware and Indiana); and that eleven supposedly egalitarian states located beyond the Mississippi River outlawed them (Arizona, California, Colorado, Idaho, Nebraska, Louisiana, Nevada, Oklahoma, Oregon, Texas, and Utah). Four western states also barred Anglo/Mongolian marriages (Arizona, California, Oregon, and Utah), and Nevada additionally proscribed Anglo/Indian and Anglo/Chinese unions.[79] Western legislatures continued to add racial groups to state rolls as legislators deemed it necessary. Filipinos, for example, joined the prohibited list in California as late as 1933.[80]

Clearly antimiscegenation codes and statutes revealed the tightening of Anglo westerners' feelings regarding people of color, but how effectively these laws constrained intermarriage is questionable. For one thing antimiscegenation legislation was obviously enforced erratically, for court records reveal the existence of children of intermarriages. These blended-ancestry offspring occasionally petitioned courts to legitimate their parents' marriages so they might inherit property and other assets. Documents from *In re Walker's Estate* (1896) show that Juana Walker, a resident of Pinal County, Arizona, unsuccessfully petitioned a court to validate the 1871 marriage of her Anglo father, John Walker, to her mother, a Pima Indian woman named Chur-ga, so Juana could inherit Walker's estate.[81] Accounts of journalists, travelers, and settlers disclosed the widespread incidence of other intermarriages, especially between whites and blacks, Indians and blacks, and Indians and whites.[82]

A second factor calls into question the effectiveness of western antimiscegenation codes and statutes: even after western legislatures eliminated such laws, intermarriage rates remained low. If legal restrictions had comprised the primary deterrent to intermarriage, presumably rates of intermarriage would have risen dramatically once legal constraints disappeared. The lack of such growth suggests that the occurrence of intermarriage derived more from unbalanced sex ratios, propinquity of groups, and contact between group members than from constraining legislation.[83]

Of course western antimiscegenation laws prevented some couples from marrying, but these laws were perhaps more significant in creating legal tangles for people who defied them. Spouses who misrepresented their racial heritage at the time of marriage especially ended up in legal difficulties. A significant number of annulment and divorce cases came before western courts after one spouse discovered Native American, African American, or Asian ancestry in his or her mate. In Oklahoma in 1908, an Anglo woman, Alexandria Lewis, sued her African American husband,

Albert Lewis, for divorce. She charged that he had misrepresented himself as an Osage Indian. After she discovered his African American background, she requested a divorce. Alexandria apparently expected the court to extend sympathy to her; she not only asked the court to end a marriage only four months old, but requested $6 per week alimony.[84]

During the Red Scare years of the early 1900s, public interest in comparable "miscegenation" cases mounted. In 1919 when growing intolerance led to twenty-five race riots, one western divorce case especially reverberated through the Anglo and African American press. That year Nebraskan Francis Patrick Dwyer learned that his wife, Clara McCary Dwyer, supposedly had "negro blood in her veins." Francis subsequently filled suit for annulment of his marriage. Nebraska legal stipulations allowed this; until 1913 Nebraska had prohibited marriage between Anglos and persons of one-fourth or more black ancestry, but in that year legislators changed the law to read people having "one-eighth or more negro, Japanese or Chinese blood."[85]

Clara Dwyer fought her husband's annulment petition, probably to protect her child's legitimacy. When the court found for her, Clara sued Francis for divorce on the basis of desertion and cruelty. Although she won her plea, the prevailing issue was whether Clara indeed had "black blood" in her veins rather than the fairness and morality of antimiscegenation restraints. Because of widespread sentiment against mixed marriages, Nebraska did not repeal this legislation until 1963.[86]

Legal nightmares involving intermarried couples left a legacy of bitterness among westerners of color. From earlier encounters, people of color had already developed a low opinion of Anglo "justice." Native Americans often believed that Anglos seldom respected or obeyed Anglo laws. In Washington Territory Anglo men with wives in the East or Europe migrated westward, represented themselves as single men, and married Indian women. When Native American women, who believed themselves married in white eyes, discovered they were not, shame engulfed them and their families. Native Americans thus concluded that Anglos applied their laws at will to benefit themselves.[87]

Oklahoma Indians observed other white settlers who similarly applied Anglo laws in self-serving ways. Frequently Anglo migrants married Indian women by tribal custom only, which allowed them flexibility should they want to leave their marriages. But when the U.S. government offered land allotments and other rights to spouses of Cherokee Indians, these men suddenly demanded civil marriage ceremonies.[88]

Other Native Americans judged Anglo legal proscriptions absurd, yet accepted the necessity of complying with them in order to function in an Anglo-dominated world. As recently as the 1960s, a legal advice column in the *Navajo Times* ridiculed Anglo law but advised its readers to obey it. A Native American columnist counseled his readers that, according to Anglo regulations, if a woman's husband died and she lacked that "little piece of paper"—a marriage license—Anglo judges might "say the children were not of [her] husband." Because this license evidently made love and children legal, it seemed wiser to go along with the "white man's law" and buy a marriage license even when marrying according to tribal custom. The column ended on a pragmatic note: "Make it easier for your children to live in the white man's world. Don't brand them as 'illegitimate' in the white man's world."[89]

Given some westerners' jaundiced view of Anglo law and the uses to which Anglos put their codes and statutes, antimiscegenation legislation easily confirmed their opinion that Anglo law primarily served the interests of Anglos. Even when the Supreme Court decision in *Loving v. Virginia* (1967), struck down antimiscegenation laws and made it illegal to restrict intermarriage, the decision could not obliterate decades of bitterness regarding such constraints.[90]

Of course had peoples of color come to dominate western society, they probably would have passed into law their own prejudices against Anglos and each other. Anglo American settlers held no exclusive claim to racial prejudice in the West; other instances abounded. Between 1693 and 1823, for example, the Spanish government attempted to enforce a caste system in colonial New Mexico. Later during the 1880s and 1890s, Chickasaw Indians prohibited marriages between Chickasaws and African Americans.[91]

But because Anglos had achieved dominance and had legislated their bigotry into antimiscegenation codes, peoples of color felt victimized and misused. In addition, westerners of color understandably resented the implications of inferiority inherent in such legislation. Thus even though antimiscegenation statutes fell short of preventing intermarriage, such restrictions left a legacy of resentment among westerners of color, passions that would not soon dissipate.

When an Apple Marries an Orange

If mixed-heritage couples withstood the myriad family, community, and legal pressures that confronted them and decided to marry, they soon

learned that people opposed intermarriage on grounds other than prejudice. Many westerners justifiably believed that intermarried couples would
confront difficulty in surmounting their differences, especially racial dissimilarities. In fact the principle often proved accurate that when disparate people—the proverbial apple and orange—married, a certain amount
of strife would ensue. In turn such conflict created a higher divorce rate
among intermarried couples than among intramarried ones.[92]

On the most basic level, intermarried couples' dissimilar physical features frequently drew stares from passersby. At family gatherings one spouse
or the other stood out from the group. Unfortunately many westerners
were less than tactful or kind about such matters and harassed an intermarried
couple with everything from thoughtless remarks to blunt questions.[93]

The opposite situation (being mistaken for a member of a spouse's group)
also proved unsettling. Eastern missionary Elaine Goodale Eastman, who
married a Sioux physician, was frequently identified as an Indian. Curious
people's responses ranged from asking her "Can you talk American?" to
automatically discounting her opinions regarding Indian reform because
they assumed Eastman's Sioux connections biased her ideas. The Eastmans
proved incapable of successful intermarriage and eventually separated.[94]

Intermarried couples also encountered residential and employment limitations throughout the West. When one spouse was a person of color, the
couple often had to live in a community of color. Life on an Indian reservation, in an urban ghetto, or in a barrio usually provided a lower standard
of living than the couple might have liked or been able to afford. Moreover one spouse sometimes realized that his or her status as an intermarried person negatively affected job prospects and economic mobility. This
employment liability created yet another predicament for an intermarriage, because marriages with lower incomes experienced higher divorce
rates. Thus if an intermarriage was circumscribed economically, it became
more vulnerable to divorce on that score.[95]

Yet another economic problem frequently bedeviled intermarried
couples and their families. Among some groups who formed extended family
units, people presumed that the highest wage-earner in a family would
help support the others. As a result Native American and Spanish-speaking extended families often expected Anglo spouses to contribute to their
maintenance. During the 1880s an Anglo man who had married a Native
American woman supplied housing, board, and clothing not only for his
own children, but for a number of other family members. Although the

man himself expressed no regret, the man's mother said that her son "would have been better off financially if he'd had a white wife."[96]

Communication posed another obstacle to intermarried couples. Members of different groups not only expressed themselves in distinctive ways but held specific expectations regarding appropriate responses. One spouse might offend another through innocent miswording of a query or offering thoughtful silence as a reaction instead of a heartfelt explanation. People from some cultures preferred intense discussion, while others believed in remaining taciturn. Communication was further impeded when a couple lacked a common language; speaking in one's second language could easily lead to misstatements or misunderstandings. According to recent studies, however, educational levels sometimes offset such communication difficulties.[97]

If religious dissimilarities were part of a couple's divergence, additional disruptions often occurred. A Protestant married to a Roman Catholic, for example, encountered the church's dictum that children of such a union must be raised as Catholics. In mid-nineteenth-century San Antonio, Anglo men married to Spanish-speaking women found that the church's rule usually prevailed; such wives customarily baptized their children as Catholics and reared them as such.[98] Other doctrinal and philosophical quandaries could arise between an intermarried pair, especially if each spouse expressed strong attachment to his or her religious beliefs. Much like Roman Catholics, Jews and Mormons usually exhibited determination and tenacity in religious matters. It is little wonder, then, that Jewish/gentile and Catholic/Mormon marriages experienced a notable failure rate.[99]

Discrepancies in cultural values formed yet another barrier between intermarried spouses. Even mates of the same religion quarreled if they held disparate cultural values. Irish and Italian Catholics, for example, varied on such issues as ideal family size, divorce laws, and women's roles. In contrast to the usual belief that younger generations displayed more leniency in their attitudes, Irish and Italian youngsters frequently fell further apart in their thinking than their parents.[100] Among Native American, Chicano, and Anglo youth in rural New Mexico, attitudes also diverged on such questions as ideal age of marriage and preferred family size.[101]

Dissimilarities resulting from cultural values pervaded every aspect of marriage. Culturally induced convictions affected something as elementary as body image and what comprised "fat" and "thin." Cultural beliefs also complicated expectations surrounding sexuality, frequency of sex, and specific sexual practices.[102] Diverse backgrounds also shaped spouses' ideas concerning gender roles. If one mate came from a traditional culture based on patriarchy and the other from one with partnership marriage, the gender expectations of each could create a virtually unbridgeable chasm.[103]

Moreover diverse mates brought with them to marriage a broad range of ideas regarding the negotiation of marital change. Strategies ranged from submission, obliteration (ignoring problems), compromise, and consensus to physical violence, murder, and divorce.[104] Even ideas regarding the possibility of divorce differed according to cultural background. Group members developed opinions concerning dissolution of marriage largely on the basis of their group's experience with it; these experiences varied from traditional ease of divorce among North Alaska Eskimos to customary difficulty of divorce among Catholics to increasing divorce among African Americans.[105]

Allied to the issue of cultural values was that of loyalty. The degree to which one spouse or the other felt tied to his or her group of origin could divide an intermarried pair. As a case in point, when an Oklahoma Indian named Ella Coody Robinson learned that her husband, a native Texan, wanted to move closer to his father, she resisted leaving her Cherokee roots. Although Ella finally consented to move to Texas, she was unhappy and unwell there. She explained that when she contracted malaria, her husband "was forced to let me come back to the Cherokee Nation to my mother's." Ella never returned to Texas, even though her husband eventually died there. Near the end of her life, Ella boasted that "with the exception of the four years I spent in Texas, I have spent the entire 91 years of my life in the Cherokee Nation."[106]

Intermarriages seemed to function better when one spouse renounced his or her cultural loyalties. In a representative case, Alice Brown Davis's father, a physician from Scotland, first encountered Seminole society in 1832 when, as a U.S. government physician, he accompanied Seminoles along the Trail of Tears to the West. He soon courted and married Lucy Redbird, of the royal Tiger clan, then settled among the Seminole and assisted the tribe for the rest of his life. In 1874, when his daughter Alice met and married an Anglo, George Rollins Davis, Davis similarly adopted the Seminole people and their problems.[107]

In a comparable case Cave Johnson Couts of Tennessee first entered California as a military officer during the Mexican War. In California, Couts courted and, in 1852, married Ysidora Bandini of San Diego. Couts soon resigned his military commission; the former conqueror became a ranchero instead. Cave and Ysidora lived with the Bandini family while he developed Rancho Guajome, which eventually encompassed 20,000 acres. Couts not only designed his ranch house in traditional hacienda style, but soon established it as a cultural mecca in the San Diego area. Known for his devotion to his large family and to Spanish customs, Couts, and his marriage, endured and flourished.[108]

Finally children constituted a predicament for intermarried mates. Questions regarding offsprings' welfare carried tremendous cultural implications: in what schools and what ways should children be educated, whom should they date, whose cultural identity and loyalties should they adopt? In addition providing children with an accepting community brought heartbreak to many parents. In the Punjabi-Chicana marriages in California's Imperial Valley mentioned above, dilemmas regarding children often appeared. Such marriages, which generally produced large numbers of children, unintentionally denied their offspring knowledge of one family language or another, acceptance from other children and community members, and lack of full cultural identity.[109]

Intermarriage as Assimilation or as Agent of Cultural Change

Given this dismal tale of western intermarriage, one must question whether intermarriage had any redeeming values. Numerous historians and, to a lesser extent, sociologists have long maintained that the chief benefit of intermarriage lay in its propensity to assimilate people socially, economically, and politically into the dominant society.[110]

Recent multicultural perspectives and methodologies, however, have raised serious reservations about the utility and validity of assimilation theory. First, the assimilation model sets up an adversary situation, which assumes that one spouse adopts the other's ways. Such a scheme presumes the existence of two clear-cut sets of customs, the dominant and the minority. But scholars now believe in gradations of culture, as well as cultural differences according to era, generation, and region.[111]

Second, the assumption that intermarriage fostered one spouse's cultural absorption of the other is suspect, in that this idea has encouraged investigators to envision assimilation where little or none at all occurred. On closer examination it is obvious that instances of intermarried spouses who resisted assimilation proliferated throughout the West. For example in 1841 mutual resistance to absorption and resulting hostility ruptured the family and business relationships of John Rowland and William Workman. Taking their Spanish-heritage wives and children with them, Rowland and Workman left their successful Taos distillery to move to California, where they hoped to escape family and community pressure, protect their enterprises, and conserve their way of life.[112]

Rowland's and Workman's wives accompanied them to California, perhaps under duress, but other Spanish-heritage spouses resisted change. Instead these mates preferred to retain Catholicism, maintain an extended family network, and continue to speak Spanish. Not only did non-Anglo spouses favor their own culture, but many resented Anglo assumptions of superiority. Other non-Anglo mates interpreted assimilation as an aggressive policy degrading their own culture. Consequently some non-Anglo spouses, especially Asians, not only resisted absorption into Anglo society, but actively worked to preserve Asian ways.[113]

A final problem with assimilationist theory is that scholars apply it to all groups, which is an invalid approach. As noted above in another context, intermarriage in fact fostered absorption primarily when people married spouses only slightly different from themselves, as in the case of a German marrying a native-born American. In marriages between Anglos and persons of color, assimilation ensued far less often, probably because westerners of color had been segregated, colonized, and judged so different and inferior that they indeed felt inassimilable.[114]

Thus the widespread presumption that intermarriage led to assimilation appears not only mistaken, but misguided as well. More precisely to think in terms of one group absorbing the other discounts the role of economics, urbanization, social status, and group size in intermarriage and in the assimilation process. It would be more accurate and constructive to explore intermarriage as an agent of cultural change. Although one spouse's culture absorbed the other in some marriages, and one mate resisted assimilation in other marriages, a third pattern also existed. Neither assimilationist nor pluralistic, this model merged both cultures to create a new form.

Those western intermarriages that developed this third model proved flexible enough to maintain connections to their families and cultures of origin and to develop ties between mates. In other words neither of the spouses deserted their own culture, yet as a family they also developed an additional blended culture. As Minnesotan Patti Fong Woodson described her marriage to an Anglo man, "I have an opportunity to maintain both cultures for myself and my children." When she experimented with combining these cultures in her family life, Woodson explained that her husband was "very pleased to go along with me."[115]

Maintaining one's heritage while producing a common culture occurred especially among younger generations of westerners. Rather than simply adopting both Chicano and American customs, second- or third-generation Chicanos born in the United States who married Anglos generated a distinctive, third set of customs. Similarly mixed-heritage offspring in Hawaii constructed new cultural identities. Instead of feeling compelled to chose one parent's group or the other, younger generations developed a unique blend.[116]

Conclusion

Given this account of the stresses and strains on intermarriages in the American West, it is almost superfluous to ask why intermarriage proved so difficult. Marriage itself is a demanding undertaking, fraught with challenges even during the best of times. Add to marriage the pressures of intermarriage, and it is little wonder that western intermarriage exhibited a higher divorce rate than intramarriage.

Currently intermarriage continues to increase at a slow pace in the western United States. Even in culturally diverse states such as Hawaii, New Mexico, and Texas, where the presence of dissimilar peoples suggests widespread intermarriage due to necessity, growth of cross-cultural courtship and marriage is less than phenomenal. In Hawaii, for example, racial hierarchies remain strong and influence courtship patterns, while less-favored and more-favored groups of marriage partners continue to exist.[117] At the same time, the divorce rate of western intermarried couples continues to outdistance that of intramarried spouses. As recently as the 1980s, the Hawaiian divorce rate averaged approximately 10 percent more for intermarriages than for intramarriages.[118]

In the continental United States, New Mexico and Texas provide similar, if less widely studied, examples. Although marriages between peoples of Spanish background and Anglos have risen slightly since 1970, data indicate that Chicano/Anglo couples who wish to intermarry face barriers that do not confront homogeneous couples. Intermarried spouses also experience additional pressures as a result of the mixed nature of their union. Such marriages suffer a higher failure rate than do intramarriages in both states.[119]

It seems reasonable, then, to conclude that the obstacles western intermarriage encountered together with these marriages' subsequent failure rate, provided an important causal factor in the West's rising divorce rate. Marrying across racial and other lines was possible in the West, but such marriages were seldom easy or stable.

13

A Native American mother-in-law and Anglo in-law (far left) in Montana in 1925
with three young "mixed blood" descendants and other Anglo friends and in-laws.
(Courtesy UNM Press, private collection)

14

Despite the diversity of western peoples, Anglo settlers, missionaries, teachers, and officials tended to impose their beliefs and practices on others. (Courtesy Montana Historical Society)

15

Such factors as harsh living conditions and many children put stresses on western families. For others, such as these Mormon settlers in Arizona during the 1880s, religious beliefs helped hold them together.
(Courtesy Museum of New Mexico, negative no. 15615)

Mr & Mrs S. Boggs.

16

Other married couples, like this one in Dodge County, Minnesota, might suffer racial prejudice and economic discrimination. (Courtesy Minnesota Historical Society)

17

Other westerners, like Polly Bemis of Idaho, might face discrimination and thus pressure on her marriage because she married a man of another race, in this case Anglo homesteader Charlie Bemis.
(Courtesy Idaho Historical Society)

$50 REWARD !

Reward of $50.00 will be paid by Zepheniah Smith for the re-
covery or information leading to the recovery of Mrs. Nannie
Bell Smith; age 26 years, height about 5 feet 4 inches, weight 120
pounds, brown eyes, dark brown hair. Disappeared from her
home near Trousdale, Okla., Oct., 20, 1905. Was traced to Oklahoma City, Okla. Will likely seek employment such as light
house work, as health would not permit her to do hard work.
Was in very poor health at time of disappearance. The above
picture is good of her taken about a year ago.

ADDRESS ALL INFORMATION TO

ZEPHENIAH SMITH
Trousdale, Okla.

Box No. 3.

OKLAHOMAN PRINT OKLAHOMA CITY

18

*When marriages broke down, many westerners deserted their spouses. Here an
abandoned Oklahoma husband seeks information in 1905 regarding his wife.
(Courtesy Oklahoma Territorial Museum, Guthrie)*

19

During Oklahoma's days as an Indian Territory, dissatisfied Anglo couples had to apply for divorces to the Cherokee National Council in Tahlequah. The Council also granted divorces to Cherokees. (Courtesy Glenda Riley, private collection)

20

*Law offices in Guthrie, Oklahoma, where
disenchanted spouses sought divorces, especially during the 1890s.
(Courtesy Glenda Riley, private collection)*

21

Opposite Top: Minnehaha Courthouse in Sioux Falls, South Dakota, which gained notoriety for granting "easy" divorces during the late nineteenth century.
(Courtesy Glenda Riley, private collection)

22

Opposite Bottom: In the twentieth century, the West became infamous for "quickie" marriages, especially in Las Vegas, even of couples who had divorced only hours before.
(Courtesy Glenda Riley, private collection)

23

Below: Youngsters emulate the adults in their lives, and for western children this also has meant copying their styles of marriage and divorce.
(Courtesy Glenda Riley, private collection)

4

Separating, Deserting, Divorcing

This concluding essay returns to the question posed at the study's outset: Why is the divorce rate higher in the American West than elsewhere? Although a number of suggestions have been posited, this chapter adds that the American West contained every characteristic that sociologists and historians identify as underlying factors of divorce. These include urbanization, industrialization, stress of modern life, men's and women's entry into the paid labor force, women's changing roles, and the gradual broadening of divorce laws and judicial decisions regarding divorce.[1]

Recently several sociologists have emphasized westerners' mobility as a basis of divorce, while historians have enlarged the list of causes even further by professing that changes in the patriarchal family, rising expectations of marriage, and gender imbalances between husbands and wives also created marital tensions and often resulted in divorce.[2]

But this essay also argues that two additional factors existed in the West, which combined with others to propel the region's divorce rate upward. One of these involved lenient western attitudes toward divorce. More than any other regional group in history, westerners have long exhibited a willingness to break unsatisfactory marital bonds and seek potentially more satisfying ties despite the costs. Then as now, divorce fit well with widely expounded ideas regarding western democracy, individualism, change, and reform. Divorce permitted people to make choices and reorder their lives when they deemed it necessary. Divorce also allowed the pursuit of personal happiness as a desirable goal. Although it is unlikely that democratic ideals directly caused divorce, these principles encouraged and justified rationales for divorce.[3]

A second influence on the West's divorce rate was the growth of economic and other opportunities for women. Although historians often assume that western women encountered fewer employment opportunities than women in other regions of the United States, and that western women faced numerous social and legal restraints, divorce statistics suggest otherwise. Western women of all classes and backgrounds sought divorces in greater numbers than women in other sections of the United States. Thus the factors propelling western women into seeking divorces demand further analysis.[4]

Western Attitudes toward Divorce

Ease of Divorce

Divorce—and especially lenient divorce—had a long-term history in the American West. Native Americans were the first inhabitants to institute easy divorce there. Although some Native groups experienced little divorce,[5] numerous others believed that a married couple's satisfaction comprised the main consideration in marriage. Marital separation was frequently uncomplicated, based upon the dissatisfaction of either or both spouses, or simply on mutual consent. During the latter half of the nineteenth century, the U.S. Bureau of Indian Affairs formally recognized such Indian-custom separations and divorces. Although the seeming casualness of such divorces mocked orthodox Anglo teachings regarding marriage and divorce, BIA officials accepted verbal testimony by spouses, family members, or friends as sufficient "grounds" for divorce.[6]

French- and Spanish-speaking settlers, who were usually Roman Catholic, introduced a different set of attitudes regarding marriage and divorce. They generally eschewed divorce, yet recognized that marital strife occurred. Consequently French courts, from the lower Louisiana Territory at least as far north as Ste. Genevieve, issued a significant number of divorces of bed and board, part of a long-standing tradition. As early as 1728, Louise Jousset La Louire of New Orleans petitioned the council for a divorce of bed and board, complaining that her husband had "dissipated" her considerable dowry, kicked and beaten her, and hit her with a hammer, stick, and other heavy objects. Despite her husband's rebuttal of these charges, the council ruled for Louise and ordered that her husband return Louise's dowry and give her additional property and goods.[7]

In an upper Louisiana case, Pelagre Carpentier Vallé presented even more damning charges. To a Ste. Genevieve court she testified that her husband drank, beat her, gambled, kept a mulatto mistress, and squandered their joint property. Pelagre too received property and other assets to support herself and her two children.[8] These and other cases established important precedents that eventually influenced nineteenth-century western divorce law.

Spanish-speaking peoples who settled in the Southwest, then known as El Norte, also resisted absolute divorce. Rather than emphasizing individual rights, such societies focused upon maintaining families. Still discontented couples could petition for annulments or divorces of bed and board. In California in 1844, for example, a Monterey court separated Juan Romero and Juana Hernandez who, being illiterate, made their marks on the document. Although a high proportion of such separations ended in reconciliation, their very existence established important legacies for western society: a belief in publicly airing marital grievances; court intercession to protect one spouse, usually the wife; and a growing number of policies and laws regulating marital dissolution.[9]

Other viewpoints regarding marriage and divorce gradually entered the West. Because nineteenth-century African American slaves were typically denied access to Anglo law, they created their own rituals. African American churches sometimes granted "divorces" to unhappy slave spouses or to slaves whose mates had been sold, while slave communities sanctioned the dissolution of other unions. Additionally slave owners ordered couples to part. In Oklahoma a Creek slave holder bought a slave woman and "married" her to one of his male slaves. But when the couple failed to have children, their owner "divorced" them and sold the woman to another Oklahoma planter.[10]

When Anglo settlers arrived on the western scene, many brought casual values regarding marriage and divorce with them. Although such Anglos as conservative Europeans, Catholics, and others remained committed to the concept of marriage as a lifetime undertaking, others believed in the contractual nature of marriage and thus in marriage's potential to end in divorce. At the same time, even though Anglo settlers carried established ideas and institutions westward, most refused to be bound by them. Instead they revised customary procedures when it suited their purposes. In addition western settlers frequently acted in haste. Because they were anxious to establish government and other institutions, they often skipped time-consuming deliberations. Haste set the stage for the adoption of permissive divorce statutes and short residency requirements on more than one occasion.[11]

Thus western states and territories soon gained notoriety for their broadminded, or as some said, decadent divorce laws. The West was widely known for divorce laws that were, according to an 1867 observer, "very liberal; seldom compelling men or women to remain in marriage bonds which they wish severed."[12]

A number of western men reinforced the idea that the West favored lenient divorce. Reuben Ward of Howard County, Missouri, maintained that "just cause and good provocation" forced him and his wife to "tear" themselves "asunder," yet in a whimsical notice in the Missouri *Intelligencer* on 19 June 1824, he advised his wife to "set thy cap for another and a more happy swain, while I roam through the world sipping honey from the bitter or sweet flowers that chance may strew in my path."[13] With this lighthearted farewell, Ward joined thousands of others who left their homes and spouses behind them.

Many western women also publicized western divorce. In 1853 Abby Mansur of California began to search for a richer husband than the one she had, explaining that "it is all the go here, for Ladys to leave there [sic] Husbands, two out of three do it." Similarly Sarah Wooley grew disgusted with her husband's penchant for other women. In 1885 she felt she could no longer "conform to Samuel's image of a wife as a meek, passive slave" and agreed to a divorce. Later yet, when in 1902 Grace Fairchild found her husband "ill-fitted for the life of a pioneer," she divided their land and built a successful ranch to support her and her nine children.[14]

The American West provided such a hothouse environment for divorce that the western divorce rate rose faster than that in northeastern or southern states. In 1908 U. S. Commissioner of Labor Carroll D. Wright reported that "the divorce rate increases as one goes westward." Wright and the staff of the United States Census Bureau collected divorce statistics, which revealed that the ratio of divorces to population increased faster in western states than in any other region of the United States. This situation existed well before extreme ease of divorce in such western states as Nevada and California helped drive up the West's tally. During the late nineteenth century, then, even though intraregional variations existed and the West contained conservative pockets, divorce occurred more frequently in the West than in the North and South:

	North Atlantic Division	South Atlantic Division	North- Central Division	South- Central Division	Western Division
	Table 4.1	Divorces Per 100,000 People			
1870	26	8	43	18	56
1880	29	13	56	37	83
1890	29	21	73	63	106
1900	39	33	95	97	131[15]

The growth of divorce in the West was even more telling when rates in the western division were combined with two other largely trans-Mississippi areas, the south-central and north-central divisions, which comprised the two next-highest divisions in the nation. The western division encompassed Arizona, California, Colorado, Idaho, Montana, Nevada, New Mexico, Oregon, Utah, Washington, and Wyoming; the south-central division included Indian Territory, Oklahoma Territory, and Texas; and the north-central division contained Indiana, Illinois, Iowa, Kansas, Michigan, Minnesota, Missouri, Nebraska, North Dakota, Ohio, South Dakota, and Wisconsin.

Undoubtedly some Americans interpreted high rates of divorce in these states and territories as a temporary development resulting from stresses of migration and settlement. But Commissioner Wright pointed out that the spiraling divorce rate was a western rather than a frontier phenomenon. Although it seemed reasonable to expect divorce rates to stabilize as western areas became more settled, Wright noted that "no such tendency" was "apparent in the figures for divorce, and, in fact, an opposite tendency" appeared "to be at work."[16] In Wright's view, high rates of divorce in the West seemed likely to continue rather than abate.

Wright's prophecies came to pass. The percentage distribution of divorce according to divisions of the United States in the early twentieth-century indicated that the trans-Mississippi West—which included most of the central divisions as well as the western division—ranked highest and generally continued to rise at a faster rate than other regions:

Table 4.2	Percent Distribution by Division in Selected Years				
	North Atlantic Division	South Atlantic Division	North-Central Division	South-Central Division	Western Division
1916	13.5	6.5	40.3	24.3	5.2
1930	12.5	7.8	38.3	23.9	7.5
1940	12.9	12.4	30.6	24.7	19.3
1950	11.2	13.9	28.1	25.0	21.8[17]

Desertion and Divorce

Desertion soon emerged as a phenomenon in the West as well, which in turn persuaded many westerners to support permissive divorce. During the nineteenth and early twentieth centuries, a significant number of abandoned spouses in eastern and central states obtained divorces after their spouses went westward. Police "wanted" posters from the 1890s indicate that numerous mates, especially husbands, used westward migration as an opportunity to leave their families behind.

Abandoned wives sought information through wanted posters regarding absent husbands or offered rewards. A Mrs. Robert Archibald of Elgin, Illinois, listed her fifty-two-year-old husband among the missing and offered a $100 reward for his return. The wife of forty-one-year-old Peter Hempler of Chicago, Illinois, swore out a warrant for "wife and child abandonment" and offered a "liberal reward" to the person who apprehended her husband. Of course some women were too poor to offer rewards. The wife of thirty-year-old Frank Limbrack of Owensboro, Kentucky, searched for her husband because she and her children were "in destitute circumstances," while the wife of forty-one-year-old George W. Roach of Harrisburg, Illinois, explained that her poverty occurred overnight: her husband took with him $1,400, "every cent of money she had," when he deserted.[18]

Beginning during the mid-1880s, however, a higher proportion of abandoned spouses lived in the West and obtained divorces in western jurisdictions than in other regions. For one thing, a sizable number of western settlers obtained divorces because their spouses refused to migrate with them. A wife who remained in a couple's former home was considered a deserter in jurisdictions whose laws stated that a husband's domicile constituted the family domicile. A typical case was that of Berne Ball. In 1895 he divorced his wife of twenty-eight years on the ground of desertion, after she refused to migrate from New York City to Logan County, Oklahoma.[19]

For another thing, western settlers themselves experienced desertion. In police wanted posters, abandoned mates often expressed their hope that deserters would return, even though circumstances surrounding abandonment made it clear that the deserters had little interest in doing so. An especially poignant broadside came from the wife of Walter Davis of Sherman, Texas. It began with an eye-catching plea: "For Humanity's Sake, Help Me Locate Walter L. Davis." Davis's wife then told a strange tale about his disappearance. From Walter's letters, she had learned that kidnappers had forced him to "work in some mine unknown to him." In these letters, which Davis mailed "on the trains between Fort Smith, Arkansas, and Oklahoma City" and which "arrived tolerably regular," Davis explained that he was unable to send his address because he was unaware of his location. Davis's wife concluded her appeal by offering a reward for information about Davis, the money to be paid by Davis's father.[20]

Evidently because the West offered enormous anonymity and mobility, it also inspired women to desert their husbands in large numbers. An Oklahoma Territory divorce case indicated that one man sought a divorce on the ground of his wife's prolonged absence, explaining that she had "gone over-land in a wagon west to some Western state."[21] A police wanted poster revealed that another Oklahoma husband believed a well-built, dark-haired, mustachioed hypnotist had "exercised his power" over his wife and spirited her away. He offered a generous reward for information about his attractive, well-dressed, and healthy-complexioned wife and the spell-casting hypnotist.[22]

The husband of twenty-two-year-old May Walker of Pueblo, Colorado, issued a poster stating that May had disappeared in the company of seventeen-year-old Mabel Wade, a "very good looking girl" and asking anyone who had seen the pair to contact him. And S. D. Gilbert of Smithville, Texas, offered a reward of $50 for the return of twenty-two-year-old Carrie Gilbert, after she left town suspiciously dressed in a "long grey cloak, hat and heavy black veil."[23]

Democratizing Divorce

Westerners, who frequently espoused a belief in equality of opportunity, demonstrated this principle by democratizing divorce. More than in other regions, western legislatures and courts proved themselves willing to grant divorces to all types of people. Even American Indian councils gave white-style divorces. Articles in the *Cherokee Advocate* and records of the Cherokee National Council during the 1880s indicate that the council enacted several "Acts Granting Divorces." After the passage of an 1881 divorce statute, Cherokee circuit and district courts also granted divorces in Indian Territory, later part of Oklahoma Territory. Grounds for divorce were adultery, imprisonment of three years or more, willful desertion for one year, extreme cruelty by violence or other means, and habitual drunkenness.[24]

After Oklahoma Territory formed in 1890, Indian couples increasingly availed themselves of white divorce courts. When Luke Bearshield divorced his wife, Nellie, in 1893, a Guthrie newspaper declared he was the first Indian to obtain a "legal," meaning an Anglo, divorce. During subsequent years, other Indians sought divorces from white courts. One of these involved the common-law wife of Eastman Richard, who petitioned for a divorce, custody of their two children, and $40,000 alimony.[25]

African Americans, who now married according to Anglo law, also turned to white courts to dissolve marriages. Although court records seldom specify the race of petitioners, newspaper accounts of divorces often do so. In 1893 a Guthrie, Oklahoma, newspaper noted that Aaron Jordan divorced his wife, Sarah, because she refused to leave Arkansas and join him in Oklahoma; both were African American. A few years later, a Vinita, Oklahoma, paper reported that Laura Brookins divorced her husband because of his abusive behavior; again both were African American.[26]

People representing all jobs, professions, and social classes also requested divorces from western courts. Divorce records from Oklahoma Territory during the 1890s show that male divorce seekers held jobs ranging from homesteader to well-to-do merchant, while female petitioners worked as everything from housewives to keepers of boardinghouses. Newspaper accounts from the 1890s indicate that divorce also touched the lives of professional and business people: a professor, two judges, a colonel, a "wealthy German," and a district leader of the Republican party.[27]

Nineteenth-Century Divorce Mills

By the late nineteenth century, western divorce mills further encouraged the growth of casual attitudes toward divorce. Of course numerous Americans expressed outrage concerning the soaring divorce rate, especially in the West. Even before Census Bureau findings proved that the West had the highest divorce rate in the nation, northerners and southerners already believed that the West was rapidly leading the nation into moral and social decline.

Frequent reports of outrageous western divorce trials and free-wheeling divorce mills that granted quick divorces to migratory divorce seekers from stricter jurisdictions reinforced these impressions.[28] Then in 1885 Samuel W. Dike, secretary of the National Divorce Reform League, pointed out that divergent divorce laws made divorce mills and migratory divorce possible. "The divorce broker," he wrote, "sits in his office, and from the compilations prepared for his use, assigns his applications to one State or another as may best suit each case."[29]

Even many westerners judged divorce mills as immoral and the height of laxity and permissiveness. Thus some of them opposed divorce mills, but others actively supported them. People with vested interests in divorce, including attorneys, merchants, hotelkeepers, and divorce seekers themselves, defended the right of western divorce mills to operate.

Utah became the first trans-Mississippi state to gain the reputation of being a divorce mill. The state drew criticism partly as a result of Mormon policies concerning divorce.[30] Beginning in 1847 Mormon church leaders regularly granted divorces. Because church officials lacked the legal power to terminate marriages, they claimed they limited themselves to divorcing polygynous couples whose marriages fell within church jurisdiction. Brigham Young reportedly granted over sixteen hundred divorces between 1847 and 1876. Although Young theoretically opposed divorce, because it contradicted Mormon beliefs in eternal marriage, he willingly terminated contentious and other unworkable marriages. In a single day, Young relieved George D. Grant of three wives; a few weeks later, he parted Grant from a fourth.[31]

As news of Mormon church divorces reached the non-Mormon world, public outrage against Mormons flared. After 1852, when the first Utah territorial legislature adopted a statute permitting probate courts to grant divorces, many people became highly critical of Utah's civil divorces as well. The 1852 Utah Territory statute proved objectionable because, in addition to listing the usual grounds of impotence, adultery, willful desertion, habitual drunkenness, conviction for a felony, and inhumane treatment, it included an omnibus clause. According to this provision, judges could grant divorces "when it shall be made to appear to the satisfaction and conviction of the court that the parties cannot live in peace and union together and that their welfare requires a separation." In addition the 1852 statute contained a loose residency requirement: a court need only be satisfied that a petitioner was "a resident of the Territory, or wishes to become one."[32]

As a result of the 1852 statute, civil divorces were easy to obtain in Utah Territory. Discontented mates could even receive a divorce on the same day they applied for it. Also, unlike those in most other jurisdictions, Utah judges accepted collusion—an agreement to divorce between husband and wife. A married couple could appear in court, testify that they agreed to divorce, and receive a decree. Such was the situation on 12 February 1856, when John and Sarah Wardall petitioned for a divorce in a Washington County probate court and requested that John receive custody of the two oldest boys, Sarah custody of their daughter and youngest boy, and that they split two beds, four pillows, two bolsters, and other household equipment down the middle.[33] Reportedly the non-Mormon town of Corinne even offered divorce papers already signed by a county judge, with blank spaces for names of the spouses.[34]

It is little wonder, then, that when Jacob Smith Boreman, a non-Mormon from Virginia, became United States district court judge in the Salt Lake City region in 1872, he was shocked by Utah divorce laws and procedures. He especially expressed surprise that judges accepted collusion and that divorce seekers could file petitions, enter proof of grounds, and receive divorce decrees "all on the same day."[35]

Boreman himself heard a portion of one of the most dramatic divorce cases in Mormon history. In 1873 Ann Eliza Webb Young brought suit against her husband, Brigham Young. Young seemed willing to divorce Ann Eliza, but unwilling to pay the requested alimony: $20,000 in court costs plus $200,000 to support Ann Eliza and her children. Young, who had once offered to divorce any wife who wished to leave him, fought Eliza's petition by arguing that their marriage was illegal because it was polygynous and thus unrecognized by United States law. According to Boreman, Young believed that if he won, he would be free from alimony. If he lost, plural marriage would have gained legal recognition; thus, if a judge denied Ann Eliza a divorce, he would have nevertheless declared the Youngs' plural marriage valid.

After an 1874 federal law moved Utah divorce cases from probate to district courts, Boreman became the presiding judge in the case of *Young v. Young.* He ordered Brigham Young to pay temporary alimony to Ann Eliza, but had to imprison Young to make him pay. In 1877 another district court dismissed the suit, because its judge refused to recognize Brigham Young's plural marriage to Ann Eliza. Consequently she failed to gain a divorce decree and alimony, while Brigham Young failed to get recognition for plural marriage.[36]

Despite Utah's lenient divorce laws, it remains unclear whether the state deserved its reputation as a divorce mill. Between 1867 and 1886, Utah courts granted 4,078 divorces. Of these, 1,267 couples had married in Utah. It is impossible to know how many of the remaining 2,811 cases involved migratory divorce seekers or those who were converts anxious to join the Latter-day Saints after they freed themselves from mates opposed to becoming Mormon. High migration rates into Utah during these years, however, suggest that most divorces were obtained by would be converts rather than migratory divorce seekers.[37]

During the early 1890s, divorce mills allegedly emerged in the Dakotas as well. Members of the House of the Dakota territorial legislature introduced divorce into the region in 1862, when they granted divorces to Minnie Omeg from her husband, C. Omeg, and to General William Tripp from his wife, Sarah A. Tripp. Other divorce seekers soon requested legislative divorces from the House.

Dakota legislators felt harried and distracted by these petitions and complained that divorce diverted time and energy from other business. Thus, in the 1865–66 session, the Dakota legislature shifted primary jurisdiction for divorce to courts. In this first territorial divorce law, Dakota legislators also established adultery and life imprisonment as grounds for divorce and required that petitioners be residents of the territory when the adultery or imprisonment occurred. In its 1866–67 session, the Dakota Territorial Legislature specified seven grounds for divorce, set the residency requirement at ninety days in the county where the suit was filed, and recognized the practice of notifying a defendant by public notice rather than personal service. In 1877 legislators reduced the grounds to six, but added the flexible ground of neglect and broadened the plea of cruelty to include "mental suffering." In addition a new clause stated that the ninety-days' residence could be established in any county.[38]

During the 1880s, Dakota Territory experienced an economic boom and increased immigration. Consequently in 1889 an enabling act divided Dakota Territory into two states, South Dakota and North Dakota. South Dakota's legislature retained six grounds for divorce and the ninety-day residency requirement.[39] South Dakota courts also reportedly granted a

growing number of divorces. The bustling city of Sioux Falls quickly garnered renown as the newest divorce mecca in the United States. Located
on the eastern border of South Dakota, Sioux Falls provided a hub for
major railroad lines, which transported not only goods, but out-of-state
divorce seekers. As a commercial center, Sioux Falls offered an abundance
of attorneys and courtrooms. It also offered increasingly sophisticated theater, shopping, lodging, and recreational facilities. In 1893 the *Evening
Argus Leader* remarked that Sioux Falls was becoming "metropolitan with
a vengeance"; it encompassed ten gambling halls, thirty-seven "holes in
the wall," and one hundred prostitutes.[40]

Throughout the United States, Americans viewed Sioux Falls as a rol-
licking and extremely lenient "divorce colony." Charles H. Craig, editor
of the Sioux Falls *Daily Press*, supposedly gave the city that epithet; other
journalists supplied lurid details. In 1895 a Chicago journalist and an attorney visited Sioux Falls briefly, then wrote a titillating book about the
city. According to them the "Queen City" prospered "through the misery,
sin, and follies of wives and husbands." A few years later, journalist George
Fitch expanded this portrait in the *American Magazine*. In Fitch's words,
Sioux Falls boasted many "corpulent homes built from the proceeds of the
divorce industry." He estimated that the Minnehaha County court in Sioux
Falls granted from seventy-five to one hundred divorces each year.[41]

Other accounts further inflamed people's imaginations. In 1908 a novel
by a Sioux Falls dentist characterized the city as the "scene of an endless
social drama, the battle-ground upon which a giant domestic problem is
daily fought." The following year Jane Burr's "letters" described the experiences of a female divorce seeker living alone in Sioux Falls.[42]

As the city's notoriety grew, many citizens vehemently opposed the
local divorce industry. While some attorneys, hotelkeepers, and
businesspeople insisted that lenient divorce laws boosted Sioux Falls's
economy, other inhabitants railed against these laws. William Hobart Hare,
Episcopal bishop of South Dakota between 1873 and 1909, emerged as
leader of the opposition. Viewing women and men as incomplete beings
comprising a "whole" only in marriage, Hare rejected divorce as a solution
to family disharmony. He especially attacked merchants and attorneys who,
in his view, "capitalized on unhappiness" by soliciting "divorce business."[43]

In late 1890 South Dakota legislators began to debate divorce reform.
Although legislators discussed a reform bill, it never reached the floor of
the House. In 1893 the legislature passed a bill requiring six months of

residency in South Dakota before divorce proceedings could begin and one year of residency before the awarding of a final decree. Because this moderate change failed to satisfy critics, legislators introduced several stricter residency bills during subsequent sessions, but none became law.[44] In 1907 a one-year residency requirement became the focus of debate, political maneuvering, and lobbying in South Dakota. When the bill came up for a vote, both houses passed it by an unexpectedly large margin. The following year a popular referendum also supported the one-year provision. When the measure went into effect on 1 January 1909, the linchpin of South Dakota divorce mills, short residency, vanished.[45]

It is unclear whether any South Dakota cities actually qualified as divorce mills granting many quick divorces to out-of-state petitioners. The divorce rate in Minnehaha County in 1903 was extremely high, one divorce per 2.26 marriages compared to a national average of one divorce per every 7.0 marriages, and may have included many migratory decrees. But that migratory divorces were exaggerated is supported by U.S. Census Bureau statistics. These data revealed a much lower divorce rate than reported by South Dakota newspapers at the time. Census Bureau figures also indicate that divorce rates in such other central states as Kansas and Arkansas surpassed South Dakota's supposedly anomalous rate. Even a few states east of the Mississippi outdistanced South Dakota's rate, notably Indiana and New Hampshire.[46]

Despite lack of statistical proof, South Dakota's image as a divorce mecca continued to loom large in westerners' minds. Moreover between 1893 and 1899, South Dakota's northern neighbor experienced a similar but relatively short-lived phenomenon. North Dakota had shared territorial legislation with South Dakota, including a ninety-day residency requirement for divorces. Charles A. Pollack, a former Iowan who in 1884 became district attorney of Cass County, North Dakota, and served as a judge on the Cass County bench between 1897 and 1917, explained that short residency requirements were common in frontier regions. According to him, these requriements were intended to lure settlers by allowing doctors and lawyers to practice on arrival and men to vote after thirty days. A ninety-day residency requirement for divorce appeared restrictive by contrast.[47]

In line with such thinking, when North Dakota achieved statehood in 1889 it retained territorial statutes stating that divorce would be a judicial matter and that a divorce petition could be initiated after ninety days of residency in the state. An 1899 statute listed seven grounds for divorce, including the catchall grounds of cruelty and neglect. Because North Dakota was less accessible than South Dakota, these provisions failed to attract divorce seekers. But when the South Dakota legislature restricted the ease of divorce in 1893 by lengthening the state's residency requirement from three to six months, some divorce business shifted northward.[48]

Fargo, the seat of Cass County, supposedly attracted the majority of divorce seekers. This growing city on the eastern border of North Dakota offered all necessary facilities: major railroads, hotels, shops, entertainment, attorneys, courts, and newspapers.[49] By the mid-1890s, Fargo's reputation as a divorce mill rivaled that of Sioux Falls, a development that astounded and appalled many of Fargo's citizens. The Women's Christian Temperance Union especially opposed North Dakota divorce statutes. John Shanley, first Roman Catholic bishop of Fargo, proved another energetic critic, opposing divorce in general and the form it took in North Dakota in particular. During the mid-1890s, he crusaded for tighter controls on divorce.[50]

A growing number of North Dakota legislators agreed with these critics. In 1893, 1895, and 1897, the legislature considered, but failed to pass, one-year residency bills. In 1899 South Dakota's legislature approved a one-year residency requirement that became law on 1 July 1899.[51] In mid-1899, then, the divorce days of North Dakota came to a halt. But since that time, writers have repeated and enlarged tales of booming divorce mills in Fargo and other North Dakota cities.[52] U.S. Census Bureau statistics, however, fail to confirm this image; government figures indicate that Fargo courts granted fewer divorces than those in Sioux Falls. Cass County court "register of actions" books also reveal that the numbers of divorces granted in Fargo were lower than those in Sioux Falls. Overall during these years, North Dakota issued divorces at a slower pace than such other western states and territories as Alaska, Montana, and Utah, and such eastern states as Rhode Island and Maine.[53]

During the 1890s Oklahoma Territory took North Dakota's place as the premier western divorce mill. In 1890 the framers of the Organic Act, which created Oklahoma Territory, acted in haste and simply copied Nebraska's divorce provisions. Soon realizing that Nebraska statutes were unsuited to the new territory, local legislators within the year created distinct territorial divorce statutes. In one section the new statutes lodged jurisdiction for divorce in district courts and required petitioners to live in the territory for ninety days before applying for divorce. In another section they gave jurisdiction to both probate and district courts and required that a petitioner live in the territory for two years and in the county of filing for six months before applying for a divorce.[54]

Oklahoma Territory's 1890 provisions also allowed notification of proceedings by publication and provided for appeal of divorce decrees. Grounds were adultery, extreme cruelty, willful desertion, willful neglect, habitual intemperance, and conviction of a felony. Statutes stipulated that extreme cruelty meant "the infliction of grevious [sic] bodily injury or grevious [sic] mental suffering upon the other, by one party to the marriage."[55] In 1893 the Oklahoma territorial legislature revised and clarified these contradictory conditions. New provisos lodged jurisdiction for divorce exclusively in the district courts, set residency at ninety days, and specified ten grounds, including the pliant category "gross neglect of duty." To stop immediate remarriages, a new provision stated that a divorce decree would take effect six months after it was granted.[56]

Despite these changes, confusion continued to prevail in Oklahoma Territory's divorce proceedings. Beginning in 1890 probate court judges had been hearing divorce cases after ninety days of residency by the petitioner rather than two years as required in 1890. Although the 1893 reform should have closed down probate divorce business, probate court judges continued to grant divorces and require only ninety days of residency. Soon territorial newspapers maintained that Oklahoma was turning into a divorce mecca. In 1892 the *Daily Leader* reported that hundreds of divorce seekers streamed into Oklahoma to take advantage of quick and easy probate divorces. Two years later the *Daily Times Journal* asserted that Oklahoma Territory's divorce colony continued to grow in spite of recent prohibitions on probate courts.[57]

The legality of Oklahoma's probate divorces came before the Oklahoma Territorial Supreme Court in 1894. After Chief Justice Frank Dale heard a divorce appeal, *Irwin v. Irwin*, he ruled that probate courts had lost the power to grant divorces after 14 August 1893. Because Dale's decision invalidated probate divorces granted after that date, Associate Justice Henry W. Scott voted against it. Scott warned that Dale's decision would "make innocent people guilty of adultery and bigamy."[58] Public alarm flared when the Kingfisher *Free Press* predicted that hundreds of divorces would be nullified, while the Guthrie *Daily Leader* declared that those who had received a probate divorce after 14 August 1893 and had subsequently remarried were bigamists. To alleviate these problems, territorial legislators passed an act legalizing divorces granted by probate courts before 28 February 1895.[59]

Despite the confusion, Oklahoma newspapers reported that divorce seekers continued to pour into the territory.[60] During these years Guthrie emerged as the center of Oklahoma's divorce trade. One attorney even described the town as an ideal divorce "resort": scenic, warm climate, financially reasonable, and free of "crowds of loungers and gossips to listen to whatever testimony may be given."[61] Oklahoma Territory's standing as a divorce haven also provoked criticism, both inside and outside the territory. In 1893 Governor Abraham J. Seay recommended that the ninety-day residency requirement be lengthened.[62] Chief Justice Frank Dale especially denounced attorneys and businesspeople who actively solicited divorce trade. In 1894 he threatened to disbar attorneys who advertised in eastern newspapers for divorce clients and to appoint an investigatory committee to identify such lawyers.[63]

In 1896 the United States Congress intervened in Oklahoma Territory, by establishing a one-year residency requirement in territorial divorce cases. On 25 May the one-year residency bill went into force. Within a few weeks, the El Reno News optimistically stated that "the Divorce business in Oklahoma has entirely disappeared." But as late as 1908, the Daily Oklahoman disclosed that courts still disputed the precedence of the one-year law over Oklahoma's ninety-day provision.[64]

Was Oklahoma Territory a true divorce mill? Despite assertions that it "outstripped its competitors in drawing clients," government statistics fail to support this contention. Instead, figures indicate a slightly lower rate of divorce per one thousand population in Oklahoma Territory than in such western states as Montana, Texas, and Washington. East of the Mississippi River, however, only Indiana outdid Oklahoma.[65]

In all likelihood contemporary observers exaggerated the number of divorces that nineteenth-century western divorce mills granted to migratory divorce seekers.[66] Still, the apparent ease of divorce in many western areas of the United States alarmed many westerners. At the same time, lenient laws inspired other westerners to treat divorce more casually than ever.[67] Of course westerners had yet to witness the height to which Nevada would carry the divorce industry.

During the early twentieth century, Nevada became the most highly publicized destination for divorce seekers. Nevada, and especially Reno, gained a reputation as a jurisdiction that combined lax laws, leisure pursuits, and a pleasant climate. Reno began its rise to notoriety as a divorce mill largely because of Nevada's six-month residency requirement for citizenship, voting, and divorce, a provision intended to accommodate the needs of a highly mobile population of miners and entrepreneurs. In 1900 a well-known Englishman, Earl Russell, divorced his wife in Reno, married another woman, and was subsequently sued for adultery by his first wife.[68] Other well-known people soon took advantage of Nevada's six-month residency requirement and permissive grounds for divorce, including a broad, catchall cruelty provision. In 1905 the ease of Reno divorce, at least for those who could afford to travel to Nevada and spend six months there, was brought to public attention by Laura D. Corey of Pittsburgh. Corey claimed that her wealthy husband was involved with a dancer and intended to dissolve his marriage in Reno.[69]

Such publicity thrust Reno, and the American West, into the national spotlight. In 1907 William H. Schnitzer, a New York City lawyer, further publicized Reno when he established an office there and published a pamphlet describing Nevada's generous divorce provisions and Reno's attractions as a divorce mecca. Schnitzer also advertised widely in newspapers and theater programs, promising "quick and reliable action" and the "shortest residence" for divorce in the U.S. Although the Nevada Supreme Court reprimanded Schnitzer in 1911 by temporarily suspending his license, the divorce industry had taken hold in Reno.[70]

Within a few years, the inhabitants of Reno found themselves embroiled in a struggle that pitted prodivorce advocates against an antidivorce faction. In Reno patterns of resistance to easy divorce followed those in earlier divorce mills, including Sioux Falls, Fargo, and Guthrie. Women's groups, especially church societies and mothers' clubs, circulated antidivorce petitions. Ministers sermonized against easy divorce. And in 1913 Reno's major newspaper, the Nevada State Journal, insisted that, "Any work too damaging for any other state to do is certainly too damaging for Nevada to do."[71]

Next, public antidivorce protests erupted in Nevada's capital. On 7 February 1913, 160 protestors boarded the Virginia and Truckee Railroad train and traveled from Reno to the state capitol in Carson City. There these demonstrators thronged into the capitol demanding that the state legislature adopt a bill requiring one year's residency of all divorce petitioners.[72] Nevada subsequently passed a one-year residency requirement, but businesspeople and entrepreneurs created a public outcry against the one-year measure. They sorely missed the revenues, including transportation costs, legal fees, entertainment, meals, and lodging, that the divorce trade put into their pockets. When the legislature convened in January 1915, the Reno Businessmen's Association requested reinstatement of the six-month residency requirement for divorces. In spite of women's groups, clergy, and a Reno delegation's protests, a six-month residency bill passed on 17 February 1915. Although Governor Emmet D. Boyle believed the issue should go to a popular referendum, he signed the bill.[73]

The matter of short residency was far from dead in Nevada, however. Opponents of easy divorce raised the issue of a one-year residency bill again in 1922, but voters rejected the idea by three to one. Five years later Nevada reduced its residency requirement from six to three months, in a bill pushed through the legislature and hurriedly signed by Governor Fred B. Balzer before protest could arise. The *Nevada State Journal* chastised legislators and Balzer in a scathing editorial, which concluded that, "Such procedure is repugnant to the principles of free government and forms a most dangerous precedent."[74]

During the late 1920s and 1930s, then, Reno's divorce business increased dramatically. In 1926 Nevada courts granted 1,021 divorces. After the legislature lowered the residency requirement in 1927, the number of divorces almost doubled, to 1,953 that year. In 1928 Nevada courts awarded 2,595 divorces. Then in 1931, feeling under pressure from such other liberal divorce states as Arkansas and Idaho, both of which had issued divorces at a faster rate than Nevada through the second decade of the century, Nevada again reduced its residency requirement; when it appeared that Arkansas and Idaho were about to match Nevada's three-month requirement, Nevada dropped its provision to six weeks. Although the *Nevada State Journal* sarcastically declared "Revival of Gold Rush Days Predicted," again Governor Balzer signed the bill.[75]

A number of other provisions designed to attract divorce seekers to Nevada accompanied the state's six-week residency provision. A Nevada court could grant a divorce to a plaintiff on the forty-third day of residency, if the defendant filed an appearance through an attorney. In uncontested cases a court could accept the testimony of the plaintiff without corroborating witnesses. At the same time, liberal gambling provisions guaranteed that divorce seekers could amuse themselves, and spend more money, while waiting for their residencies to become final.[76]

Increasingly divorce seekers went not only to Reno, but also to Las Vegas, whose glitzy image and gambling venues attracted them. Consequently Nevada's divorce industry experienced a boom. Numbers of divorces granted in Nevada jumped form 2,609 in 1930 to 5,260 in 1931.[77]

By 1940 Nevada's divorce rate, forty-nine divorces per one thousand people, was by far the highest of all states. Still, Nevada divorces accounted for only one out of every fifty divorces granted in the United States. Because famous and wealthy people sought divorces in Nevada and garnered huge amounts of publicity, Nevada's easy divorce grew large in the public mind. Ultimately the Reno scandal, and the eventual addition of Las Vegas as a divorce center, led to a widespread image of the American West as the epitome of the land of lax divorce. Divorce mills also convinced numerous westerners to think of themselves as innovators in divorce.

Other Western Innovations

Besides producing some of the most lenient divorce provisions in the United States, the West also launched progressive notions of divorce, notably the concept of no-fault divorce. The idea of no-fault had its roots in the early twentieth century, for a growing number of Americans questioned the efficacy of "fault" divorce. As the divorce rate climbed, a growing number of people became concerned about the effects of the divorce process on spouses and children.[78]

Not until the 1940s, however, did Americans begin to discuss the possibility of replacing adversarial divorce with a nonpunitive procedure.[79] At the same time, a number of states had begun to deemphasize adversarial divorce procedures by legislative enactment. In several states statutes permitted couples to divorce after they had lived apart for a specified time; no wrongdoing need have occurred.[80] Still many people continued to advocate the elimination of adversary divorce.[81]

It was westerners who finally acted on the matter. In 1967 after studying various suggestions and the 1966 *Report of the Governor's Commission on the Family*, California legislators began to draft no-fault divorce statutes. In 1969 the California legislature approved the Family Law Act, and Governor Ronald Reagan signed the measure into law on 5 September, 1969. The bill, which went into effect on 1 January 1970, replaced

California's seven grounds for divorce with two no-fault provisions: irre-mediable breakdown of a marriage and incurable insanity. Petitioners had only to reside in California for six months before applying for a divorce. Judges could award alimony based on a spouse's need for support and the other spouse's ability to pay; courts were to divide a couples' property equally. Judges could also make child-custody decisions. And the final decree was to be known as a dissolution, rather than a divorce.[82]

California's no-fault statute marked the beginning of widespread changes in American divorce law. In 1971 another trans-Mississippi state, Iowa, became the first to follow California in adopting no-fault divorce. By August 1977 only three states retained the adversary system of divorce: Illinois, Pennsylvania, and South Dakota. Fifteen states (Arizona, California, Colo-rado, Delaware, Florida, Iowa, Kentucky, Michigan, Minnesota, Missouri, Montana, Nebraska, Oregon, Washington, and Wisconsin) stipulated ir-retrievable breakdown of a marriage as the sole ground for divorce, while sixteen others (Alaska, Alabama, Connecticut, Georgia, Hawaii, Idaho, Indiana, Maine, Massachusetts, Mississippi, New Hampshire, North Da-kota, Texas, Tennessee, Rhode Island, and Ohio) had added irretrievable breakdown to existing "fault" grounds.[83]

Rather than causing divorce rates to escalate, as is so often assumed, no-fault legislation created a number of other immediate changes in Ameri-can divorce. For example as divorce became easier to obtain, the number of people receiving annulments and legal separations dropped. Thus some of the apparent increase in numbers of divorces was simply a shift of an-nulled and separated couples to the divorce column. Moreover fewer couples escaped to lenient western jurisdictions such as Nevada to di-vorce, but stayed in their home jurisdictions instead.[84]

More fundamentally no-fault theory changed the definition of divorce from a punishment of an offending spouse to a "remedy for situations which are unavoidable and unendurable." Thus although no-fault laws attempted to preserve marriages when possible, they provided relief to dissatisfied spouses on nonjudgmental grounds.[85] They also made collusion between divorcing spouses unnecessary, because one no longer "sued" the other for divorce. As a result, numbers of male petitioners, who had no need to let their wives seek divorce while they assumed public "blame" for marital breakdown, increased considerably. Between 1966 and 1969, more than 78 percent of plaintiffs in California divorce suits were female, but in 1974 this figure dropped to slightly below 68 percent.[86]

Additionally no-fault divorces were cheaper, because such actions seldom involved high court, attorney, and other costs. A 1977 United States Supreme Court ruling, *Bates v. State Bar of Arizona*, strengthened this effect by permitting attorneys to advertise their services. Soon American lawyers advertised easy, inexpensive divorces more frequently than any other legal service. According to these advertisements, divorces could be obtained for the bargain price of from $50 to $100.[87]

Finally the West's gradual move toward, and eventual adoption of, no-fault divorce reinforced the region's image as a cauldron of change and progressive attitudes toward marriage and the family.[88] But no-fault divorce did not stand alone in this process. Another significant western trend, which also had its origins in the early twentieth century, was Hollywood stars' propensity to marry, divorce, remarry, and redivorce.

It was not until 1959 that someone totaled the score for numerous Americans who had evidenced a long-standing fascination with Hollywood stars who frequently married and divorced. In that year, a *McCall's Magazine* article exposed the marital escapades of Hollywood figures. What purported to be the first chart of Hollywood divorces ever compiled revealed that, among others, in 1934 Gloria Swanson divorced her fourth husband, in 1950 Arline Judge divorced her sixth husband, and in 1956, Artie Shaw divorced his seventh wife.[89]

Like support for no-fault divorce, acceptance of multiple divorce, especially in Hollywood, also grew. In subsequent years, such stars as Zsa Zsa Gabor, Mickey Rooney, and Elizabeth Taylor contributed heavily to Hollywood's divorce and remarriage rate. As recently as 1988, a *USA Weekend* article exposed a number of other well-known personalities who had married and divorced several times. To the query "how many marriages?" it responded: Muhammad Ali, 4; Glen Campbell, 4; Johnny Carson, 4; Joan Collins, 4; Dick Clark, 3; Doris Day, 4; Rita Hayworth, 5; Liza Minnelli, 3; Mary Tyler Moore, 3; Richard Pryor, 5; Jason Robards, 4; Kenny Rogers, 4; Telly Savalas, 3; George C. Scott, 5; Frank Sinatra, 4; Jane Wyman, 5; and Tammy Wynette, 5.[90]

Given that the West embraced everything from long-term divorce to divorce mills, no-fault divorce, and multiple divorce, it is little wonder much of the regional also evidenced liberal attitudes and policies toward divorce. In turn these permissive attitudes and policies contributed to the West's immoderate divorce rate.

Western Women's Economic and Judicial Opportunities
From Wage-Work to Entrepreneurship

Western women's growing economic and other opportunities also affected the climbing divorce rate in the American West. Although historians of western women often maintain that those living in the West encountered fewer wage and entrepreneurial opportunities than women living in the northeastern and southern sections of the United States, two sets of statistics refute this claim. In the first place, U.S. census figures show that more western women than northeastern and southern women petitioned for divorce, which suggests that western women felt capable of supporting themselves and their children on their own. In the second place, social science research has demonstrated that women with economic autonomy, ranging from Native Americans living in tribal groups to Anglos living in urban areas, more readily sought divorces than women who had no means of support.[91]

One must ask, then, how the idea that western women could not support themselves originated? For one thing, the assumption that fewer western women worked for wages than women in other areas of the country probably originated with U.S. Census Bureau figures. In 1890 census data indicated that 13 percent of western women worked outside their homes, as compared to 17 percent nationally. Such figures make it appear that most western women had less economic opportunity open to them.

But the way in which census takers classified "employment" and how such labels affected western women demands further examination. During the nineteenth century, census takers categorized men and some women as gainfully employed if they earned a direct income (as did farmers) or a cash wage (as did factory workers). Clearly an industrializing society that measured individuals by money earned created the census grouping "gainfully employed." If a person earned money, he or she was gainfully employed; if a person did not earn money, he or she fell under the section "not gainfully employed."

Such divisions proved far more meaningful for western men than women. Male farmers, laborers, mechanics, merchants, and entrepreneurs won bread for their families by earning cash for their labor. Many western women worked just as hard as men, yet no cash wage, no pay check, rewarded their industry. Although women's labor in fields, family businesses, making extra goods for sale, and working as slaves contributed to a family's sustenance, the women performing work were considered unemployed.

Case history after case history proves that women's labor expanded beyond domestic duties, yet still went unrewarded in terms of cash.

One representative case was that of Sarah Royce, who performed unpaid work in a California mining camp. When she and her husband arrived in Weaverville, a number of men convinced her husband to join them in opening a store. According to Sarah, because "it had not been thought necessary for all the men of the firm to devote their time to the store," two of them continued mining. Thus "when a large number of customers came together," Sarah agreeably "helped to serve them."[92]

Farther north another wife who contributed to the family business was an African American woman in Yakima, Washington. As a young girl she learned the barbering trade from her guardian and served as a barber in her husband's shop. After she married another barber and the couple relocated to Seattle, she helped in his shop, contributing to the family business but drawing no wage.[93]

Yet another woman who assisted in earning the family income but earned no money of her own lived in Durant, Oklahoma. During the 1870s this woman's husband, a Choctaw missionary, earned only $400 a year. To bring in additional income, he taught a subscription school; she helped him teach. He also opened an orphanage in his home; his wife cared for the children, taught them to speak English, and made clothes for them out of cast-offs sent from other missions.[94] Similarly an El Reno, Oklahoma, woman assisted her missionary husband in his work with Kiowa and Comanche Indians, often riding horseback ten or twelve miles on cold winter nights to attend to ailing Kiowa patients.[95]

Another peculiarity of the census occurred in the category "farmer," in which census takers included only women who farmed on their own; a married woman who ran the family farm while her husband worked elsewhere was not usually counted as a farmer.[96] Nor were women who worked on family farms alongside their fathers, brothers, and husbands regarded as farmers or as gainfully employed; they were considered farm wives, daughters, sisters, or mothers. Yet a Gallatin Gateway, Montana, woman remembered that she "helped hay, and . . . stack grain and anything that had to be done on the farm" and "worked with the cattle."[97]

Census takers also tended to overlook women ranchers and trail hands, although anecdotal evidence reveals that both single and married women engaged in both occupations. In Montana, Wyoming, and Texas, documented cases existed of women who ran ranches and drove their cattle to market or worked as partners with their husbands, doing everything from cooking to wrangling cattle.[98]

Nor did census takers record slave women as agricultural and other types of workers. African American slave women worked in the fields, helped build roads, cut down stands of timber, and performed other necessary labor on farms and plantations. A former Texas slave remembered that during the 1850s her mother was the plantation cook.[99] Yet none of these women qualified for the category "gainfully employed."

Still the U.S. census is not totally at fault for long-standing misinterpretations of western women's work. Media, popular culture, and even some western historians have contributed to mistaken beliefs regarding women's wage work. As a consequence of scholarly neglect and popular stereotypes, it is necessary to diverge slightly to indicate that western women indeed worked in an incredible variety of paid occupations.

For example because society often dismissed women who sold companionship and sexual services to men with a sniff of its collective nose, it is easy to forget that the work of such women constituted employment. One variation of western women who provided entertainment for men were the ubiquitous hurdy-gurdy girls, who appeared from Montana to California. A California woman of the 1850s explained that troupes moved from gold camp to gold camp where, for a stiff fee, women drank and danced with men deprived of female company: "every dance brought to the house fifty cents for drinks and fifty-cents to the girl."[100]

Most of these hurdy-gurdy girls were also prostitutes, as were most dance hall girls. Prostitutes also worked in hotels, boardinghouses, brothels, and cribs, especially in such cattle towns as Abilene, Wichita, and Dodge City in Kansas, where males outnumbered females by two or three to one, and in mining camps from Nevada to California, where men could outnumber women by as much as fifteen or twenty or one. The majority of these women were typically, but not always, unmarried, usually in their teens and twenties. Census data, police records, newspapers, and other sources demonstrate that the calling attracted both white women and women of color.[101]

Brothel districts, often called tenderloins, developed in other kinds of towns as well. In the railroad town of Grand Island, Nebraska, evidence from newspapers, court dockets, plat maps, and city directories show that prostitution thrived during the late nineteenth century. Sometime in the mid-1880s, a husband-wife team built Grand Island's first brothel. Grand

Island's "burnt district" grew and flourished until the turn of the century, when the city council passed restrictive laws.[102]

Western women also held a huge variety of other paid jobs, which, unlike prostitution, seldom appear in popular culture or even in most western histories. Among other things, women worked as actresses, agricultural laborers, artists and illustrators, authors and lecturers, bakers, barkeepers, book agents, boot and box makers, cigar makers, clergy, clerks and copyists, coal and wood dealers, confectioners, dairymaids, distillers, domestic workers, editors, environmental advocates, glove makers, government employees, gun and lock smiths, hair dressers, hunters and trappers, journalists and novelists, laundresses, librarians, mantua makers, miners, musicians, rag pickers, saleswomen and peddlers, shepherds, shop clerks and shopowners, photographers, postmasters, tailoresses and seamstresses, teamsters, telegraph operators, umbrella and parasol makers, and morticians.[103]

Western women also entered the professions in significant numbers. In 1890 14 percent of western women became professionals, as compared to 8 percent nationally. Teaching especially attracted western women. Because western society often saw teaching as a logical extension of women's childcare skills, and offered lower pay than most men were able to accept, women teachers not only outnumbered men teachers throughout the West, but also outnumbered women teachers in the Northeast and South. Laura Brown, who began her teaching career in Custer County, Montana in 1886, was representative. A local rancher and member of the school board loaned Brown a horse and told her that she would receive $65 per month. "Was I ever thrilled," she recalled, "seventeen years old and earning so much!" Brown added, "I earned it all right."[104]

Other women teachers combined teaching with additional economic endeavors, especially farming or homesteading. Sarah Jane Price of Nebraska saved money from her small salary and bought a farm. She ran the farm and continued to teach. Other teachers took what additional employment they could find; during the summer of 1885 one even became a cook on a trail drive.[105]

Some western women also continued to teach after marriage. Although numerous school districts required a woman's resignation when she married, others did not. Married women teachers were especially common in areas experiencing teacher shortages and in families suffering cash deficits. A Washington state woman explained that when she accompanied her husband to Spokane in 1888, they encountered what she described as "boom times in the Coeur d'Alene mining district." After the Big Chief mine "swallowed" the couple's savings, the woman and her husband took teaching jobs to "get money enough to go on with."[106]

Teaching attracted women of color as well. For instance an early Kansas newspaper noted that there was at least one African American woman teacher in the Exoduster town of Nicodemus, Kansas, in 1878.[107] Although less is known about Hispanic and Asian teachers, anecdotal evidence indicates that many existed in the West. An early example was Apolinaria Lorenzana who, as a young woman, worked as a tutor in Santa Barbara, California, probably sometime during the 1820s.[108]

In addition to teaching, women earned income through appointive and elected offices in education. They especially served as county superintendents of schools, a demanding job requiring travel to inspect outlying schools and teachers. In Park County, Montana, women served as superintendents from the county's beginning in 1887. In another Montana county during the 1880s, Mary Johnstone served first as principal and then as county superintendent. In Sacramento, California, Sarah Mildred Jones, an African American teacher, also achieved a position of leadership.[109]

Another profession that western women entered in greater numbers than usually believed was that of physician. In the Dakota Territory during the 1880s, German-born and trained Friede Feige practiced medicine, while her minister husband homesteaded. A South Dakota doctor, Abbie Ann Jarvis, acquired medical training at the Women's Medical College in Chicago where, in 1898, she graduated fourth in a class of twenty-four students. On the west coast, Lavinia Goodyear Waterhouse became a successful hydropathic physician in Sacramento.[110]

Women doctors existed in other regions of the West as well. In twentieth-century Washington state, Dr. Mary Perkins of Steilacoom began her medical practice in 1903.[111] In Hawaii Dr. Kong Tai Heong was the first Chinese woman doctor to practice. Trained at the Canton Medical School in China, Dr. Heong and her husband, Dr. Li Khai Fai, emigrated to Hawaii in 1896. The couple established the first Chinese hospital in Honolulu, then went into private practice in 1910.[112]

Besides excelling in the professions, western women also proved their mettle as individual entrepreneurs. Entrepreneurial-minded women started businesses ranging from boardinghouses and hotels to millinery shops and brothels. Often these women succeeded financially, including western women of color who had to overcome prejudice against both gender and race. In Colorado African American Clara Brown profitably invested in mines, while in California African American Mary Ellen Pleasant established a small fortune by running boardinghouses, restaurants, and laundries.[113]

This overview of western women in paid employment, professions, and business only hints at the vastness and diversity of western women's gainful employment. For every one of the women mentioned here, thousands more held some form of wage work during part or all of their adult lives. In the words of one married African American woman in Washington state who had held a range of jobs, "I've worked all my life, hard work . . . ."[114]

These western women not only knew how to earn income, but also how to take care of themselves. Those who divorced turned their economic skills into full-time support for themselves and their children. In 1888 for example, a Jewish woman named Fannie Marks, who had married David Marks in their native Poland in 1863, petitioned for a divorce in San Diego because of her husband's gambling. Mother of thirteen children, Fannie expanded her boardinghouse operation to support herself and her family.[115] In Nebraska Dr. Georgia Arbuckle Fix's husband occasionally drove her to housecalls in his buckboard wagon before she divorced him in the early 1900s.[116] Also during the early twentieth century, Martha Waln of Ten Sleep, Wyoming, left her alcoholic husband, taking with her only $50 and a horse. To support herself and her five children, she first served as a postmaster and ran a small shop in her home. Next she became a peddler, then joined the Watkins Medicine Company as a traveling salesperson. Waln later returned to Ten Sleep to found a retail store and finally bought a small ranch.[117]

Divorced women also took up land to support themselves and their children. During the 1880s a recently divorced women with a four-year-old daughter boarded a train for Montana, where she chose a 360-acre claim, boasting a 14-by-16 foot shack with two windows, a door, and a shingled roof. Similarly Kate E. May, a divorced Oklahoma woman, joined a land run to obtain a homestead to support herself and her four-month-old child.[118]

Because census figures are inexact and comparative data is nonexistent, it is impossible to know if more western women held paid employment than women in other regions. It is clear, however, that far more western women had the resources to support themselves than is usually supposed; thus divorce would not have loomed as an economic impossibility to such women. It is little wonder then that Commissioner Carroll Wright discovered that western women obtained more divorces than women in other sections of the country, as well as more than western men.

As a national average, women received approximately two-thirds of divorces granted, and men received one-third.[119] Because the West accounted for more divorces than other regions, however, women in western states and territories were awarded at least two-thirds of decrees. Women received more than two-thirds of divorces in California, Colorado, Iowa, Kansas, Minnesota, Montana, Nebraska, Nevada, Washington, and Wyoming.[120]

These divorcing women also received alimony more frequently than women in northeastern and southern states. Most women who requested alimony were plaintiffs rather than defendants, for it was widely believed that a guilty wife forfeited her claim to a husband's earnings if her misbehavior brought the marriage to an end. Clear regional differences existed in the application of this principle. Massachusetts judges awarded alimony in 6.1 percent of cases, but Utah judges did so in 32.1 percent. Alabama courts awarded alimony in 1.9 percent of cases, but Nebraska courts did so in 20.1 percent.[121]

Even when a man initiated the divorce and proved his wife guilty, western judges sometimes awarded alimony to female defendants. One such case was that of Lorenzo B. Lyman, who filed for divorce from his wife, Fannie, on 30 August 1891, in Oklahoma Territory. Although Fannie lived in Montana, she quickly arrived at the Guthrie courtroom, where she testified that Lorenzo had refused to support her and her two children, one of whom was an epileptic. She had supported herself and the children by taking in boarders and running an employment agency. Fannie then countersued, charging abandonment and asking for custody of the children, a $2,000 lump-sum settlement, and $600 per year. The court found for Fannie and awarded her custody, alimony, and a portion of the couple's joint property. In another case David Hughes sued his wife, Mary, on the ground of adultery in 1897, also in Oklahoma Territory. Mary appeared in court, where she denied the charge, asked for $50 per month alimony, and gave the court a detailed description of two amputations of her arm, the result of David shooting her "without any cause." David got a divorce, but Mary received $1000 alimony and $50 in attorney's fees.[122]

Generally, however, alimony awards proved insufficient to western women's needs. Presumably those who had worked during their marriages would continue to do so after they divorced. Divorce records revealed that a large number of divorcing women had earned income and had sometimes supported their husbands as well. In 1891 Susie Gleason told an Oklahoma territorial court she had been "compelled to support herself" because her husband drank excessively and failed to provide, while Lina Weyach said she had worked as a washerwoman during the course of her marriage. Later that year seamstress Jennie Zeller stated that, despite her willingness to financially support him, her habitual drunkard husband had abandoned her. In 1893 Marian Quick said she had earned her own living and provided "board" for her abusive husband. A few days later, Phoebe Wise testified that she worked as a hired girl and laundress. In 1895 Grace Rowland and Belle Beck mentioned supporting themselves after their husbands' abandonment, but they neglected to specify their jobs. Also in that year, Adolfine Schwart explained that she "washes & sewes [sic] for others." In 1899 Eva Bowers noted that she had "worked for her own living" because her husband refused to support her. The following month Martha Condron maintained that she supported herself and her alcoholic husband by working as a dressmaker.[123]

Women who had not worked before seeking divorces found what jobs they could, ranging from giving piano lessons to clerking in shops and claiming homesteads.[124] When Anna Nelson Page divorced her husband in 1905, she moved to Grand Forks, North Dakota, where she supported herself and her son by working as Society Editor for the *Herald*. In 1911 Page purchased the Devils Lake *Inter-Ocean* and in 1915 established the Grand Forks *Independent*.[125]

Economic skills were especially important to divorced western women because they had a slightly better chance of getting child custody than did women in southern and northeastern states. Between 1887 and 1906, Census Bureau figures showed that women nationally received custody at a three-to-one ratio to men. In western states, however, women received custody at a noticeably higher ratio, especially in California, Colorado, Idaho, Iowa, Kansas, Michigan, Minnesota, Montana, Nebraska, Nevada, Utah, and Washington.[126]

Obviously western divorce was far from a nirvana for women. Alimony awards were often small, one-time sums, and child-custody decisions were erratic. Consequently many women remained in difficult marriages because they were unable to support themselves and feared losing their children. One especially touching case was that of Lena Tow, who left her

husband and took their three small children to Montana. After her borrowed funds ran out and she failed to find a job, Lena dejectedly returned
to her husband in Norway, Iowa. A despairing Kansas woman took another tack; she simply waited for her verbally abusive, alcoholic husband
to die.[127] But thousands of western women grasped their courage and their
limited funds in their hands and sued for divorce.

Changing Popular and Judicial Scruples

Alongside economic opportunities, changing moral standards in the
late-nineteenth- and early-twentieth-century West urged women toward
divorce, which increasingly garnered widespread support. Especially on
the west coast, Progressives joined with feminists and other reformers in
calling for the freedom of choice to stay in a marriage or leave it.[128]

At the same time, the rising divorce rate itself played a role in westerners'
revision of older values. Even though the West's divorce rate had risen
steadily, numbers of divorces awarded throughout the nation reached an
unexpected high by the end of the nineteenth century: perhaps as many
as ten to twelve marriages per thousand ended in divorce in the United
States as a whole.[129] During the first decade of the twentieth century, the
divorce rate continued to experience an unprecedented increase.[130] The
sheer force of numbers of divorces convinced some westerners, and
compelled others, to accept the institution's increasing ubiquity in
western society.

Obviously not all westerners supported "modern" ideas regarding divorce. A significant number continued to view marriage as a religious sacrament lasting for a lifetime. But millions of others accepted the idea of
permissive divorce. Besides radicals, rebels, and reformers, a growing number of average, middle-class women embraced the idea of divorce.[131] On
18 May 1913, for example, a western woman named Sara Bard Ehrgott
boarded a ship in Portland, Oregon, with her sister, Mary, and her four-
year-old daughter, Kay. The party sailed to San Francisco, where Sara spent
$62.70 on three train tickets to Goldfield, Nevada. Faced by her husband's
opposition to a divorce, Sara Ehrgott had resolved to go to Nevada to
obtain a divorce, preferably in a town far from "the unpleasant notoriety
of Reno." During the train's Sacramento stop, Sara mailed a letter to
her husband telling him of her plans. When the trio arrived in Goldfield, the party discovered what Sara described as a "typical mining
town," but to her amazement and delight, Goldfield's hotel boasted

running water, bathtubs, electricity, and "excellent food." After settling into the hotel, Sara met with an attorney to initiate a divorce suit against her husband, Albert.[132]

When Sara Ehrgott met with her attorney in Goldfield on 23 May 1913, he told Sara that she could get her a divorce decree in less than the required six months, if her husband would give his consent. Although Sara felt euphoric—"what a wonderful relief it would be if I could have this case come up at once and not have to endure this dreary six months waiting"—Albert continued to oppose her. Sara thus rented a small four-room house for $20 a month, where she and her daughter lived until a Goldfield court granted her divorce in early 1914, after what Sara termed "long, unnecessary delays."[133]

Sara Ehrgott was in the forefront of a growing number of western women who rejected the idea of marriage as a lifetime sacrament. Also she had earned income as a lecturer and writer. Thus although her husband had not committed a marital crime (adultery, desertion, nonsupport, or cruelty), Sara decided she no longer loved him. Moreover she loved another man, California attorney Charles Wood.[134]

Both Charles and Sara adhered to, and attempted to promulgate, a new morality, in that they believed it was unethical to force two people to live together when they wished to divorce. Wood especially felt baffled by people who failed to see that free divorce was "best for society and the race." In Wood's view, every couple forced to remain together despite altered feelings was "a cancer" and "every refusal of freedom leads to falsities."[135] Less philosophical than Charles, Sara had simply seized the opportunities the West offered in employment and liberal divorce, thus dissolving her relationship to one man and establishing a tie to another.

Conclusion

During the late nineteenth century, many Americans came to believe that the growing willingness of westerners, especially women, to divorce indicated a pressing need for reevaluation. In calling for divorce reform, these Americans maintained that such long-held American values as individualism, freedom from tyranny, and a search for personal happiness had flourished in the American West, and had gotten out of hand.

During the early twentieth century, nationwide concern regarding divorce intensified. Even conservative, religiously oriented people began to divorce in growing numbers. In the twentieth-century West, divorce among those of Spanish heritage climbed. Even though Hispanics divorced less than Anglos and African Americans, probably as a result of their adherence to Roman Catholic beliefs, they divorced in greater numbers than their parents and grandparents had.[136] Mennonites divorced at a slower pace than westerners overall, but at a faster rate than Mennonites living in the Canadian West.[137]

Certainly westerners had put their oft-professed beliefs in equality and the pursuit of happiness into practice, at least in the area of divorce. By the turn of the twentieth century, almost any westerner could divorce, and more did so than in any other region of the United States.

Epilogue

The previous essays have offered a number of answers to the dilemma of why the American West had, and still has, the highest divorce rate in the world. The first essay argued that historical competition between cultures caused courtship to break down in the American West, so that the selection process became increasingly incoherent and ineffective. The second essay maintained that even though numerous factors united western couples, those same factors could just as easily stress western marriages as much as or even more than they held them together. The third indicated that although the West offered great opportunities for intermarriage, accompanying barriers and opposition helped create a significant failure rate among intermarriages. The concluding essay added that the West manifested every characteristic identified as a causal factor of divorce, including urbanization and women's changing roles, as well as demonstrating liberal attitudes toward divorce and offering western women expanding economic, moral, and judicial choices.

Obviously the answer to the West's unusually high divorce rate is a complicated one. But studying the issue through cultural layering (the analysis of courtship, marriage, intermarriage, and divorce across western cultures) has illuminated a heretofore unexplored dimension: the great diversity of cultures in the American West, with their tendency to clash rather than blend, created a chaotic environment in which to court and marry. Looking at cultural layering another way, the process is like an artist working in watercolors. When one color is layered over another, an entirely new color emerges. So it is with cultural layering in this study; overlaying culture after culture has produced a fresh portrayal of western marriages and divorce.

145

What then can be done to help concerned westerners lessen family instability? On the one hand, perhaps nothing can be done. The West has provided a giant petri dish for the growth of divorce. A rising divorce rate is a well-entrenched, historical pattern. It is thus conceivable that American society, with the West in the lead, is undergoing a transition to such a revolutionary type of family form that we would not identify it as a family at all. If so, historians and other scholars of the mid-twenty-first century will look back on earlier developments and wonder why we bemoaned divorce and why we could not identify the passage in which we participated.

One the other hand, the astonishing growth of divorce has left in its wake a huge legacy of information and experience, tools that we can use to create what one historian has called "an ethically responsible transition from present to future."[1] In particular the history of western divorce points to several areas that demand increased attention from legislators, jurists, policymakers, and individuals.

Examples of reforms suggested here could be adopted with potential advantage by all states in all regions, but in the West they have special pertinence. Because more western families break apart than those in other regions do, western jurisdictions must lead the way in seeking remedies. No single revision proposed here is a panacea, but taken together they send the message that marriage, and divorce, are serious business, not to be undertaken lightly.

For one thing, courtship demands reconsideration. In this era of public debate regarding family values, politicians and journalists emphasize marriage and divorce. But what about courtship? It might be far more productive to focus on what happens before people marry—and eventually divorce. If courtship is supposed to result in the selection of a compatible mate for a lifetime, western courtship is a failure. Thus contemporary western courtship requires rethinking, for selecting a lifetime companion is a critical matter.

Once upon a time, the process of choosing a spouse was a family affair. But by the beginning of the twentieth century, courtship had shifted, assisted by the automobile, from family parlors to anonymous public places and secluded apartments. In addition throughout much of the West, Anglo culture not only layered itself over others, but ignored or even destroyed many of those cultures' ways in the process. Customs such as the courting walk or parental involvement became laughable to many westerners and frequently disappeared.

It is easy to say that parents and others must reassert themselves in courtship decisions, but historical evidence supports the opposite pattern. Perhaps such information *should* come from the home, but it frequently does not. To fill the void, one thinks of three other types of people already heavily involved in family dynamics and outcomes: educators, clergy, and political leaders.

Teachers at all levels can help. After the rise and fall of "marriage and family" courses during the 1960s, family-oriented instruction virtually disappeared from school and college curriculums. Today's teachers are often overtaxed, yet thousands are willing to pick up where parents leave off, or give up. Educators and counselors can support the ideal of lifetime marriage and help people avoid divorce by expanding programs intended to educate people before and during marriage.

In the West teachers have a special opportunity, for they can draw upon the region's many cultures for illustrations. Multicultural education would be enriched by inclusion of units regarding courtship, marriage, and family customs across cultures. The point is not to convince people of all cultures to accept one model, but to help them understand that many customs exist and offer a variety of benefits.

The point is also to force people to think about what they desire in marriage and to seek a spouse who has similar expectations. As the end of the twentieth century nears, some westerners cling to traditional views of marriage, while others embrace new marital models and redefine marriage accordingly. In 1986 one popular magazine described a contemporary prototype, a marital state called the "new togetherness." It "takes as its criterion the success of the separate life," supports the "independence of husband and wife," and enables "both partners to function well and happily outside the home." Such spouses would, as another proponent of this type of marriage phrased it, combine "enduring love with self-development."[2]

Whether they decided to adopt this or other ideals, most westerners would benefit greatly from being forced to examine and adjust their expectations of marriage and to weigh the pros and cons of contemporary models. Knowing what one expects and what one wants in both a mate and a marriage is one way to reduce the likelihood of divorce.

Clergy and officials are another key to improved courtship. They must, as Catholic priests routinely do, require waiting periods and premarital counseling. An Oregon man admitted that although he resisted a priest's teachings through six months of counseling, he felt better prepared and happier in marriage than if the priest had simply performed the ceremony.[3]

Of course the world will never be perfect. Despite advice and education, some people will rush into marriage for myriad reasons. Some will grab an unsuitable mate because they fear being alone. Others will follow the romantic messages pumped out by music, television programs, and movies. And many clergy and officials will shrug and marry couples in haste, while Nevada wedding chapels will marry on the spot, no questions asked.

As a result, legislation is necessary. Marriage must be harder to get. People who worry about the West's divorce rate frequently suggest that divorce should be more difficult to obtain; but divorce is only the seal that marks the legal termination of a bad marriage. The availability of divorce is seldom the cause of a marriage's disintegration; rather, the fact that a mismatched couple wed in the first place led to martial problems and eventually to divorce. Although laws cannot force people to choose compatible partners, legal restraints can force people to wait before marrying. Like a gun license, a marriage license must have a cool-down period, for both weapons and matrimony create potentially explosive situations. Mandatory premarital counseling is another possibility. Perhaps people seeking marriage licenses can be forced to think while they are waiting.

The institution of western marriage needs assistance as well. Private and public agencies must help reduce the stresses on contemporary marriages. Education, counseling, and marriage enrichment workshops are already in place and growing, but married couples require more help. For instance two-job couples with children must have reasonable, quality childcare. In 1990 an article in *Newsweek* called the state of daycare in the United States "haphazard." Its authors pointed out that no federal regulations exist to cover daycare: "the government offers consumers more guidance choosing breakfast cereal than child care."[4]

Many policymakers fear that by supporting childcare, federal and state governments would appear to encourage women to bear fewer children and to put children increasingly in the hands of others while women themselves work outside their homes. Officials hesitate to send what seems to be an antifamily message. In fact provision and regulation of reliable childcare facilities with properly paid employees would proclaim a profamily stance. Because most women will hold jobs, either by choice or necessity, services women provided when at home, especially childcare, must be provided by others. If the federal government refuses to undertake this task, then the states must. State provision and regulation of childcare would assist two-job marriages involving children to remain stable and in force.

The mechanism of divorce also needs attention and refinement—or perhaps replacement. Because both adversary divorce and no-fault divorce have proven problematic, it is time to devise an entirely new form of divorce.[5] California, quickly followed by Iowa, led the no-fault revolution. Now that the no-fault system has revealed serious imperfections, these and other western states have an opportunity to pioneer a new pattern of divorce.

It might be helpful to separate the granting of a divorce decree or dissolution from decisions concerning child custody, alimony, and division of property. Let one court grant the divorce and another determine custody and financial arrangements. As long as custody of children and spousal support are tied to the divorce process, divorcing spouses are encouraged to use their children as weapons in their battles. Clearly using children in this way increases their bitterness about their parents' divorce and biases them against their future prospects of achieving happy, lifetime marriages.[6]

Moreover, alimony, property, and childcare awards must be equitable to all parties involved and must be effectively enforced. Intended or not, divorce has punished, and often still punishes, divorcing men and women. Because husbands and wives fail to achieve the ideal of lifetime marriage, their suffering somehow seems justified. But divorce has especially hurt, and continues to hurt, women, many of whom are still economically dependent upon men. Because women, the long-time protectors of home and family, fail to hold crumbling marriages together, their misfortunes can seem particularly just.

Adequate support for divorcing women and their children has remained a puzzling and unresolved issue. Today preventing divorced women and their children from entering the ranks of the destitute demands developing an equitable means of dividing a divorcing couple's assets, a means that recognizes the contributions of each partner to the marriage, even when only one is employed outside the home or earns less than the other.[7] This requires the enactment of statutes to guide courts in making such decisions and in reassessing what constitutes assets and contributions. A man's work experience is an asset; a woman's homemaking skills a contribution. Both must be taken into account and valued at the time of divorce.

Moreover division of social security benefits and pensions in divorce also needs more regulation. Despite the pioneering work of Colorado Congresswoman Pat Schroeder and the innovative Foreign Service Act of 1980, which provided the first model for the division of pension benefits in case of divorce, many decisions regarding retirement benefits rest in the hands of state courts, who are permitted, but not required, to divide such assets between divorcing partners. As a result, a wife who has a legal right to part of her husband's military pension may not receive it. In addition even if a wife receives a portion of her husband's retirement benefits, she often discovers that it is virtually impossible to collect.[8] Uniform strict standards for dividing this form of marital property and an effective payment method are equally necessary.

In some cases divorcing men may also need to make claims on their wives' financial resources and on joint property, including pensions and other retirement benefits, especially if they have fewer marketable skills than their wives and receive custody of the couple's children. Women's financial postdivorce support to former spouses, and especially to children, also requires equitable guiding principles and an enforcement mechanism.

Divorced westerners also require expanded counseling and other services funded by private organizations and agencies, local and state governments, and the federal government. Once divorced, westerners continue to require care and support. Mediation and counseling programs, educational and vocational courses, and job placement bureaus for divorcing women and men are already widespread. They encourage divorcing individuals to reject an adversary mentality, to take the best actions for both spouses and their children, to allow themselves some transition and recovery time before establishing new romantic relationships, to determine what they can learn from divorce, and to deal effectively with their children and their new financial situations.

These programs need expansion as well as increased funding for a number of reasons. In particular, current programs cannot serve everyone who needs help. Also the current failure rate of remarriages is appallingly high, adding further to the West's divorce rate. Yet one of the rationales for divorce is that it allows men and women to contract new marriages that might succeed. If the success rate of remarriages is to rise and a higher number of blended families are to remain intact, divorced people must be consoled, counseled, and reconstructed before entering a new marriage. Most are unable do this themselves; they must have outside help.

To be effective, counseling and other postdivorce services must develop several important components. A concerted outreach would inform low-income, non-English-speaking, illiterate, and other people that such resources exist. Tailoring services to meet the needs of particular westerners, including Chicanos and Asian Americans, who are experiencing rising divorce rates, would make counseling more useful.[9] Other programs designed for people in cross-cultural marriages could help them learn where they went astray and how to resolve their differences with others more constructively in the future. And providing free or inexpensive childcare would allow both female and male custodial parents to take advantage of these resources without detriment to children.

Counseling and other services must also develop an awareness of gender differences in clients. Men and women need different advice and forms of assistance. For instance many women must learn how to be a single parent while entering, or reentering, the job market. Specialized counseling is necessary if these women are to master such transitions successfully.[10]

Finally children of divorce need, and deserve, more study and more counseling services. Currently the extent and nature of damage sustained by children of divorce is unclear. Although some experts continue to maintain that children are capable of adjusting to the demands of divorce, others argue that they suffer long-term harm.[11] Far more studies must be funded and undertaken if we are to understand, and avoid or repair, the harm done to children of divorce and to reshape the divorce process so it is less traumatic to children. At the same time, counseling services for children of divorce and people who work with them must be expanded.[12] In the West it is especially important that such counselors speak a child-of-divorce's native language and understand his or her culture.

Granted, many changes have taken place in western courtship, marriage, intermarriage, and divorce. During the late twentieth century, the West initiated and implemented such reforms as no-fault divorce. Individual western states have also tried to remedy such problems as awarding of alimony, division of property, custody of children, child support, and postdivorce education and services. Yet more changes need to occur.

Fears about the demise of the American family need not hold us back; the family has remained vital in the face of rising divorce rates. Rather than declining as has so often been predicted, western families have survived, in some form, even the most liberal divorce policies. Eskimo societies of North Alaska, which allow free divorce, provide an especially dramatic case in point. Despite the ease of divorce, Eskimo people continue to marry, while divorced spouses and children form new family units.[13]

Other westerners have also maintained their faith in marriage and the family. Part of the vitality of these institutions comes from their ability to expand and encompass a two-parent, two-child model as well as blended, single-parent, complex, gay and lesbian, and "skip-generation" families.[14] Perhaps then the key to survival of families as we know them is to give up our nostalgic attachment to the idealized nuclear family, which had little relevance to most western cultures in any event, and to embrace a broader definition of "family."

If western families are to survive in some form, they need help now. Just because cultural diversity has proven more detrimental than helpful in the past does not mean it will do so in the future. In fact contemporary awareness of differences and the willingness to analyze and work with dissimilarities could lead instead to increased harmony and less family instability in the West.

Notes

Introduction

1. Linton C. Freeman, "Marriage without Love: Mate-Selection in Non-Western Societies," in Robert F. Winch, Robert McGinnis, and Herbert R. Barringer, eds., *Selected Studies in Marriage and the Family* (New York: Holt, Rinehart and Winston, 1962), 439–42, and Kathleen Gough, "The Origin of the Family," *Journal of Marriage and the Family* 33 (November 1971): 760–71.

2. John Demos, *Past, Present, and Personal: The Family and the Life Course in American History* (New York: Oxford University Press, 1986); Eliza K. Pavalko and Glen H. Elder, Jr., "World War II and Divorce: A Life-Course Perspective," *American Journal of Sociology* 95 (March 1990): 213–34; and Maris A. Vinovskis and Laura McCall, "Changing Approaches to the Study of Family Life," in Joseph M. Hawes and Elizabeth I. Nybakken, eds., *American Families: A Research Guide and Historical Handbook* (New York: Greenwood Press, 1991), 15–23. A discussion of other early approaches appears in Richard N. Adams, "An Inquiry into the Nature of the Family," in Gertrude Dole and Robert L. Carnetro, eds., *Essays in the Science of Culture* (New York: Thomas Y. Crowell Company, 1960), 30–49. An example of life-cycle research is Florence Kaslow, "The Sociocultural Context of Divorce," *Contemporary Family Therapy* 3 (December 1991): 583–607.

3. An example is M. F. Nimkoff and Russell Middleton, "Types of Family and Types of Economy," *American Journal of Sociology* 66 (1960): 215–55.

4. Two instances are, Selma Berrol, "Immigrant Working-Class Families," 219–45, and Margaret M. Caffrey, "Women and Families," 223–57, in Hawes and Nybakken, eds., *American Families*.

5. Karen Anderson, "African American Families," 259–90, and Nancy Shoemaker, "Native American Families," 291–317, in Hawes and Nybakken, eds., *American Families*.

6. As early as 1981, Lawrence Stone maintained that no national or regional family type existed. See Stone, "Family History in the 1980s," *Journal of Interdisciplinary History* 12 (Summer 1981): 51–87. Yet scholars continue to speak of, study, and characterize "the" American family, as do Rudy Ray Seward, *The American*

Family: A Demographic History (Beverly Hills, CA: Sage Publications, 1978), and Arlene F. Saluter, *Changes in American Family Life: Current Population Reports* Series P-23, No. 163 (Washington, DC: Government Printing Office, 1989), which present statistical profiles of "the" American family without recognition of racial, cultural, regional, or other diversities.

7. Roger A. Kessinger, *Marriage Licensing Laws: A State by State Guide* (Kila, MT: Kessinger Pub. Co., 1990), 92, 141, 210, 259, 302.

8. Kessinger, *Marriage Licensing Laws*, 71, 160, 166, 247.

9. Kessinger, *Marriage Licensing Laws*, 266, 295,

10. Stephanie Coontz, *The Social Origins of Private Life: A History of American Families, 1600–1900* (London: Verso, 1988), 317–24, and Kathleen Neils Conzen, "A Saga of Families," in Clyde A. Milner, II, Carol A. O'Connor, and Martha A. Sandwiess, eds., *The Oxford History of the American West* (New York: Oxford University Press, 1994), 315–57.

11. John Modell, "Historical Reflections of American Marriage," in Davis and Grossbard-Schechtman, eds., *Contemporary Marriage*, 182–83, and Ellen K. Rothman, *Hands and Hearts: The History of Courtship in America* (New York: Basic Books, 1984).

12. Joseph M. Hawes and Elizabeth I. Nybakken, "The Study of the American Family," in Hawes and Nybakken, eds, *American Families*, 8–9.

13. Hawes and Nybakken, "The Study of the American Family," 4–5, and Shoemaker, "Native American Families," in Hawes and Nybakken, eds., *American Families*, 196–300. See also Sylvia Junko Yanagisako, "Mixed Metaphors: Native and Anthropological Models of Gender and Kinship Domains," in Jane Fishburne Collier and Sylvia Junko Yanagisako, eds., *Gender and Kinship: Essays toward a Unified Analysis* (Stanford, CA: Stanford University Press, 1987), 86–118, and John H. Moore, "The Dialects of Cheyenne Kinship: Variability and Change," *Ethnology* 27 (1988): 253–69.

14. Freeman, "Marriage without Love," 442-45.

15. Joy Hendry, "Japan: Culture Versus Industrialization as Determinant of Marital Patterns," in Kingsley Davis and Amyra Grossbard-Shechtman, eds., *Contemporary Marriage: Perspectives on a Changing Institution* (New York: Russell Sage Foundation, 1985), 197–220, and G. Robina Quale, *A History of Marriage Systems* (New York: Greenwood Press, 1988), 1–13.

16. For instance, in Steven Mintz and Susan Kellogg, *Domestic Revolution: A Social History of American Family Life* (New York: Free Press, 1988), xviii–xix, the authors identify three principal forces for change in American families—economy, demography, and transformations in women's roles—but fail to consider regional differences in these factors.

17. One instance of a study of a specific western group is Douglas Monroy, *Thrown among Strangers: The Making of Mexican Culture in Frontier California* (Berkeley: University of California Press, 1990).

18. Tamara K. Hareven, "The History of the Family and the Complexity of Social Change," *American Historical Review* 96 (February 1991): 111–19.

19. Kessinger, *Marriage Licensing Laws*, 172.

20. United States Department of Commerce and Labor, *Marriage and Divorce, 1867–1906*, 2 vols.(reprint, Westport, CT: Greenwood Press, 1978), 1.14–5, 70–71. See also, Mary Somerville Jones, *An Historical Geography of Changing Divorce Law in the United States* (Ph.D. diss., University of North Carolina, Chapel Hill, 1978), 59–60.

Chapter 1

1. Anna Moore Shaw, *A Pima Past* (Tucson: University of Arizona Press, 1974), 54–55. For Apache customs, see Ruth McDonald Boyer and Narcissus Duffy Gayton, *Apache Mothers and Daughters: Four Generations of a Family* (Norman: University of Oklahoma Press, 1992), 185–86.
2. Edeen Martin, "Frontier Marriage and the Status Quo," *Westport Historical Quarterly* 10 (March 1975): 100.
3. Frances R. Conley, "Martina Didn't Have a Covered Wagon," *The Californians* 7 (March/August 1989): 54.
4. Blaine T. Williams, "The Frontier Family: Demographic Fact and Historical Myth," in Harold M. Hollingsworth, ed., *Essays on the American West* (Austin: University of Texas Press, 1969), 40–65. Consult also, John C. Hudson, "The Study of Western Frontier Populations," in Jerome O. Steffen, ed., *American West: New Perspectives, New Dimensions* (Norman: University of Oklahoma Press, 1979), 44–45.
5. Originally appeared in the *Lexington* (Missouri) *Express*, reprinted in the *Liberty Weekly Tribune*, vol. 12, no. 41, 18 February 1859, p. 1, available at the Jackson County Historical Society, Independence, Missouri.
6. Fuller discussions of the role of love appear in William J. Goode, "The Theoretical Importance of Love," 455–70, and Hugo G. Biegel, "Love: Courtly, Romantic, and Modern," 510–17, in Robert F. Winch, Robert McGinnis, and Herbert R. Barringer, eds., *Selected Studies in Marriage and the Family* (New York: Holt, Rinehart and Winston, 1962), 455–70; E. S. Turner, *A History of Courting* (New York: E. P. Dutton, 1955); Morton M. Hunt, *The Natural History of Love* (New York: Alfred A. Knopf, 1959); Ellen K. Rothman, *Hands and Hearts: The History of Courtship in America* (New York: Basic Books, 1984); and Helen E. Fisher, *Anatomy of Love: The Natural History of Monogamy, Adultery, and Divorce* (New York: W. W. Norton and Co., 1992).
7. Michael Grossberg, *Governing the Hearth: Law and the Family in Nineteenth-Century America* (Chapel Hill: University of North Carolina Press, 1985), 35, 39, 56; Rothman, *Hands and Hearts*, 103–10; and John D'Emilio and Estelle B. Freedman, *Intimate Matters: A History of Sexuality in America* (New York: Harper & Row, 1988), 75.
8. Mary Johnstone Powers, *A Pioneer Woman's Reminiscences* (Helena: Montana Historical Society, 1947).
9. Maud Parshall Norris, interview, 1938, vol. 67, no.9837, Indian-Pioneer Papers, Western History Collections, University of Oklahoma Library, Norman.
10. "Betty Powers" Interview in George P. Rawick, ed., *The American Slave* (Westport, CT: Greenwood Pub. Co., 1972), 5:191. See also, Deborah Gray

White, *Ar'n't I a Woman? Female Slaves in the Plantation South* (New York: W. W. Norton, 1985), 150.

11. "Emma Taylor" Interview in Rawick, ed., *The American Slave* 5:75.

12. D'Emilio and Freedman, *Intimate Matters*, 98–99, and "Taylor" Interview, Rawick, ed., *The American Slave* 5(4):75.

13. Regarding Minnesota, see David Vassar Taylor, "The Blacks," in June Drenning Holmquist, ed., *They Chose Minnesota* (St. Paul: Minnesota Historical Society Press, 1981), 73.

14. A rich literature exists on Exodusters, including Arvarh E. Strickland, "Toward the Promised land: The Exodus to Kansas and Afterward," *Missouri Historical Review* 69 (July 1975): 405–12, and Nell Irvin Painter, *Exodusters: Black Migration to Kansas After Reconstruction* (New York: Alfred A. Knopf, 1977). For Colorado, see W. Sherman Savage, *Blacks in the West* (Westport, CT: Greenwood Press, 1976), 84–85.

15. Sucheta Mazumdar, "In the Family," in Asian American Studies Center, University of California, Los Angeles, and Chinese Historical Society of Southern California, *Linking Our Lives: Chinese American Women of Los Angeles* (Los Angeles: Chinese Historical Society of Southern California, 1984), 29.

16. Alice Chai, "Korean Women in Hawaii, 1903–1945," in Nobuya Tsuchida, ed., *Asian and Pacific American Experiences: Women's Perspectives* (Minneapolis: Asian/Pacific American Learning Resource Center, University of Minnesota, 1982), 77.

17. David Beesley, "From Chinese to Chinese American: Chinese Women and Families in a Sierra Nevada Town," *California History* 67 (September 1988): 170–73.

18. Shu-Ching Lee, "China's Traditional Family, Its Characteristics and Disintegration," in Winch et al., *Selected Studies*, 138–51, and Sally M. Miller, "California Immigrants: Case Studies in Continuity and Change in Societal and Familial Roles," *Journal of the West* 33 (July 1993): 25–34.

19. Marvin R. Koller, "Residential and Occupational Propinquity," in Winch et al, *Selected Studies*, 472–77. Early theories stressing other factors are discussed in Richard Centers, *Sexual Attraction and Love: An Instrumental Theory* (Springfield, IL: C. C. Thomas Publisher, 1975); Robert A. Lewis, "A Developmental Framework for the Analysis of Premarital Dyadic Formation," *Family Process* 11 (March 1972): 17–48; and Bernard Murstein, "Stimulus-Value-Role: A Theory of Marital Choice," *Journal of Marriage and the Family* 32 (August 1970): 465–81.

20. Sarah Winnemucca Hopkins, *Life Among the Piutes [sic]: Their Wrongs and Claims* (New York: G. P. Putnam Sons, 1883), 49.

21. Jay Miller, ed., *Mourning Dove: A Salishan Autobiography* (Lincoln: University of Nebraska Press, 1990), 49.

22. A fair, detailed description of a fandango is found in, Caleb Coker, ed., *The News from Brownsville: Helen Chapman's Letters from the Texas Military Frontier, 1848–1852* (Austin: Texas State Historical Association for the Barker Texas History Center, 1992), 53.

23. Sarah Deutsch, *No Separate Refuge: Culture, Class, and Gender on an Anglo-Hispanic Frontier in the American Southwest, 1880–1940* (New York: Oxford University Press, 1987), 42–43.

24. Patricia Preciado Martin, *Images and Conversations: Mexican Americans Recall a Southwestern Past* (Tucson: University of Arizona Press, 1983), 25.
25. Martin, *Images and Conversations*, 53, 99.
26. Jack E. Eblen, "An Analysis of Nineteenth-Century Frontier Populations," *Demography* 2, no. 4 (November 1965): 399–411.
27. From Association of American Women broadside, reproduced in Joan Swallow Reiter, *The Women* (Alexandria, VA: Time-Life Books, 1978): 50.
28. Stephanie Cooper Shulsinger, "The Mercer Girls," *American West* 8 (July 1971): 28–29.
29. *Waterloo* [Iowa] *Courier*, 3 April 1860. By way of contrast see Susan Steinfirst and Barbara B. Moran, "The New Mating Game: Matchmaking Via the Personal Columns in the 1980s," *Journal of Popular Culture* 22 (Spring 1989): 129–39.
30. Mari Sandoz, *Old Jules Country* (New York: Hastings House, 1965), 300–301.
31. Sandoz, *Old Jules Country*, 300–301.
32. Emery S. Bartlett, "The Bartlett Family of Poweshiek County, Iowa," December, 1911, Iowa Historical Archives, Des Moines.
33. Robert J. Chandler, "'What One Writes Lives Forever': Notes on Frank Rumrill's Gold Rush Experience," *Western Express* 43 (October 1993): 18–22.
34. Ella T. Wilson, "Sketch of Isabella Diehl," undated, Pioneer Daughters Collection, South Dakota State Historical Resource Center, Pierre.
35. Mrs. Andrew Odegaard, "Biography of Emma Odegaard," undated, Pioneer Daughters Collection, South Dakota State Historical Resource Center, Pierre.
36. See, for example, Wilson Cape, "Population Changes in the West North Central States, 1900–1930," *North Dakota Historical Quarterly* 6 (1932): 276–91.
37. Auguste Carlier, *Marriage in the United States*, (reprint, New York: Arno Press, 1972), 32.
38. Mrs. Will Bangs, "My Homesteading Days," undated, Historical Society of Montana Library, Helena.
39. Becky Berry, "Grandma Berry's Ninety Years in Oklahoma," *Chronicles of Oklahoma* 45 (1967): 61–62.
40. Berry, "Grandma Berry's Ninety Years," 61–62.
41. Emily Butcher, "Diary, 1896–99," Manuscript Department, Kansas State Historical Society, Topeka.
42. D'Emilio and Freedman, *Intimate Matters*, 98.
43. Emancipation Slave Contract, 19 December 1853, Joint Collection of the University of Missouri/Western Historical Society Manuscripts—Columbia and State Historical Society of Missouri Manuscripts, Columbia.
44. Beesley, "From Chinese to Chinese American," 174.
45. Yuji Ichioka, "*Amerika Nadeshiko*: Japanese Immigrant Women in the United States, 1900–1924," *Pacific Historical Review* 49 (May 1980): 342.
46. Mary S. Henshall, "Pioneer Portraits: Henry and Fumiko Fujii," *Idaho Yesterdays* 19 (Spring 1975): 23.
47. Ichioka, "*Amerika Nadeshiko*," 341–57, and Mei T. Nakano, *Japanese American Women: Three Generations, 1890–1990* (Berkeley: Mina Press Publishing, 1990), 24–29.

48. Akemi Kikumura, *Through Harsh Winters: The Life of a Japanese Immigrant Woman* (Novato, CA: Chandler and Sharp Publishers, Inc., 1981), 29.

49. Chai, "Korean Women," in Tsuchida, ed., *Asian and Pacific American Experiences*, 77.

50. Chai, "Korean Women," 78.

51. Doña Apolinaria Lorenzana, "Reminiscences," 1878, Bancroft Library, University of California, Berkeley. Another instance is found in Sarah Cline, "The Spiritual Conquest Reexamined: Baptism and Christian Marriage in Early Sixteenth-Century Mexico," *Hispanic American Historical Review* 1 (August 1993): 453–80.

52. Guadalupe Vallejo, "Ranch and Mission Days in Alta California," *Century Illustrated Monthly Magazine* 41 (December 1890): 183–92.

53. Coker, *The News from Brownsville*, 33.

54. Shaw, *A Pima Past*, 137–50.

55. Mary Matovich, "Merry Christmas, Children, 1956," Montana State University Library Special Collections, Bozeman.

56. Virginia Sutter, "Today's Strength From Yesterday's Tradition—The Continuity of the American Indian Woman," *Frontiers* 6 (Fall 1981): 56.

57. August B. Hollingshead, "Dating in Elmtown," in Winch et al, *Selected Studies*, 502–5.

58. Beverly Hungry Wolf, *The Ways of My Grandmothers* (New York: William Morrow and Co., 1980), 200–201. Also discussed in James Mooney, *Myths of the Cherokee and Sacred Formulas of the Cherokees* (reprint, Nashville, TN: Charles Elder, 1972), 481–82, original available at the John Vaughan Library, Northeastern Oklahoma State University, Tahlequah, Oklahoma.

59. Fannie J. Bell, interview, undated, no number, vol. 7, Indian-Pioneer Papers, Western History Collections, University of Oklahoma Library, Norman.

60. Norine Dresser, "Marriage Customs in Early California," *Californians* 9 (November/December 1991): 48.

61. Phyllis A. Dinkel, "Old Marriage Customs in Herzog (Victoria), Kansas," *Western Folklore* 19, 2 (April 1960): 99–105.

62. John Sirjamaki, *The American Family in the Twentieth Century* (Cambridge: Harvard University Press, 1955), 39.

63. Odegaard, "Biography."

64. Quoted in Marion S. Goldman, *Gold Diggers and Silver Miners: Prostitution and Social Life on the Comstock Lode* (Ann Arbor: University of Michigan Press, 1981), 40.

65. Margaret Ronan, ed., *Frontier Woman: The Story of Mary Ronan* (Helena: University of Montana Publications in History, 1973), 44.

66. Homer E. Socolofsky, ed., "The Private Journals of Florence Crawford and Arthur Capper, 1891–1892," *Kansas Historical Quarterly* 30 (Spring 1964): 16–17, 47.

67. John Wade Geil, ed., "Babe and Gabriel: An Oregon Courtship," *Oregon Historical Quarterly* 87 (Summer 1986): 117–66. See also Karen Lystra, *Searching the Heart: Women, Men, and Romantic Love in Nineteenth-Century America* (New York: Oxford University Press, 1989).

68. Lela Barnes, ed., "North Central Kansas in 1887–1889: From the Letters of Leslie and Susan Snow of Junction City," *Kansas Historical Quarterly* 24 (Winter 1963): 372, 377.

69. Quotation from *The Parlor Letter Writer* (New York: James Miller, n.d.), 11. The Bledsoe-Hain correspondence is found in Marilyn Ferris Motz, "'Thou Art My Last Love': The Courtship and Remarriage of a Rural Texas Couple in 1892," *Southwestern Historical Quarterly* 93 (April 1990): 457–73.

70. Ellen K. Rothman, "Sex and Self-Control: Middle-Class Courtship in America, 1770–1870," *Journal of Social History* 15 (Spring 1982): 409–25, and Rothman, *Hands and Hearts*.

71. Annegret Ogden, "Love and Marriage: Five California Couples," *The Californians* 5 (July/August 1987): 8.

72. Daniel Scott Smith and Michael S. Hindus, "Premarital Pregnancy in America, 1640–1971: An Overview and Interpretation," *Journal of Interdisciplinary History* 5 (Spring 1975): 537–70.

73. David J. Langum, "*Californio* Women and the Image of Virtue," *Southern California Quarterly* 59 (Fall 1977): 245–50. For perceptions of New Mexican women, see Lewis H. Garrard, *Wah-To-Yah and the Taos Trail* (Glendale, CA: Arthur H. Clark, 1938), 238; Fray Angélico Chávez, "Doña Tules, Her Fame and Her Funeral," *El Palacio* 57 (August 1950): 227–34; and Beverly Trulio "Anglo-American Attitudes toward New Mexican Women," *Journal of the West* 12 (April 1973): 299–339.

74. James M. Lacy, "New Mexican Women in Early American Writings," *New Mexico Historical Review* 34 (January 1959): 41–51.

75. Thomas D. Hall, *Social Change in the Southwest, 1350–1880* (Lawrence: University Press of Kansas, 1989), 155. For a slightly different perspective, consult, Ramón A. Gutiérrez, *When Jesus Came, the Corn Mothers Went Away: Marriage, Sexuality, and Power in New Mexico, 1500–1846* (Stanford, CA: Stanford University Press, 1991).

76. D'Emilio and Freedman, *Intimate Matters*, 97–98.

77. D'Emilio and Freedman, *Intimate Matters*, 75–77.

78. Daniel Scott Smith, "The Dating of the American Sexual Revolution: Evidence and Interpretation," in Michael Gordon, ed., *The American Family* (New York: St. Martin's Press, 1978), 426–38.

79. Louise Sophia Gellhorn Boylan, "My Life Story," 1867–83, Iowa State Historical Society, Iowa City.

80. Joan M. Jensen, "The Death of Rosa: Sexuality in Rural America," *Agricultural History* 67 (Fall 1993): 1–12.

81. Peter Ling, "Sex and the Automobile in the Jazz Age," *History Today* 39 (November 1989): 18–24. See also Beth L. Bailey, *From Front Porch to Back Seat: Courtship in Twentieth Century America* (Baltimore: Johns Hopkins University Press, 1988).

82. Quoted in "Aboriginal Courtship," *Nation* 134 (April 20, 1932): 456. See also Hungry Wolf, *The Ways of My Grandmothers*, 190–91.

83. Seymour Parrer, "Cultural Rules, Rituals, and Behavior Regulation," *American Anthropologist* 86 (September 1984): 584–600.

84. Goode, "The Theoretical Importance of Love," in Winch et al., *Selected Studies*, 463–69.

85. Shaw, *A Pima Past*, 30.

86. Terry P. Wilson, "Osage Women, 1870–1980," in Sucheng Chan, Douglas Henry Daniels, Mario T. García, and Terry P. Wilson, eds., *Peoples of Color in the American West* (Lexington, MA: D. C. Heath, 1994), 184–85.

87. Frank B. Linderman, *Red Mother* (New York: John Day, 1932), 130–31.

88. Miller, ed., *Mourning Dove*, 50–51.

89. Wilson, "Osage Women," 184–85.

90. Dresser, "Marriage Customs in Early California," 46.

91. Deutsch, *No Separate Refuge*, 43, and Janet Lecompte, "The Independent Women of Hispanic New Mexico, 1821–1846," *Western Historical Quarterly* 12 (January 1981): 23.

92. Rosalind Z. Rock, "'Pido y Supplico': Women and the Law in Spanish New Mexico, 1697–1763," *New Mexico Historical Review* 65 (April 1990): 146.

93. Eblen, "An Analysis of Nineteenth-Century Frontier Populations," 412–13, and Michael J. O'Brien, "Social Dimensions of Settlement," in Michael J. O'Brien et al., *Grassland, Forest, and Historical Settlement* (Lincoln: University of Nebraska Press, 1984), 210–30.

94. Grossberg, *Governing the Hearth*, 19–20. A fuller discussion is found in Glenda Riley, *Divorce: An American Tradition* (New York: Oxford University Press, 1991), chap. 4.

95. Caroline Phelps, "Diary, 1832," Iowa State Historical Society, Iowa City.

96. Florence Marshall Stote, "Of Such is the Middle West," undated, Manuscript Department, Kansas State Historical Society, Topeka.

97. Michele Shover, "The Blockhead Factor: Marriage and the Fate of California Daughters," *Californians* 7 (September/October 1989): 32–39.

98. See, for example, Phelps, "Diary."

99. *Dubuque* [Iowa] *Visitor*, 18 May 1836; *Waterloo* [Iowa] *Courier*, 5 June and 31 July 1861; and *Fairfield Ledger*, 15 December 1870. Other examples appear in, William J. Petersen, "Boys, Keep away from Muslin," *Palimpsest* 50 (November 1969): 637–48.

100. *Iowa News* [Dubuque], 16 September and 2 December 1837, and *Burlington* [Iowa] *Daily Hawk-Eye*, 24 February 1859.

101. S. F. Cook, *The Conflict between the California Indian and White Civilization: IV. Trends in Marriage and Divorce Since 1850* (Berkeley: University of California Press, 1943), 24–25.

102. Geoffrey May, *Marriage Laws and Decisions in the United States* (New York: Sage Foundation, 1929), 12–13.

103. Mary Ann Hafen, *Recollections of a Handcart Pioneer of 1860* (Lincoln: University of Nebraska Press, 1983), 49–55.

104. Mary Annetta Coleman Pomeroy, "My Life Story," 1939, Arizona Historical Society, Tucson. For a recent discussion of such beliefs, see Seymour Cain, "More Wives Than One: The Mormon Doctrine and Practice of Plural Marriage," *Journal of Unconventional History* 2, no. 1 (Fall 1990): 70–83. A study of the effect of

Mormon religious beliefs on contemporary courtship can be found in Mary Riege Laner, "Unpleasant, Aggressive, and Abusive Activities in Courtship: A Comparison of Mormon and NonMormon College Students," *Deviant Behavior* 6, no. 2 (April/June 1985): 145–68.

105. George D. Smith, "Mormon Plural Marriage," *Free Inquiry* 12 (Summer 1992): 32–37.
106. Lecompte, "The Independent Women of Hispanic New Mexico," 23, and Jane Dysart, "Mexican Women in San Antonio, 1830–1860: The Assimilation Process," *Western Historical Quarterly* 7 (October 1976): 365–75. A more modern view of cohabitation is Edmund L. Van Deusen, *Contract Cohabitation: An Alternative to Marriage* (New York: Grove Press, Inc., 1974).
107. Margaret Mead, *Male and Female* (New York: Wm. Morrow and Co., 1949), 195.
108. John Sirjamaki, *The American Family in the Twentieth Century* (Cambridge: Harvard University Press, 1955), 55.
109. Martin King Whyte, *Dating, Mating, and Marriage* (New York: Aldine de Gruyter, 1990).

Chapter 2

1. Robert F. MacKinnon, Carol E. MacKinnon, and Mary L. Franken, "Family Strengths in Long-Term Marriages," *Lifestyles: A Journal of Changing Patterns* 7 (Winter 1984): 115–26.
2. George Devereux, "The Social and Cultural Implications of Incest among the Mohave Indians," *Psychoanalytic Quarterly* 8 (1939): 510–33. Apache wedding customs are discussed in, Ruth McDonald Boyer and Narcissus Duffy Gayton, *Apache Mothers and Daughters: Four Generations of a Family* (Norman: University of Oklahoma Press, 1992), 5–6.
3. Rosalind Z. Rock, "'Pido y Suplico': Women and the Law in Spanish New Mexico, 1697–1763," *New Mexico Historical Review* 65 (April 1990): 155, and Janet Lecompte, "The Independent Women of Hispanic New Mexico, 1821–1846," *Western Historical Quarterly* 12 (January 1981): 29, 32.
4. Lecompte, "The Independent Women of Hispanic New Mexico," 26. This issue is discussed in more detail in, Gloria Ricci Lothrop, "Rancheras and the Land: Women and Property Rights in Hispanic California," *Southern California Quarterly* 86 (Spring 1994): 59–84.
5. Decree authorizing Delores Romero de Correa to sell property in the city of Los Angeles, March 9, 1872, in California Courts, Los Angeles County Collection, Huntington Library, San Marino, California.
6. Contract of Marriage between Thomas Alexandre Morgan and Azelie Brosset, 22 January 1839, Cane River Collection, Historical New Orleans Collection, New Orleans. Another case from the 1800s is St. Julien de Tournillon and Mary Brown Jones, An Irish Catholic Immigrant, Marriage Contract, 23 July 1832, Kuntz Collection, Special Collections, Tulane University, New Orleans. An example from the 1600s is found in Heloise H. Cruzat, trans., "Marriage Contract," *Louisiana Historical Quarterly* 17 (1934): 242–45.
7. Dolores Egger Labbé, *Women in Early Nineteenth-Century Louisiana* (Ph.D. diss., University of Delaware, 1975), 58–71.

8. Susan C. Nicholas, Alice M. Price, and Rachel Rubin, *Rights and Wrongs: Women's Struggle for Legal Equality* (Old Westbury, NY: Feminist Press, 1979), 22–31.

9. John Sirjamaki, *The American Family in the Twentieth Century* (Cambridge, MA: Harvard University Press, 1955), 33–37.

10. Steven Mintz and Susan Kellogg, *Domestic Revolutions: A Social History of American Family Life* (New York: Free Press, 1988), 126.

11. Sarah Winnemucca Hopkins, *Life Among the Piutes* [sic]: *Their Wrongs and Claims* (New York: G. P. Putnam Sons, 1883), 49.

12. Jay Miller, ed., *Mourning Dove: A Salishan Biography* (Lincoln: University of Nebraska Press, 1990), 55–56.

13. Raymond S. Brandes (trans.), "*Times Gone By in Alta California:* The Recollections of Señora Doña Juana Machado Alípaz de Wrightington," *Californians* 8 (November/December 1990), 43–57.

14. Sarah Deutsch, *No Separate Refuge: Culture, Class, and Gender on an Anglo-Hispanic Frontier in the American Southwest, 1880–1940* (New York: Oxford University Press, 1989), 44.

15. "Jenny Proctor" Interview in George P. Rawick, ed., *The American Slave*, (Westport, CT: Greenwood Publishing Co., 1972), 5:217, and Deborah Gray White, *Ar'n't I a Woman? Female Slaves in the Plantation South* (New York; W. W. Norton, 1985), 44.

16. Grace A. McGrew, "Pioneer Women—Anna Hill Plummer," 1936, Nisqually Plains Room, Pacific Western University, Tacoma.

17. No author, "Biographical Sketch of Mrs. William A. Valentine," undated, Pioneer Daughters Collection, South Dakota State Historical Research Center, Pierre; and Vera M. Lockard, letter to "Dear Mother," 2 January 1913, held by Norma Hassman, Cedar Falls, Iowa, copy in Glenda Riley's possession. See also "Lucie Emma Dickinson Lott, Her Story," undated, South Dakota State Historical Resource Center, Pierre.

18. "Polly Colbert" Interview, Rawick, The American Slave, 7:33, and Woodie Howgill, ed., "Honeymoon across the Plains: The Ellen Bell Tootle Diary," *Heritage of the Great Plains* 16 (Summer 1983): 11–17.

19. Nettie Sanford, *Early Sketch of Polk County* (Newton, IA: Chas. A. Clark, 1874), 33.

20. "Interview with Mrs. C. W. Callerman," Oklahoma City, Oklahoma, 1937, Indian-Pioneer Papers, Western History Collection, University of Oklahoma Library, Norman. An additional account of a shivaree is found in, James L. Thane, Jr., "The Governor's Lady Writes Home to Ohio," *Montana: The Magazine of Western History* 24 (July 1974): 19.

21. Works Progress Administration, "From an Interview with Mrs. Louise Pillisier," *Told by the Pioneers* (n.p.: n.p., 1938), 146.

22. Lola Harvey, *Derevnia's Daughters: Saga of an Alaskan Village* (Manhattan, KS: Sunflower University Press, 1991), 294.

23. Lucie Cheng and Suellen Cheng, "Chinese Women of Los Angeles, A Historical Survey," 21, and Feelie Lee and Elaine Lou, "Traditions and Transitions," 59, in Asian American Studies Center, UCLA, and Chinese Historical Society of Southern California, *Linking Our Lives: Chinese American Women*

of Los Angeles (Los Angeles: Chinese Historical Society of Southern California, 1984), 21.

24. See for example Robert H. Lowie, "Marriage and Family Life among the Plains Indians," *Scientific Monthly* 34 (January/June 1932): 462–64.

25. Steven Mintz, *A Prison of Expectations: The Family in Victorian Culture* (New York: New York University Press, 1983), 103–46.

26. Ruth B. Moynihan, Susan Armitage, and Christiane Fischer Dichamp, eds., *So Much To Be Done: Women Settlers on the Mining and Ranching Frontier* (Lincoln: University of Nebraska Press, 1990), 6–8, 289–90.

27. Faye Cashatt Lewis, *Nothing to Make a Shadow* (Ames: Iowa State University Press, 1971), 34, 70.

28. Dorothea Lummis, letter to "Dearie Boy," 26 or 27 April 1884, Huntington Library, San Marino, CA.

29. Noah M. Glatfelter, "Letters from Dakota Territory, 1865," *Bulletin of the Missouri Historical Society* 18 (January 1962): 104–34.

30. Quoted in Andrew J. Rotter, "'Matilda for God's Sake Write': Women and Families on the Argonaut Mind," *California History* 48 (Summer 1979): 135–36; N. A. C., letter to "Dear Wife," original held by Alan H. Patera, Lake Grove, Oregon; and E. A. Wiltsee Collection, letter to wife Elizabeth Prentiss, Wells Fargo Archives, San Francisco.

31. Mollie Dorsey Sanford, *Mollie: The Journal of Mollie Dorsey Sanford in Nebraska and Colorado Territories, 1857–1866* (Lincoln: University of Nebraska Press, 1976), 152–53.

32. "Charley Jackson—He Walked Freedom's Long Road," (St. Paul) *Pioneer Press*, 12 February, 1968, Mattie V. Rhodes and Family Papers, Archives-Manuscripts Division, Minnesota Historical Society, St. Paul.

33. Eva Bell Neal, "Biography," undated, Archives-Manuscripts Division, Minnesota Historical Society, St. Paul.

34. Glatfelter, "Letters," 105.

35. Sarah Tracy, "The Brides of Pioneers," 1898, Special Collections, Montana State University Library, Bozeman.

36. José E. Limón, *Mexican Ballads, Chicano Poems: History and Influence in Mexican-American Social Poetry* (Berkeley: University of California Press, 1992), 335–38, 140–60, 173–74; Cheryl J. Foote, "Changing Images of Women in the Western Film," in Richard W. Etulain, ed., *Western Films: A Brief History*, (Manhattan, KS: Sunflower University Press, 1983), 64–71; and Howard Movshovitz, "The Still Point: Women in the Westerns of John Ford," and Corlann Gee Bush, "The Way We Weren't: Images of Women and Men in Cowboy Art," *Frontiers* 7 (1984): 68–72, 73–78.

37. Paul R. Spickard, "Work and Hope: African American Women in Southern California during World War II," *Journal of the West* 33 (July 1993): 70–79.

38. Emma Vignal Borglu, "The Experience at Crow Creek, a Sioux Indian Reservation at South Dakota," 1899, South Dakota State Historical Resource Center, Pierre. Differences between Native American and Anglo definitions of gender roles are found in Karen Sacks, "State Bias and Women's Status," *American Anthropologist* 78 (September 1976): 565–69.

39. Valerie Sherer Mathes, "A New Look at the Role of Women in Indian Society," *American Indian Quarterly* 2 (Summer 1975): 136. See also Evelyn Blackwood, "Sexuality and Gender in Certain Native American Tribes: The Case of Cross-Gender Females," *Journal of Women in Culture and Society* 10 (1984): 27–42.

40. Beverly Hungry Wolf, *The Ways of My Grandmothers* (New York: Wm. Morrow., 1980), 59–60, 69.

41. Deutsch, *No Separate Refuge*, 44–45, and Sarah Deutsch, "Women and Intercultural Relations: The Case of Hispanic New Mexico and Colorado," *Signs* 12 (Summer 1987): 719–39.

42. Christine N. Marín, *The Chicano Experience in Arizona* (Tempe: Arizona State University Libraries, 1991), 11–19.

43. Katharine Harris, "Sex Roles and Work Patterns among Homesteading Families in Northeastern Colorado, 1873–1920," *Frontiers* 7 (1984): 43–49, and *Long Vistas: Women and Families on Colorado Homesteads* (Niwot: University Press of Colorado, 1993). Also useful is Mary E. Cookingham, "Combining Marriage, Motherhood, and Jobs before World War II: Women College Graduates, Classes of 1905–1935," *Journal of Family History* 9 (Summer 1984): 178–95.

44. Maureen Ursenbach Beecher, "Women's Work on the Mormon Frontier," *Utah Historical Quarterly* 49 (Summer 1981): 276–90.

45. Labbe', *Women in Early Nineteenth-Century Louisiana*, 61–61; Paula Petrik, "Capitalists with Rooms: Prostitution in Helena, Montana, 1865–1900," *Montana: The Magazine of Western History* 31 (Spring 1981): 28–41; Anne M. Butler, *Daughters of Joy, Sisters of Misery: Prostitutes in the American West, 1865–1890* (Champaign: University of Illinois Press, 1985); and Mary Murphy, "The Private Lives of Public Women: Prostitution in Butte, Montana, 1878–1817," *Frontiers* 7 (1984): 30–35.

46. This principle is demonstrated in Meeda M. S. Mashal, "Marital Power, Role Expectations and Marital Satisfaction," *International Journal of Women's Studies* 8 (January/February 1985): 40–46.

47. Priscilla K. Buffalohead, "Farmers, Warriors, Traders: A Fresh Look at Ojibway Women," *Minnesota History* 48 (Summer 1983): 241; and Miller, *Mourning Dove*, 60–61.

48. Mario T. García, "The Chicana in American History: The Mexican Women of El Paso, 1880–1920—A Case Study," *Pacific Historical Review* 49 (May 1980): 315–37, and *Desert Immigrants: The Mexican of El Paso, 1880–1920* (New Haven: Yale University Press, 1981); Richard Griswold del Castillo, *Between Borders: Essays on Mexicana/Chicana History* (Encino, CA: Floricanto Press, 1990), "Chicano Families in the Southwest, 1910–1945," in Sucheng Chan, Douglas Henry Daniels, Mario T. García, and Terry P. Wilson, eds., *Peoples of Color in the American West* (Lexington, MA: D. C. Heath, 1994), 208–13.

49. Stella M. Drumm, ed., *Down the Santa Fé Trail and into Mexico: The Diary of Susan Shelby Magoffin, 1846–1847* (New Haven: Yale University Press, 1926), 175.

50. Margaret Ronan, ed., *Frontier Woman: The Story of Mary Ronan* (Helena: University of Montana Publications in History, 1973), 80–95; and Francis A. Long, *A Prairie Doctor of the Eighties* (Norfolk, NE: Nebraska Home Publishing, 1937), 161–80.

51. Patricia Preciado Martín, *Images and Conversations: Mexican Americans Recall a Southwestern Past* (Tucson: University of Arizona Press, 1983), 65. See also Lela Barnes, ed., "North Central Kansas in 1887–1889: From the Letters of Leslie and Susan Snow of Junction City—Concluded," *Kansas Historical Quarterly* 24 (Winter 1963): 403–28.

52. Courtney Reeder Jones, "Memories of Wupatki: Life in an Ancient Ruin," *Journal of the Southwest* 35 (Spring 1993): 3–52.

53. Mariam Clayton, "Reminiscences," 1961, Manuscript Department, Kansas State Historical Society, Topeka.

54. Sarah Bessey Tracy, "Diary," 1869, Special Collections, Montana State University Libraries, Bozeman.

55. Eun Sik Yan, "Korean Women of America: From Subordination to Partnership, 1903–1930," *Amerasia* 11 (Fall/Winter 1984): 1–28.

56. Nobuya Tsuchida, ed., *Asian and Pacific American Experiences: Women's Perspectives* (Minneapolis: Asian/Pacific American Learning Resource Center, 1982), 96–98; and Mei T. Nakano, *Japanese American Women: Three Generations, 1890–1990* (Berkeley: Mina Press Publishing, 1990), 147–48. Consult also Valerie Matsumoto, "Desperately Seeking 'Deirdre': Gender Roles, Multicultural Relations, and Nisei Women Writers of the 1930s," *Frontiers* 12 (1991): 19–32.

57. Dorotea Valdez, "Reminiscences," June 27, 1874, Bancroft Library, University of California, Berkeley.

58. Doña Jesus Moreno de Soza, "Reminiscences," 1939, Arizona Historical Society, Tucson; and "Belle Chigley Interview," vol. 21 #4930, 1937, Indian-Pioneer Papers, Western History Collection, University of Oklahoma Library, Norman. To gain an understanding of the problems of raising other people's children, see Nan Cauer Maglin and Nancy Schniedewind, eds., *Women and Stepfamilies: Voices of Anger and Love* (Philadelphia: Temple University Press, 1989).

59. Valdez, "Reminiscences," and Charles R. King, "The Woman's Experience of Childbirth on the Western Frontier," *Journal of the West* 29 (January 1990): 76–84.

60. M. Guy Bishop, "Preparing to 'Take the Kingdom': Childrearing Directives in Early Mormonism" *Journal of the Early Republic* 7 (Fall 1987): 275–90.

61. Julie Roy Jeffrey, *Converting the West: A Biography of Narcissa Whitman* (Norman: University of Oklahoma Press, 1991).

62. Julia Lovejoy, "Letters," 1828–1864, Kansas State Historical Society, Topeka; and no author, "Biography of Grace Fitzgerald West," 1984, Historical Society of Montana, Helena.

63. Quoted in John H. More, "The Developmental Cycle of Cheyenne Polygyny," *American Indian Quarterly* 15 (Summer 1991): 313.

64. More, "The Developmental Cycle of Cheyenne Polygyny," 311–26.

65. Quoted in Elinore Pruitt Stewart, *Letters of a Woman Homesteader* (Lincoln: University of Nebraska Press, 1961), 265. Discussion of polygyny is found in, George D. Smith, "Mormon Plural Marriage," *Free Inquiry* 12 (Summer 1992): 32–37, 60; Michael S. Raber, "Family Life and Rural Society in Spring, Utah: The Basis of Order in a Changing Agrarian Landscape," in Jessie L. Embry and Howard A. Christy, eds., *Community Development in the American West* (Provo, UT: Brigham

Young University, 1985), 135–61; M. Guy Bishop, "Eternal Marriage in Early Mormon Marital Beliefs," *Historian* 3 (Autumn 1990): 77–78; and Kathryn M. Daynes, *Plural Wives and the Nineteenth-Century Mormon Marriage System: Manti, Utah, 1849–1910* (Ph.D. diss., Indiana University, 1991).

66. Quoted in Mary J. Tanner, letter, 19 October 1880, Bancroft Library, University of California, Berkeley. For other women who stated they liked plural marriage, see Mrs. F. D. Richards, "Reminiscences," 1880, Nancy N. Tracy, "Narrative," 1880, Mary Horne, "Migration and Settlement of the Latter-day Saints," 1884, and Eliza Roxey Snow, "Sketch of My Life," 1885, Bancroft Library; and Mary Ann Hafen, *Recollections of a Handcart Pioneer of 1860* (Lincoln: University of Nebraska Press, 1981). Women's views of polygyny are discussed in Jessie L. Embry and Martha S. Bradley, "Mothers and Daughters in Polygamy," *Dialogue* 18 (Fall 1985): 99–107. A twentieth-century, non-Mormon view of plural marriage is found in Larry L. Constantine and Joan M. Constantine, *Group Marriage: A Study of Contemporary Multilateral Marriage* (New York: Macmillan Co., 1973); and Edgar W. Butler, *Traditional Marriage and Emerging Alternatives* (New York: Harper & Row, 1979).

67. For example, see Barbara J. Koerpel, *Family of Origin Variables and Length of Courtship as Related to Mate Selection Patterns and Marital Satisfaction* (Ph.D. diss., Florida State University, 1986); and Ann Croft and Michael Craft, *Handicapped Married Couples* (London: Routledge & Kegan Paul, 1979).

68. G. Robina Quale, *A History of Marriage Systems* (New York: Greenwood Press, 1988), 287. Also useful is Robert J. Gough, "Close-Kin Marriage and Upper-Class Formation in Late-Eighteenth-Century Philadelphia," *Journal of Family History* 14 (1989): 119–36.

69. Richard W. Davis, "'We Are All Americans Now!': Anglo-American Marriage in the Later Nineteenth Century," *Proceedings of the American Philosophical Society* 135 (1991): 140–75.

70. A recent study is Yu-Wen Ying, "Marital Satisfaction among San Francisco Chinese-Americans," *International Journal of Social Psychiatry* 37 (1991): 201–13. Another that approaches the same issue from a different perspective is Betty Lee Sung, "Chinese American Intermarriage," *Journal of Comparative Family Studies* 21 (3)(Autumn 1990): 337–53.

71. Labbé, *Women in Early Nineteenth-Century Louisiana*, 58–71.

72. Quale, *History of Marriage Systems*, 273–74.

73. Haiming Liu, "The Trans-Pacific Family: A Case Study of Sam Chang's Family History," *Amerasia Journal* 18 (1992): 10–13.

74. S. F. Cook, *The Conflict Between the California Indian and White Civilization: IV. Trends in Marriage and Divorce Since 1850* (Berkeley: University of California Press, 1943), 2–3, 13–14, 29. See also Terry P. Wilson, "Osage Women, 1870–1980," in Chan et al., *Peoples of Color in the American West*, 190–97.

75. Lecompte, "The Independent Women of Hispanic New Mexico," 27; and Rock, "'Pido y Suplico,'" 148.

76. Jane Fishburne Collier, "Rank and Marriage: Or, Why High-Ranking Brides Cost More," in Jane Fishburne Collier and Sylvia Junko Yanagisako, eds., *Gender and*

Kinship: Essays toward a Unified Analysis (Stanford, CA: Stanford University Press, 1987), 209–20.

77. Letters between Benjamin and Mary Farrar, 1820, Benjamin Farrar Collection, Special Collections, Tulane University Library, New Orleans; and Louise Jouset la Loire v. Surgeon Pierre de Manade, Separation Suit, 15 February 1928, Louisiana State Museum, New Orleans.

78. Prostitution is discussed in, Rex C. Myers, "An Inning for Sin: Chicago Joe and Her Hurdy-Gurdy Girls," *Montana: The Magazine of Western History* 27 (April 1977): 24–33; Carol Leonard and Isidor Wallimann, "Prostitution and Changing Morality in the Frontier Cattle Towns of Kansas," *Kansas History* 2 (Spring 1979): 34–53; Elliott West, "Scarlet West: The Oldest Profession in the Trans-Mississippi West," *Montana the Magazine of Western History* 31 (Spring 1981): 16–27; and Anne P. Diffendal, "Prostitution in Grand Island, Nebraska, 1870–1913," *Heritage of the Great Plains* 26 (Summer 1983): 1–9.

79. A critique of temperance reformers appears in Gerald Schoenewolf, "The Feminist Myth about Sexual Abuse," *Journal of Psychohistory* 18 (Winter 1991): 331–41. Alcoholism and spousal abuse are discussed in, Myra C. Glenn, "Wife-Beating: The Darker Side of Victorian Domesticity," *Canadian Review of American Studies* 15 (Spring 1984): 17–33; Jerome Nadelhaft, "Wife Torture: A Known Phenomenon in Nineteenth-Century America," *Journal of American Culture* 10 (Fall 1987): 39–59; and Robert Griswold, "Sexual Cruelty and the Case for Divorce in Victorian America," *Signs* 11 (Spring 1986): 629–41.

80. A number of drunken husbands are described in, Caleb Coker, ed., *The News from Brownsville: Helen Chapman's Letters from the Texas Military Frontier, 1848–1852* (Austin: Texas State Historical Association for the Barker Texas History Association, 1992), 80–81.

81. Mrs. B. L. Dunlap, letter to "My dear Sister," 14 December 1830, Dunlap Family Papers, Special Collections, Tulane University Library, New Orleans. See also Marie Magdelaine, petition, 3 June 1728, Louisiana State Museum, New Orleans; and *Hardy v. Hardy*, 1743, and *Perry v. Perry*, 1743, in "Records of the Superior Council of Louisiana," *Louisiana Historical Quarterly* 12 (1929): 138–42, 153–61.

82. Jo Anne Wold, *The Way It Was: Of People, Places, and Things in Pioneer Interior Alaska* (Anchorage: Alaska Northwest Publishing Co., 1988), 110.

83. Mrs. R. O. Brandt, "Social Aspects of Prairie Pioneering: The Reminiscences of a Pioneer Pastor's Wife," *Norwegian-American Studies* 7 (1933): 1, 11.

84. Kathryn Ericson, "Jeopardy: The Muus vs. Muus Case in Three Forums," *Minnesota History* 50 (Winter 1987):299–308.

85. Melody Graulich, "Violence against Women in Literature of the Western Family," *Frontiers* 7 (1984): 14–20; and U.S. Commissioner of Agriculture, *Annual Report, 1862* (Washington, DC: U.S. Government Printing Office, 1863), 462–70.

86. Melody Graulich, "Every Husband's Right: Sex Roles in Mari Sandoz's *Old Jules*," *Western American Literature* 18 (Spring 1983): 3–20; and Betsy Downey, "Battered Pioneers: Jules Sandoz and the Physical Abuse of Wives on the American Frontier," *Great Plains Quarterly* 12 (Winter 1992): 31–49.

87. Pauline Nebher Diede, *Homesteading on the Knife River Prairies* (Bismarck, ND: Germans from Russia Heritage Society, 1983), and Akemi Kikumara, *Through Harsh Winters: The Life of a Japanese Immigrant Women* (Novato, CA: Chandler & Sharp Publishers, 1981), 32–33.

88. James Grove, "Mark Twain and the Endangered Family," *American Literature* 57 (October 1985): 377–94. For a later phenomenon, see Darrell Y. Hamamoto, "Kindred Spirits: The Contemporary Asian American Family on Television," *Amerasia Journal* 18 (1992): 35–53.

89. de Soza, "Reminiscences."

90. Elaine Tyler May, *Great Expectations: Marriage and Divorce in Post-Victorian America* (Chicago: University of Chicago Press, 1980); and Glenda Riley, *Divorce: An American Tradition* (New York: Oxford University Press, 1991), 85–107.

91. Labbé, *Women in Early Nineteenth-Century Louisiana,* 64–65; and Riley, *Divorce,* 87–89.

92. Robert L. Griswold, "Law, Sex, Cruelty, and Divorce in Victorian America, 1840–1900," *American Quarterly* 38 (Winter 1986): 721–45.

93. Anita M. Baldwin, fragment of a note, 1915, Baldwin Collection, 1876–1936, Huntington Library, San Marino.

94. Labbé, *Women in Early Nineteenth-Century Louisiana,* 62.

95. Daniel Dustin, letter to "Dear John [Dustin]," 2 November 1853, Edward Wiltsee Collection, Wells Fargo Archives, San Francisco.

96. "Esther Easter" Interview, in Rawick, *The American Slave,* 7:89.

97. "Storeman in San Francisco," St. Joseph *Adventure,* 10 October 1849; and Works Progress Administration, "Elizabeth Lotz Treat Longmire," *Told by the Pioneers,* 3:70. Other examples are Mrs. E. A. Van Court, "'We surely thought a hoodoo was over us,'" 18–27, Mrs. Lee Whipple-Haslem, "'Turbulence and evil of every description,'" 28–37, and Mrs. A. M. Green, "'I resolved to try and be cheerful,'" 124–46, in Moynihan et al., *So Much to Be Done.*

98. Dean L. May, "People on the Mormon Frontier: Kanab's Families of 1874," *Journal of Family History* 1 (Winter 1976): 169–92.

99. Joanna Stratton, "Making the Best of Hard, Hard Times," *Redbook* 155 (October 1980): 25, 27, 193–94; and Kathleen Conzen, "A Saga of Families," in Clyde Milner, II, Carol A. O'Connor, and Martha A. Sandweiss, eds., *The Oxford History of the American West,* (New York: Oxford University Press, 1994), 315–58.

100. For examples of spouses living on their own for long periods of time, see Mary Elizabeth Lee, "An Inspired Principle and a Remarkable Lady," 1949, Bancroft Library, University of California, Berkeley; William F. Schmidt, ed., "The Letters of Charles and Helen Wooster: The Problems of Settlement," *Nebraska History* 46 (June 1965): 121–37; David M. Kiefer, ed., "Over Barren Plains and Rock-Bound Mountains," *Montana: The Magazine of Western History* 22 (Winter 1972): 16–29; Ruth Seymour Burmester, ed., "Jeffries Letters," *South Dakota History* 6 (Summer 1976): 316–23; Constance L. Lieber, "'The Goose Hangs High': Excerpts from the Letters of Martha Hughes Cannon," *Utah Historical Quarterly* 48 (Winter 1980): 37–48; Kenneth W. Godfrey, Audrey M. Godfrey, and Jill Mulvay Derr, eds., *Women's Voices: An Untold History of the Latter-day Saints,*

1830–1900 (Salt Lake City, UT: Deseret Book Co., 1982), 65–81; and Anna Langhorne Waltz, "West River Pioneer: A Woman's Story, 1911-1915," *South Dakota History* 17 (Summer 1987): 140–69. For the ways in which war has affected marital dynamics, see Samuel H. Preston and John McDonald, "The Incidence of Divorce within Cohorts of American Marriages Contracted Since the Civil War," *Demography* 16 (February 1975): 1–25; and Carol K. Bleser and Frederick M. Heath, "The Impact of the Civil War on a Southern Marriage: Clement and Virginia Tunstall Clay of Alabama," *Civil War History* 30 (September 1984): 197–220.

101. Christiane Fischer, "A Profile of Women in Arizona in Frontier Days," *Journal of the West* 16 (July 1977): 42–53; and Erwin N. Thompson, "The Summer of '77 at Fort Lapwai," *Idaho Yesterdays* 21 (1977): 11–15. For army families in particular, see Kate Hogan, "Letters," 1868, and Matt Lagerberg, "Army Life at Fort Lincoln," 1935, State Historical Society of North Dakota, Bismarck; Nellie Rankin, "A Pioneer Family," 1936, Wyoming State Archives, Museum, and Historical Department, Cheyenne; Alice Mathews Shields, "Army Life on the Wyoming Frontier," *Annals of Wyoming* 13 (October 1941): 331–43; Robert M. Utley, "Campaigning with Custer," *American West* 144 (July/August 1977): 4–9, 58–60; Joan Ingalles, "Family Life on the Southwest Frontier," *Military History Texas Southwestern* 14 (1978): 203–13; Miller J. Stewart, "Army Laundresses: Ladies of the 'Soap Suds Row,'" *Nebraska History* 61 (Winter 1980): 421–36; Sandra L. Myres, "Evy Alexander: The Colonel's Lady at McDowell," *Montana: The Magazine of Western History* 24 (Spring 1974): 26–33; and Myres, "Romance and Reality on the American Frontier: Views of Army Wives," *Western Historical Quarterly* 13 (October 1982): 409–27.

102. Eulallia Pérez, "Reminiscences," 1877, Bancroft Library, University of California, Berkeley.

103. Sarah E. Olds, *Twenty Miles From a Match: Homesteading in Western Nevada* (Reno: University of Nevada Press, 1978), 15–17.

104. "Josie Jordan" Interview, in Rawick, *The American Slave*, 7:161.

105. Dupoux, letter to "Madame Chalmette," 12 November 1834, in "Letters of Baron Jopseh X. Pontalba to His Wife," Special Collections, Tulane Library, New Orleans.

106. James E. Davis, *Frontier America, 1800–1840: A Comparative Demographic Analysis of the Settlement Process* (Glendale, CA: Arthur H. Clark, 1977), 121–33; and "William Mathews" Interview, in Rawick, *The American Slave*, 5:7.

107. Sarah Winnemucca Hopkins, "'My people will never believe me again,'" in Moynihan et al., *So Much to Be Done*, 203–13.

108. Liu, "The Trans-Pacific Family," 13–29.

109. Consuelo Rocha, "Interview," 19 September 1979, American Heritage Center, University of Wyoming, Laramie.

110. Limón, *Mexican Ballads, Chicano Poems*, 36–38; and Foote, "Changing Images of Women in Western Film," 64–71.

111. Miller, ed., *Mourning Dove*, 66.

112. Yuji Ichioka, "*Amerika Nadeshiko*: Japanese Immigrant Women in the United

States, 1900–1924," *Pacific Historical Review* 49 (May 1980): 349–54; Tsuchida, *Asian and Pacific American Experiences*, 78; and Asian American Studies Center, UCLA, and Chinese Historical Society of Southern California, *Linking Our Lives: Chinese American Women of Los Angeles* (Los Angeles: Chinese Historical Society of Southern California, 1984), 44. Also helpful but dated in interpretation is Lucie Cheng Hirata, "Chinese Immigrant Women in Nineteenth-Century California," in Carol Ruth Berkin and Mary Beth Norton, eds., *Women of America: A History* (Boston: Houghton Mifflin, 1979), 223–43.

113. Marla N. Powers, *Oglala Women: Myth, Ritual, and Reality* (Chicago: University of Chicago Press, 1986), 141–60, 203–14.

114. Marín, *The Chicano Experience in Arizona*, 3–5; and Zaragosa Vargas, "Armies in the Fields and Factories: The Mexican Working Classes in the Midwest and the 1920s," *Mexican Studies* 7 (Winter 1991): 47–71. For other studies of the effects of migration upon Latinas' paid employment, see Arnoldo De León and Kenneth L. Stewart, *Tejanos and the Numbers Game: A Socio-Historical Interpretation from the Federal Censuses, 1850–1900* (Albuquerque: University of New Mexico Press, 1989), and Alejandro Portes, "From South of the Border: Hispanic Minorities in the United States," in Virginia Yans-McLaughlin, ed., *Immigration Reconsidered: History, Sociology, and Politics* (New York: Oxford University Press, 1990), 160–86.

115. Françoise Basch, "Women's Rights and the Wrongs of Marriage in Mid-Nineteenth-Century America," *History Workshop Journal* 22 (Autumn 1986): 18–40; and Elizabeth B. Clark, "Matrimonial Bonds: Slavery and Divorce in Nineteenth-Century America," *Law and History Review* 8 (Spring 1990): 25–54. A different perspective is found in Sidney Cornelia Callahan, *The Illusion of Eve: Modern Woman's Quest for Identity* (New York: Sheed and Ward, 1965).

116. Louise R. Noun, *Strong-Minded Women: The Emergence of the Woman-Suffrage Movement in Iowa* (Ames: Iowa State University Press, 1969).

117. Valerie Sherer Mathes, "A New Look at the Role of Women in Indian Society," *American Indian Quarterly* 2 (Summer 1975): 133–34.

118. Davis, *Frontier America*, 35–40.

119. *Burlington* (Iowa) *Daily Hawk-Eye*, 6 January, 1859.

120. Fanny Pringle, "A Pioneer," undated, Pioneer Daughters Collection, South Dakota State Historical Research Center, Pierre.

121. John C. Hudson, "The Study of Western Frontier Populations," in Jerome Steffen, ed., *The American West: New Perspectives, New Dimensions* (Norman: University of Oklahoma Press, 1979), 45–48. Also helpful is Deborah Fink and Alicia Carriquiry, "Having Babies or Not: Household Composition and Fertility in Rural Iowa and Nebraska, 1900–1910," *Great Plains Quarterly* 12 (Summer 1992): 157–68.

122. Geraldine P. Mineau, Lee L. Bean, and Douglas L. Anderton, "Migration and Fertility: Behavioral Change on the American Frontier," *Journal of Family History* 14 (1989): 43–61; and Lee L. Bean, Geraldine P. Mineau, and Douglas L. Anderton, "High-Risk Childbearing and Infant Mortality on the American Frontier," *Social Science History* 16 (Fall 1992): 337–63.

123. Mary Dunlava Tellefson, "Pioneer Days in Cass County," undated, State Historical Society of North Dakota, Bismarck; and Carrie Robbins, "Journal," 1887–1888, Kansas State Historical Society, Topeka. See also Sylvia D. Hoffert, "Childbearing on the Trans-Mississippi Frontier, 1830–1900," *Western Historical Quarterly* 22 (August 1991): 273–88.

124. Mrs. Christ Odegaard, "Biography," undated, Pioneer Daughters Collection, South Dakota State Historical Research Center, Pierre.

125. Sallie Davenport Davidson, "Memoirs," 1 November 1928, Montana Historical Society, Helena. Consult also Barbara Levorsen, "Early Years in Dakota," *Norwegian-American Studies* 21 (1962): 158–97, and Emma Polk, "Mother Polk's Life," undated, State Historical Society of Iowa, Iowa City.

126. Marguerite Dening, "Pioneer Life in Jackson County, South Dakota," undated, South Dakota State Historical Resource Center, Pierre.

127. Lillian A. Ackerman, "Marital Instability and Juvenile Delinquency among the Nez Perces," *American Anthropologist* 73 (June 1971): 595–603.

128. Powers, *Oglala Women*, 182–99.

129. Howard M. Bahr, "Religious Intermarriage and Divorce in Utah and the Mountain States," *Journal for the Scientific Study of Religion* 20 (1981): 251–61.

130. Sophie Trupin, *Dakota Diaspora: Memoirs of a Jewish Homesteader* (Lincoln: University of Nebraska Press, 1984), 39–40, 55–56.

131. For support of plural marriage as a widespread human practice, see Rush Nutt, "Polygamy Supposed to be a Primitive Practice and Natural to the Human Species," undated, Nutt Collection, Huntington Library, San Marino. Others who saw it as an efficacious practice among Native Americans include A. M. Stephen, "Our Forest Children," *Shingwauk Home* 4 (July 1890): 222, Albert S. Gilles, Sr., "Polygamy in Comanche Country," *Southwest Review* 51 (Summer 1966): 286–97, and Alonzo Delano, *Life on the Plains and among the Diggings* (Ann Arbor: University Microfilms, 1966), 218–19.

132. Those who criticized Mormon plural marriage include Lucy Sexton, *The Foster Family* (Santa Barbara, CA: Press of the Schouer Printing Studio, 1925), 135–36; Mrs. G. B. Ferris, *The Mormons at Home* (New York: Dix & Edwards, 1856), 116; Mrs. H. T. Clarke, "A Young Woman's Sights," 1851, Sarah Herndon, "Crossing the Plains," 1865, Sarah A. Cooke, "Theatrical and Social Affairs in Utah," 1884, Bancroft Library, University of California, Berkeley; and Jennie Kimball, "Narrative of an Overland Journey," 1876, Beinecke Collection, Yale University Library, New Haven. Those who expressed censure, or sometimes sympathy, for Mormon women include Mary Rockwood Powers, "A Woman's Overland Journal to California," 1947, California State Library, Sacramento, and Mary C. Fish, "Across the Plains," 1869, Bancroft Library. See also David J. Whittaker, "The Bone in the Throat: Orson Pratt and the Public Announcement of Plural Marriage," *Western Historical Quarterly* 18 (July 1987): 293–314; and Joan Smith Iversen, "A Debate on the American Home: The Antipolygamy Controversy, 1880–1890," *Journal of the History of Sexuality* 1 (April 1991): 585–602.

133. Emmeline B. Wells in Godfrey, Godfrey, and Derr, *Women's Voices*, 292–306; Rachel Emma Woolley Simmons, "Journal," in Daughters of the Utah Pioneers,

Heart Throbs of the West (Salt Lake City, UT: n.p., 1950), 153–208; and Riley, *Divorce*, 95–96.

134. Mary Annetta Coleman Pomeroy, "My Life Story," 1939, Arizona Historical Society, Tucson. A fuller discussion of women's attitudes toward plural marriage and scholars' interpretations is found in Glenda Riley, *Women and Indians on the Frontier, 1825–1915* (Albuquerque: University of New Mexico Press, 1984), 228–33, 236–38.

135. Roger A. Kessinger, *Marriage Licensing Laws* (Kila, MT: Kessinger Pub., 1990), 70, 95, 265.

136. Such changes are described in Robert T. Francoeur, *Eve's New Rib: Twenty Faces of Sex, Marriage, and Family* (New York: Harcourt Brace Jovanovich, 1972).

137. See for example Maggie Scarf, *Intimate Partners: Patterns in Love and Marriage* (New York: Random House, 1987).

138. Examples are found in Michael W. Yogman and T. Berry Brazelton, eds., *In Support of Families* (Cambridge, MA: Harvard University Press, 1986), especially Felton Earls, "A Developmental Perspective on Psychosocial Stress in Childhood," 29–58, and Ross D. Parke, "Fathers: An Intrafamilial Perspective," 59–68.

Chapter 3

1. August B. Hollingshead, "Cultural Factors in the Selection of Marriage Mates," in Robert F. Winch, Robert McGinnis, and Herbert R. Barringer, eds., *Selected Studies in Marriage and the Family* (New York: Holt, Rinehart and Winston, 1962), 477–89; and Suzanne K. Steinmetz, Sylvia Clavan, and Karen F. Stein, *Marriage and Family Realities: Historical and Contemporary Perspectives* (New York: Harper & Row, 1990), 163–66, 180–87, 190–95, 206–9.

2. Jacqueline Peterson, "Prelude to Red River: A Social Portrait of the Great Lakes Métis," *Ethnohistory* 25 (Winter 1978): 41–67; and Olive Patricia Dickason, "From 'One Nation' in the Northeast to 'New Nation' in the Northwest: A Look at the Emergence of the Métis," in Jacqueline Peterson and Jennifer S. H. Brown, eds., *The New Peoples: Being and Becoming Métis in North America* (Lincoln: University of Nebraska Press, 1985), 19–36.

3. See, for example, Gary A. Cretser and Joseph J. Leon, eds., *Intermarriage in the United States* (New York: Haworth Press, 1984), which included essays primarily on western peoples yet demonstrated no sense of intermarriage as a phenomenon varying by region.

4. Augustin Barbara, *Marriage across Frontiers* (Clevedon, England: Multilingual Matters Ltd., 1989), 1–7. Also consult S. Philip Morgan, Antonio McDaniel, Andrew T. Miller, and Samuel H. Preston, "Racial Differences in Household and Family Structure at the Turn of the Century," *American Journal of Sociology* 98 (January–Mary 1993): 799–828.

5. Alexander A. Plateris, *100 Years of Marriage and Divorce Statistics: United States, 1867–1967* (Rockville, MD: National Center for Health Statistics, 1973), 2–3.

6. Plateris, *100 Years of Marriage and Divorce Statistics*, 1–3.

7. Data are from *Record of Divorces, 1928–1944, Linn County, Iowa*, Linn County Courthouse, Cedar Rapids. The author gathered the statistics at the Linn County Courthouse during the summer of 1989.

8. For a study that successfully used public records to identify over three thousand intermarriages, see John H. Burma, "Interethnic Marriage in Los Angeles, 1948–1959," *Social Forces* 42 (October 1963–May 1964): 156–65.

9. Ernest Porterfield, "Black-American Intermarriage in the United States," in Gary A. Cretser and Joseph J. Leon, eds., *Intermarriage in the United States*, (New York: Haworth Press, 1984), 17–33.

10. Cases #39792, 42022, and 522353, Linn County Courthouse, Cedar Rapids, Iowa.

11. A discussion of this issue is found in, Peggy Pascoe, "Race, Gender, and Intercultural Relations: The Case of Interracial Marriage," *Frontiers* 12 (Fall 1991): 5–18.

12. Jane Dysart, "Mexican Women in San Antonio, 1830–1860: The Assimilation Process," *Western Historical Quarterly* 7 (October 1976): 365–75; Ronald C. Johnson and Germaine M. Ogasawara, "Within- and Across-Group Dating in Hawaii," *Social Biology* 35 (Spring/Summer 1988): 103–9; and Clarence Spigner, "Black/White Interracial Marriages: A Brief Overview of U.S. Census Data, 1980–1987," *Western Journal of Black Studies* 14 (Winter 1990): 214–16.

13. Mayo Hayes O'Donnell, "Angels Sang to Her," *Monterey* (California) *Peninsula Herald*, 1951; and Antonia I. Castañeda, "Gender, Race, and Culture: Spanish-Mexican Women in the Historiography of Frontier California," *Frontiers* 11 (Winter 1990): 15.

14. John A. Hussey, "The Women of Fort Vancouver," *Oregon Historical Quarterly* 92 (Fall 1991): 267.

15. Hussey, "The Women of Fort Vancouver," 266. See also Daniel T. Lichter, Diane K. McLaughlin, George Kephart, and David J. Landry, "Race and the Retreat from Marriage: A Shortage of Marriageable Men?" *American Sociological Review* 57 (December 1992): 781–99.

16. G. Robina Quale, *A History of Marriage Systems* (New York: Greenwood Press, 1988), 296–97.

17. Michael S. Coray, "Blacks in the Pacific West, 1850–1860: A View from the Census," *Nevada Historical Society Quarterly* 28 (Summer 1985): 106–8.

18. Juan L. Gonzales, Jr., "Exogamous Marriage Patterns among the Sikhs of California: 1904–1945," *International Journal of Sociology of the Family* 17 (Autumn 1987): 159–68.

19. Nobuya Tsuchida, ed, *Asian and Pacific American Experiences: Women's Perspectives* (Minneapolis: University of Minnesota Press, 1982), 177–79.

20. Beverly Hungry Wolf, *The Ways of My Grandmothers* (New York: William Morrow & Co., 1980), 70.

21. Sidney Kaplan, "Historical Efforts to Encourage White-Indian Intermarriage in the United States and Canada," *International Social Science Review* 64 (Winter 1989): 126–28.

22. Kaplan, "Historical Efforts," 129–32.

23. John S. Gray, "The Story of Mrs. Picotte-Galpin, A Sioux Heroine," *Montana: The Magazine of Western History* 56 (Summer 1986): 2–21. See also Lichter, Kephart, McLaughlin, and Landry, "Race and the Retreat from Marriage," 781–99.

24. Darlis A. Miller, "Cross Cultural Marriages in the Southwest: The New Mexico Experience, 1846–1900," *New Mexico Historical Review* 57 (October 1982):

342–45; and Rebecca McDowell Craver, *The Impact of Intimacy: Mexican-Anglo Intermarriage in New Mexico, 1821–1846* (El Paso: Texas Western Press, 1982), 12–13.

25. Quoted in Dysart, "Mexican Women in San Antonio," 371.

26. Quoted in Craver, *The Impact of Intimacy*, 23.

27. Quoted in Ted C. Hinckley, "Glimpses of Societal Change among Nineteenth-Century Tlingit Women," *Journal of the West* 33 (July 1993): 20.

28. John Mack Faragher, "The Custom of the Country: Cross-Cultural Marriage in the Far Western Fur Trade," in Lillian Schlissel, Vicki L. Ruiz, and Janice Monk, eds., *Western Women: Their Land, Their Lives* (Albuquerque: University of New Mexico Press, 1988), 199–220.

29. John E. Mayer, *Jewish-Gentile Courtships: An Exploratory Study of a Social Process* (New York: Free Press, 1961).

30. Thomas Ktsanes and Virginia Ktsanes, "The Theory of Complementary Needs in Mate Selection," in Winch et al., eds., *Selected Studies in Marriage and the Family*, 517–32; and Robert F. Winch, "Complementary Needs and Related Notions about Voluntary Mate-Selection," in Robert F. Winch and Graham B. Spanier, eds., *Selected Studies in Marriage and the Family* (New York: Holt, Rinehart and Winston, 1974), 399–409.

31. Craver, *The Impact of Intimacy*, 28–30.

32. Miller, "Cross Cultural Marriages," 336–37.

33. Douglas Monroy, *Thrown among Strangers: The Making of Mexican Culture in Frontier California* (Berkeley: University of California Press, 1990), 99–162.

34. Eleanor C. Nordyke and Richard K. C. Lee, "The Chinese in Hawai'i: A Historical and Demographic Perspective," *The Hawaiian Journal of History* 23 (1989): 196–216.

35. C. K. Cheng and Douglas S. Yamamura, "Interracial Marriage and Divorce in Hawaii," *Social Forces* 36 (October 1957): 77–84. Also useful is Beth Bailey and David Farber, *The First Strange Place: The Alchemy of Race and Sex in World War II Hawaii* (New York: The Free Press, 1992).

36. Lola Harvey, *Derevnia's Daughters: Saga of an Alaskan Village* (Manhattan, KS: Sunflower University Press, 1991), 46.

37. Ava Day, Letter to "Dear Mrs. Walker," 28 March 1964, Nebraska State Historical Society, Lincoln.

38. Interviews with Lena Barnett, 15 October 1937, vol. 14, #7838, and Stella Crouch, undated, vol. 100, #12758, Indian-Pioneer Papers, Western History Collection, University of Oklahoma Library, Norman.

39. Kenneth W. Porter, "Relations Between Negroes and Indians within the Present Limits of the United States," *Journal of Negro History* 17 (1932): 237–67; Lerone Bennett, Jr., "Red and Black: The Indians and the Africans," *Ebony* 26 (December 1970): 80; and Donald A. Grinde and Quintard Taylor, "Slaves, Freedmen, and Native Americans in Indian Territory (Oklahoma), 1865–1907," in Sucheng Chan, Douglas Henry Daniels, Mario T. García, and Terry P. Wilson, eds., *Peoples of Color in the American West* (Lexington, MA: D. C. Heath and Co., 1994), 288–99.

40. Craver, *The Impact of Intimacy,* 28–36 and Appendices 1–111, 49–60.

41. See for example interviews with Sallie Johnson Butler, undated, vol. 14, #7244; Mrs. Bill Moncrief, 27 May 1937, vol. 64, #4189; Mrs. William N. Moore, 24 August 1937, vol. 64, #7365; Alice Parker, 10 May 1937, vol. 69, #4021; Emma Jean Parker, undated, vol. 68, #7240; and Lydia Keys Taylor, 10 November 1937, vol. 89, #265, Western History Collection, Indian-Pioneer Papers, University of Oklahoma Library, Norman. Also helpful are Ella Flora Coodey Robinson, "A Cherokee Pioneer," *Chronicles of Oklahoma* 7 (December 1929): 364–74; and Lafayette Teele, "Weddings among the Indians," undated, vol. 10, Indian-Pioneer Papers, Western History Collection, University of Oklahoma Library, Norman.

42. James R. Carsklowey, in J. G. Starr Papers, Cherokee History, vol. 19: Mrs. James Bumgarner, Interview, undated, vol. 17, #12348; Joe J. Rogers, Interview, undated, vol. 98, #7101; and S. W. Ross, Interview, undated, vol. 108, #12809, Indian Pioneer Papers, Western History Collection, University of Oklahoma Library, Norman.

43. Mabel Beavers Sharpe, Interview, undated, vol. 6, # 6850, , Indian-Pioneer Papers, Western History Collection, University of Oklahoma Library, Norman.

44. Charles Throssell, "Memoirs," 1963, Throssell Collection, Nisqually Plains Room, Pacific Lutheran University, Tacoma.

45. Betty Lee Sung, "Chinese American Intermarriage," *Journal of Comparative Family Studies* 21 (Autumn 1990): 351.

46. "Nancy Winecoop," in United States Works Progress Administration, *Told by the Pioneers* (np: np, 1937), 1:114.

47. Craver, *The Impact of Intimacy,* 14–15.

48. Craver, *The Impact of Intimacy,* 16–17.

49. Mollie Beaver, Interview, 9 December 1937, vol. 6 #9409, Indian-Pioneer Papers, Western History Collection, University of Oklahoma Library, Norman. The importance of generational attitudes among specific groups is discussed in Deward E. Walker, Jr., "Measures of Nez Perce [*sic*] Outbreeding and the Analysis of Cultural Change," *Southwestern Journal of Anthropology* 223 (Summer 1967): 141–58; and Reuben Schoen, Verne E. Nelson, and Marion Collins, "Intermarriage among Spanish Surnamed Californians, 1962–1974," *International Migration Review* 12 (Fall 1973): 359–69.

50. Asian American Studies Center, UCLA, and Chinese Historical Society of Southern California, *Linking Our Lives: Chinese American Women of Los Angeles* (Los Angeles: Chinese Historical Society of Southern California, 1984), 41–42. See also Betty Lee Sung, *Chinese American Intermarriage* (New York: Center for Migration Studies, 1990), 74–86.

51. Richard Calfen, *Turning Leaves: The Photograph Collections of Two Japanese American Families* (Albuquerque: University of New Mexico Press, 1991), 170–71.

52. Harry H. L. Kitano, Wai-Tsang Yeung, Lynn Chai, and Herbert Hatanaka, "Asian-American Interracial Marriage," *Journal of Marriage and the Family* 46 (February 1984): 179–90.

53. Gary D. Sandefur, "American Indian Intermarriage," *Social Science Research* 15 (December 1986): 347–49. A discussion of whether groups develop their own

hierarchies to protect themselves or as an adaptive response to the existence of such hierarchies among more dominant groups is found in Carlos H. Arce and Armando Abney-Guardado, "Demographic and Cultural Correlates of Chicano Intermarriage," *California Sociologist* 5 (Summer 1982): 41–57.

54. Paul R. Spickard, *Mixed Blood: Intermarriage and Ethnic identity in Twentieth-Century America* (Madison: University of Wisconsin Press, 1989), 9–10, 363–64. See also "Overcoming Stereotypes," in Mark Mathabane and Gail Mathabane, *Love in Black and White: The Triumph of Love over Prejudice and Taboo* (New York: Harper Collins Publishers, 1992), 21–43.

55. B. M. Austin, Interview, 15 November 1937, vol. 3, #9189, Indian-Pioneer Papers, Western History Collection, University of Oklahoma Library, Norman.

56. Morris A. Graham and Judith Moeai, "Intercultural Marriages: An Intrareligious Perspective," *International Journal of Intercultural Relations* 9 (Fall 1985): 427–34.

57. William M. Kramer and Norton B. Stern, "Letters of 1852 to 1864 Sent to Rabbi Isaac Leeser of Philadelphia from the Far West," *Western States Jewish History* 20 (October 1988): 46–57; No author, "The First Jewish Wedding in the Territory of Arizona," *Western States Jewish History* 20 (January 1988): 126–28; No author, "A Wedding at Independence, California in 1876," *Western States Jewish History* 22 (January 1990): 112–15; and Eleanore Parelman Judd, "Intermarriage and the Maintenance of Religio-Ethnic Identity. A Case Study: The Denver Jewish Community," *Journal of Comparative Family Studies* 21 (Summer 1990): 251–68.

58. Reva Clar and William M. Kramer, "Chinese-Jewish Relations in the Far West: 1850–1950," *Western States Jewish Historical Quarterly* 15 (January 1983): 132–53.

59. Ruth McDonald Boyer and Narcissus Duffy Gayton, *Apache Mothers and Daughters: Four Generations of a Family* (Norman: University of Oklahoma Press, 1992), 4, 7, 27.

60. Robert C. Ostergren, "European Settlement and Ethnicity Patterns on the Agricultural Frontiers of South Dakota," *South Dakota History* 13 (Spring/Summer 1983): 49–82; and Marilee Richards, "Life Anew for Czech Immigrants: The Letters of Marie and Vavrín Strítecky," *South Dakota History* 11 (Fall-Winter 1981): 253–304. Also germane is Janet E. Rasmussen, "'I met him at Normanna Hall': Ethnic Cohesion and Marital Patterns among Scandinavian Immigrant Women," *Norwegian-American Studies* 32 (1989): 71–92.

61. Joseph R. Washington, Jr., *Marriage in Black and White* (Boston: Beacon Press, 1970); Joseph Golden, "Social Control of Negro-White Intermarriage," in Winch, McGinnis, and Barringer, eds., *Selected Studies in Marriage and the Family*, 1962), 496–517; and Clarence Spigner, "Black/White Interracial Marriages: A Brief Overview of U.S. Census Data, 1980–1987," *Western Journal of Black Studies* 14 (Winter 1990): 214–16.

62. Lawrence D. Rice, *The Negro in Texas, 1874–1900* (Baton Rouge: Louisiana State University Press, 1971), 263–65; and Sandefur, "American Indian Intermarriage," 347–71.

63. Susan E. Keefe and Amado M. Padilla, *Chicano Ethnicity* (Albuquerque: University of New Mexico Press, 1987), 119–27, 129–45. For a discussion of such ethnic boundaries among Japanese Americans, see John N. Tinker, "Intermarriage

and Ethnic Boundaries: The Japanese American Case," *Journal of Social Issues* 29 (1973): 49–66.

64. Everett Edington and Leonard Hays, "Difference in Family Size and Marriage Age Expectation and Aspirations of Anglo, Mexican American, and Native American Rural Youth in New Mexico," *Adolescence* 13 (Fall 1978): 393–400; Carlos H. Arce and Armando Abney-Guardado, "Demographic and Cultural Correlates of Chicano Intermarriage," *California Sociologist* 5 (Summer 1982): 41–57; and Keefe and Padilla, *Chicano Ethnicity*, 7–10, 129–33.

65. Ralph B. Cazares, Edward Murguía, W. Parker Frisbie, "Mexican American Intermarriage in a Nonmetropolitan Context," *Social Sciences Quarterly* 65 (June 1984): 626–34.

66. Caren J. Deming, "Miscegenation in Popular Western History and Fiction," in Helen Winter Stauffer and Susan J. Rosowski, eds., *Women and Western American Literature* (Troy, New York: Whitston Pub. Co., 1982), 90–99; and David D. Smits, "'Squaw Men,' 'Half-Breeds,' and Amalgamators: Late Nineteenth-Century Anglo-American Attitudes Toward indian-White Race-Mixing," *American Indian Culture and Research Journal* 15 (Fall 1991): 29–61. An anti-intermarriage novel is Charlotte M. Stanley-McKenna, *The Secret of a Birth* (N.p.: Norman L. Munro, 1884); the use of the term "squaw-man" is found in Millie M. Butler, Interview, undated, vol. 14, #10094, Indian-Pioneer Papers, Western History Collection, University of Oklahoma Library, Norman.

67. Quoted in Cecil Robinson, *With the Ears of Strangers: The Mexican in American Literature* (Tucson: University of Arizona Press, 1963), 77.

68. Robinson, *With the Ears of Strangers*, 77.

69. Hussey, "The Women of Fort Vancouver," 271–72.

70. Susan L. Johnson, "Sharing Bed and Board: Cohabitation and Cultural Difference in Central Arizona Mining Towns," *Frontiers* 7 (Fall 1984): 36–42, and quoted in Hinckley, "Glimpses of Societal Change among Nineteenth-Century Tlingit Women," 21.

71. Richard F. Burton, *The City of Saints and across the Rocky Mountains to California* (New York: Harper, 1862), 89–90.

72. Randolph B. Marcy, *Thirty Years of Army Life* (Philadelphia: Lippincott, 1866), 18, 29.

73. Karen Isaksen Leonard, *Making Ethnic Choices: California's Punjabi Mexican Americans* (Philadelphia: Temple University Press, 1992), 62–63.

74. A historical overview of opposition to black-white marriages in America is found in Washington, *Marriage in Black and White*.

75. Spickard, *Mixed Blood*, 374–75.

76. Quoted in Eugene H. Berwanger, *The Frontier against Slavery: Western Anti-Negro Prejudice and the Slavery Extension Controversy* (Urbana: University of Illinois Press, 1967), 32.

77. Berwanger, *The Frontier against Slavery*, 33–34.

78. Roger D. Hardaway, "Unlawful Love: A History of Arizona's Miscegenation Law," *Journal of Arizona History* 27 (Winter 1986): 377–90.

79. Carrol D. Wright, *Marriage and Divorce, 1867–1906*, Part I (reprint, Westport,

CT: Greenwood Press, 1978), 200–63. For a case resulting from Nevada law see Phillip I. Earl, "Nevada's Miscegenation Laws and the Marriage of Mr. and Mrs. Harry Bridges," *Nevada Historical Quarterly* 37 (Spring 1994): 1–17.

80. Staff of Asian American Studies Center, University of California, Los Angeles, "Antimiscegenation Laws and the Filipino, 1920s–1960s," in Chan et al., *Peoples of Color in the American West*, 336–44.

81. Hardaway, "Unlawful Love," 378–79.

82. W. Sherman Savage, *Blacks in the West* (Westport, CT: Greenwood Press, 1976), 189–90.

83. Constantine Panunzio, "Intermarriage in Los Angeles, 1924–33," *American Journal of Sociology* 47 (1942): 690–701.

84. "White Woman Asks Divorce from a Negro," *Oklahoma City Times-Journal*, 6 July 1908.

85. Willard B. Gatewood, Jr., "The Perils of Passing: The McCarys of Omaha," *Nebraska History* 71 (Summer 1990) 64–70.

86. Gatewood, "The Perils of Passing."

87. No author, "Early Reminiscences of a Nisqually Pioneer," in U.S. Works Progress Administration, *Told by the Pioneers*, (n.p.: n.p., 1837), 1:173.

88. Anna Kellough Wyss, Interview, 18 May 1937, vol. 101, #5847, Indian-Pioneer Papers, Western History Collection, University of Oklahoma Library, Norman.

89. Quoted in Stan Steiner, *The New Indians* (New York: Dell Publishing Company, c. 1968), 229.

90. For a historical overview of antimiscegenation law, the *Loving v. Virginia* decision, and events after the decision, consult, Robert J. Sickels, *Race, Marriage, and the Law* (Albuquerque: University of New Mexico Press, 1972).

91. Adrian Bustamante, "'The Matter Was Never Resolved': The *Casta* System in Colonial New Mexico, 1693–1823," *New Mexico Historical Review* 66 (April 1991): 143–63.

92. See for example Russell Endo and Dale Hirokawa, "Japanese American Intermarriage," *Free Inquiry in Creative Sociology* 11 (November 1983): 159–62, 166.

93. Betty Lee Sung, *Chinese American Intermarriage* (New York: Center for Migration Studies, 1990), 55–57, 87–99.

94. Kay Graber, ed., *Sister to the Sioux: The Memoirs of Elaine Goodale Eastman, 1885–1891* (Lincoln: University of Nebraska Press, 1978), 107–8, 116–20.

95. Robert L. Hampton, "Husband's Characteristics and Marital Disruption in Black Families," *Sociological Quarterly* 20 (Spring 1979): 255–66. For a discussion of wage variables in intermarriages, see Morrison G. Wong, "A Look at Intermarriage among the Chinese in the United States in 1980," *Sociological Perspectives* 32 (Spring 1989): 87–107.

96. Nannie T. Alderson and Helena Huntington Smith, *A Bride Goes West* (Lincoln: University of Nebraska Press, 1969), 185.

97. Barbara, *Marriage across Frontiers*, 58–69, and Gyung Ja Jeony and Walter R. Schumm, "Family Satisfaction in Korean/American Marriages: An Exploratory Study of the Perceptions of Korean Wives," *Journal of Comparative Family Studies* 21 (Autumn 1990): 325–36.

98. Dysart, "Mexican Women in San Antonio," 373. Also useful is Miller, "Cross-Cultural Marriages in the Southwest," 335–60.

99. Allen S. Maller, "Jewish-Gentile Divorce in California," *Jewish Social Studies* 37 (Summer 1975): 279–90; Howard M. Bahr, "Religious Intermarriage and Divorce in Utah and the Mountain States," *Journal for the Scientific Study of Religion* 20 (September 1981): 251–61; and Egon Mayer, *Love and Tradition: Marriage between Jews and Christians* (New York: Plenum Press, 1985), 151–76.

100. Miriam J. G. Bosburgh and Richard N. Juliana, "Contrasts in Ethnic Family Patterns: The Irish and the Italians," *Journal of Comparative Family Studies* 21 (Summer 1990): 269–86.

101. Edington and Hays, "Difference in Family Size and Marriage Age Expectation," 393–400.

102. Charles H. Mindel and Robert W. Habenstein, eds., *Ethnic Families in America: Patterns and Variations* (New York: Elsevier Scientific Publishing Co., 1976); and Barbara, *Marriage Across Frontiers*, 47–57, 70–84.

103. Peggy Pascoe, "Gender Systems in Conflict: The Marriages of Mission-Educated Chinese American Women, 1874–1939," *Journal of Social History* 22 (Fall/Summer 1988-89): 631–52.

104. Dugan Roman, *Inter-Cultural Marriage: Promises and Pitfalls* (Yarmouth, ME: Intercultural Press, Inc., 1988), 120–25.

105. Ernest S. Burch, Jr., "Marriage and Divorce among the North Alaskan Eskimos," in Paul Bohannon, ed., *Divorce and After* (New York: Doubleday, 1970), 152–81; James A. Sweet and Larry L. Bumpass, "Differentials in Marital Instability of the Black Population: 1970," 35 (September 1974): 323–31; Isaac W. Eberstein and W. Parker Frisbie, "Differences in Marital Instability among Mexican Americans, Blacks, and Anglos: 1960 and 1970," *Social Problems* 23 (Winter 1976): 609–21; and Thomas J. Espenshade, "The Recent Decline of American Marriage: Blacks and Whites in Comparative Perspective," in Kingsley Davis and Amyra Grossbard-Schechtman, eds., *Contemporary Marriage: Comparative Perspectives on a Changing Institution* (New York: Russell Sage Foundation, 1985), 53–90.

106. Ella Coody Robinson, Interview, 6 May 1938, vol. 77, #13833, Indian-Pioneer Papers, Western History Collection, University of Oklahoma Library, Norman.

107. Paula Waldowski, "Alice Brown Davis: A Leader of Her People," *Chronicles of Oklahoma* 58 (Winter 1980–81): 455–57.

108. Iris Wilson Engstrand and Thomas L. Scharf, "Rancho Guajome: A California Legacy Preserved," *Journal of San Diego History* 20 (Winter 1974): 1–14.

109. Leonard, *Making Ethnic Choices*, 73–78, 123–43.

110. See for example Dysart, "Mexican Women in San Antonio," 365–76; Edward Murguía, *Chicano Intermarriage: A Theoretical and Empirical Study* (San Antonio: Trinity University Press, 1982); and Sharon M. Lee and Keiko Yamanaka, "Patterns of Asian American Intermarriage and Marital Assimilation," *Journal of Comparative Family Studies* 21 (Summer 1990): 287–305.

111. The importance of trade in creating cultural adaptation is discussed in Thomas D. Hall, *Social Change in the Southwest, 1350–1880* (Lawrence: University Press of Kansas, 1989); for the effect of modernization, see R. Griswold del Castillo,

"La Familia Chicana: Social Changes in the Chicano Family of Los Angeles, 1850–1880," *Journal of Ethnic Studies* 3 (Spring 1975): 41–58; for the impact of urbanization, Steven Ruggles and Ron Goeken, "Race and Multigenerational Family Structure, 1900–1980," in Scott J. South and Stewart E. Tolnay, eds., *The Changing American Family: Sociological and Demographic Perspectives* (Boulder: Westview Press, 1992), 15–19, 25; for social status (hypergamy theory), see Larry Hajime Shinagawa and Gin Yong Pang, "Intraethnic, Interethnic, and Interracial Marriages among Asian Americans in California, 1980," *Berkeley Journal of Sociology*, 33 (1988): 95–144; and for group size, Richard D. Alba and Reid M. Golden, "Patterns of Ethnic Marriage in the United States," *Social Forces* 65 (September 1986): 202–23.

112. Craver, *The Impact of Intimacy*, 40–41.

113. Mei T. Nakano, *Japanese American Women: Three Generations, 1890–1990* (Berkeley: Mina Press Publishing, 1990), 226–27.

114. Cazares, *Generational Analysis of Chicano Intermarriage*; Avelardo Valdez, "Recent Increases in Intermarriage by Mexican American Males: Bexar County, Texas, from 1971 to 1980," *Social Science Quarterly* 64 (March 1983): 136–44; and Celestino Fernandez and Louis Holscher, "Chicano-Anglo Intermarriage in Arizona, 1960–1980: An Exploratory Study of Eight Counties," *Hispanic Journal of Behavioral Sciences* 5 (September 1983): 291–304.

115. Nelly Salgado de Snyder and Amado M. Padilla, "Cultural and Ethnic Maintenance of Interethnically Married Mexican Americans," *Human Organization* 41 (Winter 1982): 359–62; and Tuchida, ed., *Asian and Pacific American Experiences*, 177. See also William Toll, "Intermarriage and the Urban West: A Religious Context for Cultural Change," in Moses Rischin and John Livingston, eds., *Jews of the American West* (Detroit: Wayne State University Press, 1991), 164–89.

116. Keefe and Padilla, *Chicano Ethnicity* (Albuquerque: University of New Mexico Press, 1987), 6–7; Cookie White Stephan and Walter G. Stephan, "After Intermarriage: Ethnic Identity among Mixed-Heritage Japanese-Americans and Hispanics," *Journal of Marriage and the Family* 51 (May 1989): 507–19; and Cookie White Stephan, "Ethnic Identity among Mixed-Heritage People in Hawaii," *Symbolic Interaction* 14 (Fall 1991): 261–77.

117. Ronald C. Johnson and Germaine M. Ogasawara, "Within and Across Group Dating in Hawaii," *Social Biology* 35 (1–2)(Spring-Summer 1988): 103–9; D. Y. Yuan, "Significant Demographic Characteristics of Chinese Who Intermarry in the United States," *California Sociologist* 3 (Summer 1980): 184–96; Teresa Labov and Jerry A. Jacobs, "Intermarriage in Hawaii, 1950–1983," *Journal of Marriage and the Family* 48 (February 1986): 79–88; and Robert Schoen and Barbara Thomas, "Intergroup Marriage in Hawaii, 1969–1971 and 1979–1981," *Sociological Perspectives* 32 (Fall 1989): 365–82. For a counterargument (that Japanese/American intermarriage is rapidly rising) see Akemi Kikumura and Harry H. L. Kitano, "Interracial Marriage: A Picture of the Japanese Americans," *Journal of Social Issues* 29 (1973): 66–81.

118. Cheng and Ymamura, "Interracial Marriage and Divorce in Hawaii," 83–84; Ronald C. Johnson, "Group Size and Group Income as Influences on Marriage

Patterns in Hawaii," *Social Biology* 31 (Spring–Summer 1984): 101–7; and Fung Chu Ho and Ronald C. Johnson, "Intra-ethnic and Inter-ethnic Marriage and Divorce in Hawaii," *Social Biology* 37 (Spring–Summer 1990): 44–51. That similar patterns occurred among Asian Americans in California is argued in Larry Hajime Shinagawa and Gin Yong Pang, "Intraethnic, Interethnic, and Interracial Marriages among Asian Americans in California, 1980," *Berkeley Journal of Sociology* 33 (1988): 95–114.

119. Cazares, Murguía, and Frisbie, "Mexican American Intermarriage in a Nonmetropolitan Context," 626–34; Edward Murguía and W. Parker Frisbie, "Trends in Mexican American Intermarriage: Recent Findings in Perspective," *Social Science Quarterly* 58 (December 1977): 374–89; 626–34; Murguía, *Chicano Intermarriage*, 16–19, 32–35; and Nelly Salgado de Snyder and Amado M. Padilla, "Interethnic Marriages of Mexican Americans after Nearly Two Decades," Occasional Paper Number 15, Spanish Speaking Mental Health Research Center, University of California, Los Angeles, 1981.

Chapter 4

1. See, for example, Scott J. South and Glenna Spitze, "Determinants of Divorce over the Marital Life Course," *American Sociological Review* 51 (August 1986): 583–90; K. D. Breault and Augustine J. Kposowa, "Explaining Divorce in the United States: A Study of 3,111 Counties, 1980," *Journal of Marriage and the Family* 49 (August 1987): 549–58; Robert M. Counts and Anita Sacks, "Profiles of the Divorce Prone: The Self Involved Narcissist," *Journal of Divorce and Remarriage* 15 (Spring 1991): 51–74; and Lynn K. White, "Determinants of Divorce: A Review of Research in the Eighties," *Journal of Marriage and the Family* 52 (November 1990): 904–12. Suggestions for additional research are found in Sharon Price-Bonham and Jack O. Balswick, "The Noninstitutions: Divorce, Desertion, and Remarriage," *Journal of Marriage and the Family* 42 (November 1980): 959–72; and Teresa Castro Martin and Larry L. Bumpass, "Recent Trends in Marital Disruption, *Demography* 26 (February 1989): 37–51.

2. For instance, see Norval D. Glenn and Beth Ann Shelton, "Regional Differences in Divorce in the United States," *Journal of Marriage and the Family* 47 (August 1985): 641–52. Two recent and important interpretations of causes of divorce are, Elaine Tyler May, *Great Expectations: Marriage and Divorce in Post-Victorian America* (Chicago: University of Chicago Press, 1980), and Robert L. Griswold, *Family and Divorce in California, 1850–1890: Victorian Illusions and Everyday Realities* (Albany: State University of New York Press, 1982).

3. For a discussion of the role played by national attitudes in divorce rate, see Ernest W. Burgess, *The Family* (New York: American Book Co., 1945), 630.

4. The possibility that gender itself provides an underlying cause of divorce is discussed in Margaret Guminski Cleek and T. Allan Pearson, "Perceived Causes of Divorce: An Analysis of Interrelationships," *Journal of Marriage and the Family* 47 (February 1985): 179–83.

5. One person who observed little divorce among Comanches, for example, was Mrs. John Barnes, Interview, 1938, vol. 7, #9735, Indian-Pioneer Papers, Western History Collection, University of Oklahoma Library, Norman.

6. S. F. Cook, *The Conflict Between the California Indian and White Civilization Volume IV: Trends in Marriage and Divorce Since 1850* (Berkeley: University of California Press, 1943), 3–4.

7. *Louise Jousset La Loire v. Surgeon Pierre de Manade*, 15 February 1729, Records of the Superior Council of Louisiana, Louisiana Historical Center, New Orleans.

8. Carl J. Eckberg, *Colonial Ste. Genevieve: An Adventure of the Mississippi Frontier* (Gerald, MO: Patrice Press, 1985), 192–95.

9. David J. Langum, "Sin, Sex, and Separation in Mexican California: Her Domestic Relations Law," *The Californians* 5 (May/June 1987): 44–50.

10. Mary Grayson Interview, undated, Oklahoma Writers' Project, University of Oklahoma Library, Norman. For other examples see Adeline Marshall, Interview 3514, vol. 5, part 3, 47–49; Susan Merritt, unnumbered, vol. 5, part 3, 75–79; Lucinda Davis, unnumbered, vol. 4, 53–64; and Alice Douglass, unnumbered, vol. 7, 73–76, in George P. Rawick, ed., *The American Slave* (Westport, CT: Greenwood Press, 1972); and Viola Chandler, Interview, 1938, vol. 17, #13738, Indian-Pioneer Papers, Western History Collection, University of Oklahoma Library, Norman.

11. A more detailed discussion of this phenomenon is found in Glenda Riley, *Divorce: An American Tradition*. (New York: Oxford University Press, 1992), chap. 4.

12. Albert D. Richardson, *Beyond the Mississippi* (Hartford, CT: American Publishing Co., 1867), 148. That such factors as age and occupation led to higher divorce rates in the West is argued in Henry Pang, "Highest Divorce Rates in Western United States," *Sociology and Social Research* 52 (January 1968) 228–36. For the effect of high mobility on western divorce rates, see Bill Fenelon, "State Variations in United States Divorce Rates," *Journal of Marriage and the Family* 33 (May 1971):321–27. For the argument that the western environment had a similar liberalizing effect on women's rights, see Mari J. Matsuda, "The West and the Legal Status of Women: Explanations of Frontier Feminism," *Journal of the West* 24 (January 1985): 47–56.

13. *Missouri* (Franklin) *Intelligencer*, 19 June 1824.

14. Quoted in Susan Hallgarth, "'No One Should Dictate as to Ways and Means': Single Women on the Frontier," unpublished manuscript, 11–12, copy in author's possession.

15. United States Department of Commerce and Labor, *Marriage and Divorce, 1867–1906*, 2 vols.(reprint, Westport, CT: Greenwood Press, 1978), 1:14–15, 70–71. Consult also Mary Somerville Jones, *An Historical Geography of Changing Divorce Law in the United States* (Ph.D. diss., University of North Carolina, Chapel Hill, 1978), 59–60.

16. Somerville Jones, *An Historical Geography of Changing Divorce Law*, 1:14–15.

17. Alexander A. Plateris, *100 Years of Marriage and Divorce Statistics, 1867–1967* (Rockville, MD: National Center for Health Statistics, 1973), 27.

18. "Robert Archibald" Poster, 1906, "Peter J. Hempler" Poster, 1906, "Disappeared-Frank Limbrack" Poster, 1906, and "A Liberal Reward—George W.

Roach" Poster, 1906, in "Criminals Wanted," 1906, Oklahoma Territorial Museum, Guthrie, OK.

19. Case #1945, *Ball v. Ball,* filed 21 June 1895, Territorial Records, Logan County, Guthrie. A different type of desertion case is found in Paula Petrik, "Not a Love Story: *Bordeaux v. Bordeaux,*" *Montana: The Magazine of Western History* 41 (Spring 1991): 32–46.

20. "Walter L. Davis" Poster, 1905, in "Criminals Wanted," 1906, Oklahoma Territorial Museum, Guthrie.

21. Case #1966, *Hansen v. Hansen,* filed 25 July 1895, Territorial Records, Logan County, Guthrie, OK. A description of desertion cases in San Diego between 1850 and 1880 is found in Susan Gonda, "San Diego Women and Frontier Divorce," undated, San Diego Historical Society.

22. "George H. Blowers Poster," 1905, "Criminals Wanted," 1906, Oklahoma Territorial Museum, Guthrie.

23. "Mabel Wade" Poster, 1905, and "Fifty Dollars Reward" Poster by S. D. Gilbert, 1906, "Criminals Wanted," 1906, Oklahoma Territorial Museum, Guthrie.

24. For an account of early divorce practices among the Cherokee, see John Phillip Reid, *A Law of Blood: The Primitive Law of the Cherokee Nation* (New York: New York University Press, 1970), 117–18; and Renard Strickland, *Fire and the Spirits: Cherokee Law from Clan to Court* (Norman: University of Oklahoma Press, 1975), 97–102. Examples of divorce decrees are found in Cherokee National Council, vol. 270, 13 November 1880, 232–33, and dvol. 279, 22 November 1882, 14, Archives and Manuscript Division, Oklahoma Museum and Historical Society, Oklahoma City; and *Laws and Joint Resolutions of the Cherokee Nation* (Tahlequah, Cherokee Nation: E. C. Boudinot, Jr., Printer, 1887), 81; and are reported in *The Cherokee Advocate* (Tahlequah, Indian Territory), 16 November 1880, 29 September, 1 December, 8 December, 15 December 1882, and 16 February 1883. Statutes are found in *Compiled Laws of the Cherokee Nation* (Tahlequah, Indian Territory: National Advocate Printer, 1881), 287. Other tribes practiced divorce as well. See for example *Constitution, Laws, and Treaties of the Chickasaws* (Tishomingo City, OK: E. J. Foster, 1860), 102–4; *Constitution, Laws and Treaties of the Chickasaws* (Sedalia, MO: Sedalia Democrat Co., 1878), 67–69; and *General and Special Laws of the Chickasaw Nation* (Muskogee, OK: Indian Journal Steam Job Print, 1884), 19. For divorce statutes in Indian Territory, see *Annotated Statutes of the Indian Territory* (St. Paul, MN: West Pub. Co., 1899), 324–27.

25. Luke Bearshield's divorce was reported in (Guthrie) *Daily Leader,* 14 July 1893, and (Oklahoma City) *Oklahoma Times Journal,* 16 July 1893. Cinda Richard's divorce petition was related in *Daily Oklahoman* (Oklahoma City), 28 September 1913. Reports of other Indian divorces are found in (Guthrie) *Daily Leader,* 25 April 1894; (Vinita) *Indian Chieftain,* 26 November 1896; and *Vinita* (OK) *Weekly Chieftain,* 20 October 1904.

26. *Daily* (Guthrie) *Oklahoma State Capital,* 6 July 1893, and *Vinita* (OK) *Chieftain,* 1 September 1904.

27. U. S. Department of Commerce and Labor, *Marriage and Divorce,* 1:45–46. Newspaper reports of divorces are found in (Oklahoma City) *Oklahoma Times Journal,*

22 September 1893; (Guthrie) *Daily Leader*, 24 November 1893; (Oklahoma City) *Times Journal*, 4 April 1894; *Daily* (Guthrie) *Oklahoma State Capital*, 19 December 1894; *Daily Times Journal* (Oklahoma City), 15 April 1895; and *Weekly Chieftain* (Vinita, OK), 19 November 1909. Divorce even touched western governors. See Constance Wynn Altshuler, "The Scandalous Divorce: Governor Safford Severs the Tie that Binds," *The Journal of Arizona History* 30 (Summer 1989): 181–92. That divorce affected all classes of Californians is demonstrated in Griswold, *Family and Divorce in California*, 25–26, 180–81.

28. For an example of a sensationalized divorce trial, see Donald W. Hamblin, "The Sharon Cases: A Legal Melodrama of the Eighties," *Los Angeles Bar Bulletin* 25 (December 1949): 101–3, 122–23, 125–28. Another description of the Sharon trial is found in Edna Byran Buckbee, "The Story of Sarah Althea Hill," *The Pony Express* 20 (March 1954): 4, 15. Another controversial California divorce case is described in William M. Kramer and Norton B. Stern, "An Issue of Jewish Marriage and Divorce in San Francisco," *Western States Jewish History* 21 (October 1988): 46–57.

29. Samuel W. Dike, *Important Features of the Divorce Question* (Royalton, VT: New England Divorce Reform League, 1885).

30. For a detailed history of the Latter-day Saints, see James B. Allen and Glen M. Leonard, *The Story of the Latter-day Saints* (Salt Lake City: Deseret Book Co., 1976). Mormon women's accounts are found in Kenneth W. Godfrey, Audrey M. Godfrey, and Jill Mulvay Derr, eds. *Women's Voices: An Untold History of the Latter-day Saints, 1830–1900* (Salt Lake City: Deseret Book Co., 1982).

31. Eugene E. Campbell and Bruce L. Campbell, "Divorce among Mormon Polygamists: Extent and Explanations," *Utah Historical Quarterly* 46 (1978): 4–23.

32. *Utah Territorial Laws* (Salt Lake City: Capitol Printer, 1852), 82–84.

33. Probate Court Records Book, 12 February 1856, Washington County, Utah, Huntington Library, San Marino, CA.

34. *Sunstone Review*, Utah, June, 1983, 21.

35. Jacob Smith Boreman, "Curiosities of Early Utah Legislation," 1905, 40–42, Huntington Library, San Marino, CA. For a fuller discussion of Utah territorial divorce law, see Richard I. Aaron, "Mormon Divorce and the Statute of 1852: Questions for Divorce in the 1980s," *Journal of Contemporary Law* 8 (1982): 5–45.

36. Jacob Smith Boreman, "Reminiscences of My Life in Utah, On and Off the Bench, 1872-1877," Huntington Library, San Marino, CA. For a fuller discussion of the Young divorce case, see Louis J. Kern, *An Ordered Love: Sex Roles and Sexuality in Victorian Utopias: The Shakers, the Mormons, and the Oneida Community* (Chapel Hill: University of North Carolina Press, 1981), 198–200.

37. Aaron, "Mormon Divorce," 22, and Kern, *An Ordered Love*, 45–56.

38. Doane Robinson, "Divorce in Dakota," *South Dakota Historical Collection* (Pierre: Hipple Printing Co., 1924), 12:268–72; Howard R. Lamar, *Dakota Territory, 1861-1889: A Study of Frontier Politics* (New Haven: Yale University Press, 1956), 93; "Sioux Falls: The Origins of an Early Divorce Capital," *Sioux Falls Tribune*, 17 August 1893. For divorce laws see *Laws, Memorials and Resolutions of the Terri-*

tory of Dakota, 1865-66 (Yankton: G. W. Kingsbury, Printer, 1865–66), 11–14; *General Laws, Memorials and Resolutions of the Territory of Dakota, 1867* (Yankton: Bowen & Kingsbury, 1867), 45–50; George H. Hand, ed., *The Revised Codes of the Territory of Dakota, 1877* (Yankton: Bowen & Kingsbury, 1880), 215–19; A.B. Levisee and L. Levisee, eds., *The Annotated Revised Codes of the Territory of Dakota, 1883* (St. Paul, MN: West Pub. Co., 1885), 747–51; and *The Compiled Laws of the Territory of Dakota, 1887* (Bismarck: Printer for the Territory, 1887), 545–51.

39. "Enabling Act," *Laws Passed at the First Session of the Legislative Assembly of the State of North Dakota* (Bismarck: Tribune Printers, 1890), 3–13.

40. *Evening Argus Leader,* 10 January 1893. See also Myra A. Strasser, *Social and Cultural Development in 19th Century Sioux Falls, South Dakota* (M.A. Thesis, University of South Dakota, Vermillion, 1969).

41. Charles A. Smith, *History of Minnehaha County, South Dakota* (Mitchell, SD: Educator Supply Co. 1949), 373; Harry Hazel and S. L. Lewis, *The Divorce Mill: Realistic Sketches of the South Dakota Divorce Colony* (Rahway, NJ: Mascot, 1895), 5; and George Fitch, "Shuffling Families in Sioux Falls: How a Little Town has Become a Big City through its Divorce Industry," *American Magazine* 66 (September 1908): 443–45, 448.

42. Will Lillibridge, *The Dissolving Circle* (New York: Dodd, Mead, & Co., 1908), 6; and Jane Burr, *Letters of a Dakota Divorce* (Boston: Roxburgh Pub. Co., 1909).

43. Bishop William Hobart Hare, "Notes on Women," undated, Papers of Bishop William Hobart Hare, 1864–1909, Center for Western Studies, Augustana College, Sioux Falls, South Dakota, and *Missionary District of South Dakota: Journal of the Convocations with the Annual Address of the Bishop* (np: np, 1890), xi.

44. Lonnie R. Haugland, "South Dakota Divorce Legislation and Reform: 1862–1908," *The Region Today: A Quarterly Journal of the Social Science Research Associates* 2 (May 1975): 54–55.

45. Mary E. Peabody, *Zitana Duzahon: Swift Bird, The Indians' Bishop* (Hartford, CT: Church Missions Pub. Co., 1915), 61–63; Haugland, "South Dakota Divorce Legislation," 55–56; and Herbert S. Schell, *History of South Dakota* (Lincoln: University of Nebraska Press, 1968), 261–62.

46. The two analysts are Arthur G. Horton, *An Economic and Social Survey of Sioux Falls, South Dakota, 1938–39* (np: np, 1939), 81, and Robinson, "Divorce in Dakota," 275–76. Department of Labor statistics are found in, Alexander A. Plateris, *100 Years of Marriage and Divorce Statistics, United States, 1867–1967* (Rockville, MD: National Center for Health Statistics, 1973), 34–35. For other statistical interpretations, see Nelson M. Blake, *The Road to Reno: A History of Divorce in the United States* (New York: Macmillan, 1962), 123.

47. Charles A. Pollock, "The Divorce Law," undated, Pollock Collection, 1890, 1923–70, North Dakota Institute for Regional Studies, North Dakota State University, Fargo.

48. *Laws Passed at the First Session of the Legislative Assembly of the State of North Dakota* , 22, 54; and *The Revised Laws of the State of North Dakota, 1899* (Bismarck: Tribune Co., Printers, 1899), 695.

49. William H. White, "Early History and Settlements of Cass County," undated, North Dakota Institute for Regional Studies, North Dakota State University,

Fargo; and Cass County Historical Society, *Rural Cass County: The Land and Its People* (Dallas: Taylor Pub. Co., 1976), 8.

50. Elizabeth Preston Anderson, "Under the Prairie Winds," undated, in Preston Papers, 1889–1954, North Dakota Institute for Regional Studies, North Dakota State University, Fargo; and Bishop John Shanley, "Diary," 1903, Diocesan Archives of Fargo, courtesy of Reverend T. William Coyle, C.SS.R., Chancellor, Fargo, ND. For Bishop Shanley's career, see *St. Mary's Cathedral, 1899–1949* (np: np, 1949).

51. *The Revised Codes of the State of North Dakota, 1899* (Bismarck: Tribune Co., Printers, 1899), 698. See also Mariellen MacDonald Noudeck, *Morality Legislation in Early North Dakota, 1889-1914* (M.A. thesis, University of North Dakota, Grand Forks, North Dakota, 1964).

52. John Lee Coulter, "Marriage and Divorce in North Dakota," *American Journal of Sociology*, 12 (1906–7): 398–416; and Nicolai Rolfsrud Erling, *The Story of North Dakota* (Alexandria, MN: Lantern Books, 1963), 232. See also, George B. Winship, "Political History of the Red River Valley," in *History of the Red River Valley* (Grand Forks, ND: Herald Pub. Co., 1909), 1:459; "Fargo Was World's Quick Divorce Center for Two Decades," *Fargo Forum*, Diamond Jubilee Edition, 4 June 1950; William L. O'Neill, *Divorce in the Progressive Era* (New Haven: Yale University Press, 1967), 235; and Fargo-Moorhead Centennial Corporation, *A Century Together: A History of Fargo, North Dakota and Moorhead, Minnesota* (np: np, 1975), 41.

53. Government figures are found in Plateris, *100 Years of Marriage and Divorce Statistics*, 34. Cass County figures are from *Register of Actions*, Territory of Dakota, County of Cass, May 1882 to February 1885; *Register of Actions*, District Court, Cass County, North Dakota, June 1892 to October 1893 and March 1901 to April 1903. The Cass County statistics confirm that more women than men obtained divorces, but because the figures do not indicate migratory decrees, it is impossible to determine whether more women than men also secured migratory decrees.

54. *General Statutes of Oklahoma, 1908* (Kansas City, MO: Pipes-Reed Book Co., 1908), 52; and Will T. Little, L. G. Pittman, and R. J. Barker, comps., *The Statutes of Oklahoma, 1890* (Guthrie: State Capital Printing, 1891), 676–79, 903–5.

55. Little, Pittman, and Barker, *The Statutes of Oklahoma*, 903–5.

56. *The Statutes of Oklahoma, 1893* (Guthrie: State Capitol Printing, 1893), 875, 877.

57. Frank Dale (Chief Justice), *Reports of Cases Argued and Determined in the Supreme Court of the Territory of Oklahoma*, (Guthrie: Daily Leader Printing Co.,, 1896), 3:86–204; *Daily Leader* (Guthrie), 12 August 1892; and *Daily Times Journal* (OK City), 26 December 1894.

58. Dale, *Reports of Cases Argued*, 2:180–228.

59. *Kingfisher* (OK) *Free Press*, 20 September 1894; *Daily Leader* (Guthrie), 9 September 1894; *Journal of the Council Proceedings of the Third Legislative Assembly* (np: np, 1895), 515, 891; and *Territory of Oklahoma Session Laws of 1895* (np: np, 1895), 107.

60. *Edmond* (OK) *Sun Democrat*, 28 June 1895; and *Alva* (OK) *Republican*, 20 May 1896.

61. Quoted in Daniel F. Littlefield, Jr. and Lonnie E. Underhill, "Divorce Seeker's Paradise: Oklahoma Territory, 1890–1897," *Arizona and the West* 17 (1975): 23. For an example of a notice by publication, see (Oklahoma City) *Oklahoma Times Journal*, 15 July 1895.

62. Abraham J. Seay, "Governor's Message to Second Legislative Assembly of the Territory of Oklahoma Delivered January 19, 1893," *Oklahoma Territory Governors Messages and Reports, 1893-95, 1901–05* (np: np, nd), 8. For other denouncements see *Kingfisher* (OK) *Free Press*, 6 September 1894; *Daily Ardmoreite* (Ardmore, OK), 13 September 1894; and *Stillwater* (OK) *Gazette*, 19 November 1896.

63. *Daily Leader* (Guthrie, OK), 28 March 1894; and *Oklahoma* (Oklahoma City) *Time Journal*, 30 March 1894.

64. *El Reno* (OK) *News*, 7 August 1896, and *Daily Oklahoman* (Oklahoma City), 25 January 1908. Accounts of the congressional action are found in *Indian Chieftain* (Vinita, OK), 21 May 1896, and *Hennessy* (OK) *Clipper*, 4 June 1896. For revisions of divorce statutes, see *Revised Laws of Oklahoma 1910* (St. Paul, MN: West Pub. Co., 1912), 1330–37.

65. Quoted in Littlefield and Underhill, "Divorce Seeker's Paradise," 21. Government statistics are found in Plateris, *100 Years of Marriage and Divorce Statistics*, 35.

66. This view is supported in U.S. Department of Commerce and Labor, *Marriage and Divorce*, 1:15, 34.

67. Riley, *Divorce: An American Tradition*, chap. 4.

68. For Lord Russell's divorce, see Duncan Crow, *The Edwardian Woman* (New York: St. Martin's Press, 1978), 174–79.

69. George A. Bartlett, *Men, Women and Conflict* (New York: Macmillan, 1931), 11.

70. Blake, *Road to Reno*, 153–54.

71. *Nevada State Journal*, 1 February 1913.

72. *Nevada State Journal*, 8 and 18 February 1913.

73. *Nevada State Journal*, 24 February 1915.

74. *Nevada State Journal*, 19 March 1927.

75. *Nevada State Journal*, 7, 17, and 20 and 17 March 1931.

76. *Nevada State Journal*, 9 March 1931.

77. Paul H. Jacobson and Pauline F. Jacobson, *American Marriage and Divorce* (New York: Rinehart, 1959), 103–4.

78. See for example William E. Carson, *The Marriage Revolt: A Study of Marriage and Divorce* (New York: Hearst International Library, 1915), 450; Katherine F. Gerould, "Divorce," *Atlantic Monthly* 132 (October 1923): 466; and Ben B. Lindsey and Wainwright Evans, *The Companionate Marriage* (Salem, NH: Ayer Co., Pubs., 1927).

79. George Thorman, *Broken Homes* (New York: Public Affairs Committee, 1947), 15–20; Robert B. Deen, Jr., "The Present Status of Connivance as a Defense to Divorce," *Vanderbilt Law Review* 3 (December 1949): 107; and Charles H. Leclaire, "Reform—The Law of Divorce," *George Washington Law Review* 17 (April 1949): 390. For an analysis of family life during the mid-twentieth century, see Steven

Mintz and Susan Kellogg, *Domestic Revolutions: A Social History of American Family Life* (New York: Free Press, 1987), 178–95, and Elaine Tyler May, *Homeward Bound: American Families in the Cold War Era* (New York: Basic Books, 1988).

80. George Squire, "The Shift from Adversary to Administrative Divorce," *Boston University Law Review* 33 (April 1953): 141–75; Florence Perlow Shientag, "Divorce in the United States: Recent Developments," *Women Lawyers Journal* 43 (Winter 1957): 7–9, 20–21; and Somerville Jones, *An Historical Geography of Changing Divorce Laws* , 110, 138. One of the earliest states to accept separation as a ground for divorce was Louisiana. See Zue Vance, "Divorce in Louisiana: Grounds and Defenses," *Tulane Law Review* 24 (June 1950): 450–51.

81. Christopher Lasch, "Divorce and the Family in America," *Atlantic Monthly* 218 (November 1966) 57–61; Margaret Mead, "Double Talk about Divorce," *Redbook* 131 (1)(May 1968): 47–48; Henry H. Foster, Jr., "Current Trends in Divorce Law," *Family Law Quarterly* 1 (June 1967): 21–40; and Doris Jonas Freed and Henry H. Foster, Jr., "Divorce American Style," *Annals of the American Academy of Political and Social Science* 83 (May 1969): 71–87.

82. Howard A. Krom, "California's Divorce Law Reform: An Historical Analysis," *Pacific Law Journal* 1 (January 1970): 156–81. Practical advice to divorce seekers is found in Harry Walter Koch, *California Marriage and Divorce Laws* (San Francisco: Ken Books, 1969). Advice to attorneys is found in Charles W. Johnson, "The Family Law Act: A Guide to the Practitioner," *Pacific Law Journal* 1 (January 1970): 147–55.

83. Doris Jonas Freed and Henry H. Foster, Jr., "Divorce in the Fifty States: An Outline," *Family Law Quarterly* 11 (Fall 1977): 297–313; and Robert Raphael, Frederick N. Frank, and Joanne Ross Wilder, "Divorce in America: The Erosion of Fault," *Dickinson Law Review* 81 (Summer 1977): 719–31. For the effect of no-fault laws on the divorce rate, see Michael Wheeler, *No-Fault Divorce* (Boston, 1974), 30–31, 155–56; Walter D. Johnson, *Marital Dissolution and the Adoption of No-Fault Legislation* (Springfield, IL: Legislative Studies Center, Sangamon State University, 1975), 22–31; and Dorothy M. Stetson and Gerald C. Wright, Jr., "The Effects of Laws on Divorce in the American States," *Journal of Marriage and the Family* 37 (August 1975): 537–47.

84. Riley, *Divorce: An American Tradition*, 156–57.

85. Arnold O. Ginnow and Milorad Nikolic, *Corpus Juris Secundum: A Contemporary Statement of American Law as Derived from Reported Cases and Legislation* (St. Paul, MN: West Pub. Co., 1986), 36, 43–44, 59–78.

86. Lawrence M. Friedman and Robert V. Percival, "Who Sues for Divorce? From Fault through Fiction to Freedom," *Journal of Legal Studies* 5 (January 1976): 61–82.

87. Kenneth D. Sell, "Divorce Advertising—One Year after *Bates*," *Family Law Quarterly* 12 (Winter 1979): 275–83. In international advertisements, attorneys assured divorce seekers of all nationalities that they could get an American divorce cheaply, rapidly, and without traveling to the United States. In a 1988 edition of the *International Herald Tribune*, classified advertisements informed divorce seekers that some divorce attorneys even offered the services of agents in such locations as Amsterdam and Guam. These advertisements created the impression that a

floating, worldwide divorce market existed. See for example, *International Herald Tribune*, 11 August 1988. For an update of the divorce industry, see Paula Mergenbagen DeWitt, "Breaking Up is Hard to Do," *American Demographics* 14 (October 1992): 52–59.

88. Whether no-fault divorce actually helped increase the divorce rate is in question. See Douglas W. Allen, *American Economic Review* 82 (June 1992): 679–85; and H. Elizabeth Peters, *American Economic Review* 82 (June 1992): 686–93.

89. Leonard Slater, "The disgrace of Hollywood—first divorce chart ever compiled," *McCall's Magazine* 86 (March 1959): 50–52, 141–42, 145, 147. The public's interest in actors' divorces dates back to the pre–Civil War years. For example consult "Charles O'Conor and the Forrest Divorce Case," (1851 case) *New York Law Review* 3 (January 1925): 8–12.

90. "I do . . . I do!" *USA Weekend*, 29 September, 1 October 1989, 4–5.

91. Willie Pearson, Jr., and Lewellyn Hendrix, "Divorce and the Status of Women," *Journal of Marriage and the Family* 41 (May 1979): 375–87; Elaine Tyler May, *Marriage and Divorce in Los Angeles* (Ph.D. diss., University of California at Los Angeles, 1975); Katherine Trent and Scott J. South, "Structural Determinants of the Divorce Rate: a Cross-Societal Analysis," *Journal of Marriage and the Family* 51 (May 1989): 391–404; Allen M. Parkman, "Unilateral Divorce and the Labor-Force Participation Rate of Married Women, Revisited," *American Economic Review* 82 (June 1992): 671–78; and Elaine McCrate, "Accounting for the Slowdown in the Divorce Rate in the 1980s: A Bargaining Perspective," *Review of Social Economy* 50 (Winter 1992): 404–19.

92. Ralph Henry Gabriel, ed., *Sarah Royce, A Frontier Lady: Recollections of the Gold Rush and Early California* (New Haven: Yale University Press, 1932), 85.

93. Interview with Mrs. LeEtta S. King, 4 March 1976, University of Washington Library, Manuscript Collection, Seattle.

94. Interview, undated, vol. 63, #7240, Indian-Pioneer Papers, Western History Collection, University of Oklahoma Library, Norman.

95. Interview, undated, vol. 15, #9068, Indian-Pioneer Papers, Western History Collection, University of Oklahoma Library, Norman.

96. An example is Jessie E. Mudgett, Pioneer Memories Collection, Wyoming State Archives, Museum, and Historical Department, Cheyenne. Mudgett farmed because her husband worked off the farm as a bridge builder.

97. Interview with Lillie Badgley, 9 April 1982, National Endowment for the Humanities Council Oral History Project, Montana Historical Society, Helena.

98. Evelyn King, "Women on the Cattle Trail and in the Roundup," *Buckskin Bulletin* 18 (Spring 1984): 3–4, and *Women on the Cattle Trail and in the Roundup* (Bryan, TX: Brazos Corral of the Westerners, 1983); Nannie T. Alderson and Helena Huntington Smith, *A Bride Goes West* (Lincoln: University of Nebraska Press, 1969), 271–73; Georgia Kelley, "A Courageous Homesteader–Edna N. Eaton," Interview, 1936, and Eva Putnam, "Reminiscences of Pioneer Women," 1936, Wyoming State Archives, Museum, and Historical Department, Cheyenne; and Emily J. Shelton, "Lizzie Johnson: A Cattle Queen of Texas," *Southwestern Historical Quarterly* 50(3)(January 1947): 349–66.

99. Interview with Hagar Lewis, vol. 5, part 3, 5, in George P. Rawick, ed., *The American Slave* (Westport, CT: Greenwood, 1972).

100. Mrs. Lee Whipple-Halsam, *Early Days in California* (Jamestown, CA: Np, c. 1924), 26.

101. Carol Leonard and Isidor Walliman, "Prostitution and Changing Morality in the Frontier Cattle Towns of Kansas," *Kansas History* 2(1)(Spring 1979): 27–40; and Joseph W. Snell, *Painted Ladies on the Cowtown Frontier* (Kansas City, MO: Lowell Press, 1965), 3–5, 7–12.

102. Anne P. Diffendal, "Prostitution in Grand Island, Nebraska, 1870–1913," *Heritage of the Great Plains* 16(3)(Summer 1983): 1–5. Consult also Paula Petrik, "Capitalists with Rooms: Prostitution in Helena, Montana, 1865–1900," *Montana: The Magazine of Western History* 31(2)(Spring 1981): 29–34; Elliott West, "Scarlet West: The Oldest Profession in the Trans-Mississippi West," *Montana: The Magazine of Western History* 31 (2)(Spring 1981): 16–27; Paula Petrik "Strange Bedfellows: Prostitution, Politicians and Moral Reform in Helena, Montana, 1885-1887," *Montana: The Magazine of Western History* 35(3)(Summer 1985): 2–13; and Jacqueline Baker Barnhart, *The Fair but Frail: Prostitution in San Francisco, 1849–1900* (Reno: University of Nevada Press, 1986). For hurdy-gurdy girls, see Rex C. Myers, "An Inning for Sin: Chicago Joe and Her Hurdy-Gurdy Girls," *Montana: The Magazine of Western History* 27(2)(1965): 147–56. For Butte, Montana, see Mary Murphy, "The Private Lives of Public Women: Prostitution in Butte, Montana, 1878-1917," *Frontiers* 7(3)(1984): 30–35. For a thoughtful, highly informed discussion of prostitution in the American West, see Anne M. Butler, *Daughters of Joy, Sisters of Misery: Prostitutes in the American West, 1865–1890* (Champaign: University of Illinois Press, 1985).

103. Michael Bargo, "Women's Occupations in the West in 1870," *Journal of the West* 32 (January 1993): 30–45.

104. Laura Brown Zook, "Sketches of Laura Brown Zook's Early Life, 1869–1944," Montana State University Library Special Collections, Bozeman.

105. Sarah Jane Price, Diaries, 1878–95, Nebraska State Historical Society, Lincoln. Accounts of women teachers/homesteaders are Elizabeth Tyler, "Reminiscence," 1954, Montana State Historical Society, Helena; Abbie Bright, Diary, 1870/71, Kansas State Historical Society, Topeka; and Enid Bern, ed., "They had a Wonderful Time: The Homesteading Letters of Anna and Ethel Erickson," *North Dakota History* 45(4)(Fall 1978): 4–31. The teacher/trail-drive cook is Mary Hethy Bonar, Diary, 1885, State Historical Society of North Dakota, Bismarck.

106. "Mrs. Frank Reeves," in United States Works Progress Administration, *Told by the Pioneers* (np: np, 1938), 3:88.

107. Glen Schwendemann, "Nicodemus: Negro Haven on the Soloman," *Kansas Historical Quarterly* 34 (Spring 1968): 14, 26.

108. Apolinaria Lorenzana, "Reminiscence," 1878, San Diego Historical Society Archives, San Diego, CA.

109. List of County Superintendents, in "Park County Women," 1977, Montana State University Library Special Collections, Bozeman; Mary Johnstone Powers, "A

Pioneer Woman's Reminiscences," 1947, Montana Historical Society, Helena; and Larrabee, "Women of Sacramento," 7.

110. Friede Van Dalsem and Abbie Jarvis, Pioneer Daughters Collection, South Dakota State Historical Resource Center, Pierre; and "Lavinia Goodyear Waterhouse," Pacific Grove (CA) Heritage Society *Newsletter* (February/March 1989): unpaginated.

111. (Tacoma, WA) *News Tribune*, 18 July 1976, E-4.

112. Judy Yung, *Chinese Women of America: A Pictorial History* (Seattle: University of Washington Press, 1986), 39.

113. Colorado is discussed in W. Sherman Savage, *Blacks in the West* (Westport, CT: Greenwood Press, 1976), 84–85. Mary Ellen Pleasant is analyzed in Lynn M. Hudson, "A New Look, or 'I'm Not Mammy to Everybody in California': Mary Ellen Pleasant, a Black Entrepreneur," *Journal of the West* 32 (July 1993): 35–40.

114. Interview with LeEtta S. King, 4 March 1976, University of Washington Library Manuscripts Collection, Seattle.

115. Norton B. Stern, "Denouements in San Diego in 1888," *Western States Jewish Historical Quarterly* 11 (1978): 49–55. Further information concerning Jewish divorce is found in David Werner Amram, *The Jewish Law of Divorce* (New York: Hermon Press, 1968).

116. "Dr. Georgia Arbuckle Fix: Pioneer," in A. B. Wood, ed., *Pioneer Tales of the North Platte Valley* (Gering, NE: Courier Press, 1938), 188–89.

117. Paul Frizon, "The Life of Martha Waln, Pioneer of Ten Sleep, Wyoming," 1939, Wyoming State Archives, Museum, and Historical Department, Cheyenne.

118. Katharine Grant, Sketch in the Montana American Mothers Bicentennial Project, 1975–76, Montana Historical Society, Helena; and Henry Killian Goetz, "Kate's Quarter Section: A Woman in the Cherokee Strip," *Chronicles of Oklahoma* 61 (Fall 1983): 246–67.

119. U.S. Department of Commerce and Labor, *Marriage and Divorce*, 1:24.

120. U.S. Department of Commerce and Labor, *Marriage and Divorce*, 2:79–164.

121. U.S. Department of Commerce and Labor, *Marriage and Divorce*, 1:33, 99.

122. Case #1406, *Lyman v. Lyman*, filed 30 August 1891, and Case #2387, *Hughes v. Hughes*, 25 August 1897, Territorial Records, Logan County, Guthrie, OK.

123. Cases #714, *Gleason v. Gleason*, filed 2 July 1891; 736, *Weyach v. Weyach*, 29 July 1891; 798, *Zeller v. Zeller*, 18 October 1891; 1399, *Quick v. Quick*, 23 August 1893; 1410, *Wise v. Wise*, 26 August 1893; 1944, *Rowland v. Rowland*, 28 May 1895; 1984, *Schwart v. Schwart*, 3 August 1895; 1994, *Beck v. Beck*, 12 August 1895; 2681, *Bowers v. Bowers*, 17 January 1899; and 2702, *Condron v. Condron*, 15 February 1889, Territorial Records, Logan County, Guthrie, OK. Similar findings are described in Robert L. Griswold, "Apart but Not Adrift: Wives, Divorce, and Independence in California, 1850–1890," *Pacific Historical Review* 49 (May 1980): 165–87.

124. Examples are Luna Kellie, "Memoirs," undated, Nebraska State Historical Society, Lincoln; Paula M. Bauman, "Single Women Homesteaders in Wyoming, 1880–1930," *Annals of Wyoming* 58 (Spring 1986): 42; Brett Harvey Vuolo, "Pioneer Diaries: The Untold Story of the West," *Ms. Magazine* 3 (May 1975): 32–34;

and Maranda J. Cline, Diary, 1891–1907, Iowa State Historical Society, Iowa City.

125. Walter E. Kaloupek, "Alice Nelson Page: Pioneer Career Woman," *North Dakota Historical Quarterly* 13 (1946): 74–76.

126. U.S. Department of Commerce and Labor, *Marriage and Divorce,2*: 608–57. In northeastern states, men obtained custody of their children approximately one-third of the time. In southern states, where men filed for more of the divorces, they exceeded women in custody awards in the states of Alabama, Mississippi, North Carolina, and Virginia.

127. Dorothy Florence Towe (Lena's husband changed Towe to Tow) Tester, "The Circle Complete," in Montana American Mothers Bicentennial Project, 1975–76, Montana Historical Society, Helena; and Martha Farnsworth, Diaries, 1890–93, Kansas State Historical Society, Topeka. Fiction also reveals that women stuck to husbands in silent submission. For instance Robert H. Solomon, "The Prairie Mermaid: Love-Tests of Pioneer Women," *Great Plains Quarterly* 4 (Summer 1984): 143–51.

128. That the new morality appeared well before the United State's entry into World War I is argued in James R. McGovern, "The American Woman's Pre–World War I Freedom in Manner and Morals," *Journal of American History* 55 (September 1968): 315–33. Further discussion of Progressivism and divorce appears in William L. O'Neill, *Divorce in the Progressive Era* (New Haven: Yale University Press, 1967), especially 254–73. A judge who supported easier divorce is described in "The Most Difficult Problem of Modern Civilization," *Current Literature* 18 (1910): 59.

129. Ellen F. Greenberg and W. Robert Nay, "The Intergenerational Transmission of Marital Instability Reconsidered," *Journal of Marriage and the Family* 44 (May 1982): 335–47; and United States Department of Commerce and Labor, *Marriage and Divorce*, 1:14.

130. Paul C. Glick and Sung Ling Lin, "Recent Changes in Divorce and Remarriage," *Journal of Marriage and the Family* 48 (November 1986): 737–47.

131. James J. Ponzetti, Jr., Anisa M. Zvonkovic, Rodney M. Cate, and Ted L. Huston, "Reasons for Divorce: a Comparison between Former Partners," *Journal of Divorce and Remarriage* 17 (1992): 183–201.

132. Sara Bard Field, Diary, 1913, Wood Collection, Huntington Library, San Marino, CA.

133. Field, Diary, and "Notes regarding her divorce," Wood Collection, Huntington Library, San Marino, CA.

134. Sara Bard Field, "Notes concerning the letter of Charles Erskine Scott Wood to his son Erskine, written July 22, 1927," 1938, and "Notes regarding her divorce," c. 1960, Wood Collection, Huntington Library, San Marino, CA. Another California woman of the period who thought that divorce was indicated when love evaporated was Anita M. Baldwin, who divorced her second husband in 1915. Anita M. Baldwin, "Fragment of a Note Concerning her Husband," 1915, and Divorce Decree, 1 July 1915, Baldwin Collection, Huntington Library, San Marino, CA.

135. Baldwin, "Fragment of a Note" and Divorce Decree.
136. Peter Uhlenberg, "Marital Instability among Mexican Americans: Following the Patterns of Blacks?" *Social Problems* 20 (1972): 49–56; Isaac W. Eberstein and W. Parker Frisbie, "Differences in Marital Instability among Mexican Americans, Blacks, and Anglos: 1960 and 1970," *Social Problems* 23 (1976): 609–21; W. Parker Frisbie, Frank D. Bean, and Isaac W. Eberstein, "Recent Changes in Marital Instability among Mexican Americans: Convergence with Black and Anglo Trends?" *Social Forces* 58 (1980): 205–20; Richard Griswold del Castillo, *La Familia: Chicano Families in the Urban Southwest, 1848 to the Present* (Notre Dame, IN: University of Notre Dame Press, 1984), especially chap. 8, "The Contemporary Chicano Family," 112–26; and James Alan Neff, Kathleen R. Gilbert, and Sue Keir Hoppe, "Divorce Likelihood among Anglos and Mexican Americans," *Journal of Divorce and Remarriage* 15 (1991): 75–98.
137. Philip R. Kunz and Stan L. Albrecht, "Religion, Marital Happiness, and Divorce," *International Journal of Sociology of the Family* 7 (July–December 1977): 227–32; Howard M. Bahr, "Religious Intermarriage and Divorce in Utah and the Mountain States," *Journal for the Scientific Study of Religion* 20 (1981): 351–61; and Leo Driedger, Michael Yoder, and Peter Sawatzky, "Divorce among Mennonites: Evidence of Family Breakdown," *Mennonite Quarterly Review* 59 (1985): 367–82.

Epilogue

1. Hayden White, "The Burden of History," in *History and Theory* 5 (1966): 132.
2. Quotes from Avodah K. Offit, "The New Togetherness," *McCall's* (March 1986): 20, 149. See also Francesca M. Cancian, *Love in America: Gender and Self-Development* (Cambridge: Cambridge University Press, 1987), 3; and Esther O. Fisher, *Divorce: The New Freedom* (New York: Harper & Row, 1974), 1–11. For discussions of education for marriage, see Max Rheinstein, "The Law of Divorce and the Problem of Marriage Stability," *Vanderbilt Law Review* 9 (June 1956): 633–64; and Doris Jonas Freed and Henry H. Foster, Jr., "Divorce American Style," *Annals of the American Academy of Political and Social Science* 83 (May 1969): 70–88. Expectations of marriage are revealed by interviews in, Marilyn Little, *Family Breakup* (San Francisco: Tossey Buss, 1982), 17–114. That traditional views of women and marriage persist is demonstrated in Angela Corencamp, John F. McClymer, Mary M. Moynihan, and Arlene C. Vadum, *Images of Women in American Popular Culture* (New York: Macmillan, 1985), especially 201–19.
3. Interview with Rafael Mendez, 30 March 1993, Grand Junction, CO. Transcript in author's possession.
4. Quotes are found in Pat Wingert and Barbara Kantrowitz, "The Day Care Generation," *Newsweek*, special edition on "The 21st Century Family," (Winter/Spring 1990): 86–87. Four years earlier a *Newsweek* article had asserted that "child care is now an item on the national agenda." See "Changes in the Workplace," *Newsweek* (31 March 1986): 57. For discussions of the problem of childcare, see Annegret Ogden, *The Great American Housewife* (Westport, CT: Greenwood Press, 1986), 234–37; and Amy Swerdlow, Renate Bridenthal, Joan

Kelley, and Phyllis Vine, *Household and Kin: Families in Flux* (Old Westbury, CT: Feminist Press, 1981), 131–46.

5. The failures of no-fault divorce are discussed in Lenore J. Weitzman, *The Divorce Revolution: The Unexpected Social and Economic Consequences for Women and Children in America* (New York: The Free Press, 1985); and Allen M. Parkman, *No-Fault Divorce: What Went Wrong?* (Boulder: Westview Press, 1992).

6. For an elaboration on this point, see Richard Neely, "Barter in the Court," *New Republic* (10 February 1986): 13–14, 16.

7. The need for more equitable financial arrangements in contemporary divorce is discussed in Heather L. Ross and Isabel V. Sawhill, *Time of Transition: The Growth of Families Headed by Women* (Washington, DC: Urban Institute, 1975), especially 173–79; Lynne Carol Halem, *Divorce Reform: Changing Legal and Social Perspectives* (New York: Free Press, 1980), 287–92; Jean Renvoize, *Going Solo: Single Mothers by Choice* (Boston: Routledge & Kegan Paul, 1985), especially 130–38; and Terry J. Arendell, "Women and the Economics of Divorce in the Contemporary United States," *Signs: Journal of Women in Culture and Society* 13 (1987): 121–35.

8. Lenore J. Weitzman, *The Divorce Revolution: The Unexpected Social and Economic Consequences for Women and Children in America* (New York: Free Press, 1985), 113–21. See also Frances Leonard, "The Disillusionment of Divorce for Older Women," *Gray Paper* no. 6 (Washington, DC: Older Women's League, 1980), 8–9; and Henry H. Foster and Doris Jonas Freed, "Commentary on Equitable Distribution," *New York Law School Law Review* 26 (1)(1981): 47–48.

9. Many books about divorce include lists of references to resources and organizations. See for example Lucia H. Bequaert, *Single Women: Alone and Together* (Boston: Beacon Press, 1976). An argument for tailoring resources to fit a particular group's needs is found in Toni L'Hommedieu, *The Divorce Experience of Working and Middle Class Women* (Ann Arbor: University Microfilms, 1984); and Dorothy W. Cantor, "School-Based Groups for Children of Divorce," *Journal of Divorce* 1 (Winter 1977): 183–263. Examples of divorce workshops are described in David M. Young, "The Divorce Experience Workshop," *Journal of Divorce* 2 (Fall 1978): 37–47; and Young, "The Divorced Catholics Movement," 83–97. A report on workshops and other resources for children of divorce was reported in "Reading, Writing and Divorce," *Newsweek* (13 May 1985): 74.

10. For a review of the lack of gender awareness in divorce counseling, see Kristina L. Lund, "A Feminist Perspective on Divorce Therapy for Women," *Journal of Divorce* 13 (3)(1990): 57–67.

11. Judith Stern Peck, "The Impact of Divorce on Children at Various Stages of the Family Life Cycle," *Journal of Divorce* 12 (1988/89): 81–108; and Joseph Guttmann and Marc Broudo, "The Effect of Children's Family Type on Teachers' Stereotypes," *Journal of Divorce* 12 (1988/89): 315–28; and Judith S. Wallerstein and Sandra Blakeslee, *Second Chances: Men, Women, and Children a Decade after Divorce* (New York: Ticknor & Fields, 1989).

12. See for example Robert D. Allers, *Divorce, Children, and the School* (New Jersey: Princeton Books, 1982); William F. Hodges, *Interventions for Children of Divorce:*

Custody, Access, and Psychotherapy (New York: Wiley, 1986); and Marla Beth Isaacs, *The Difficult Divorce: Therapy for Children and Families* (New York: Basic Books, 1986).

13. Ernest S. Burch, Jr., "Marriage and Divorce among the North Alaskan Eskimos," in Paul Bohannon, ed., *Divorce and After* (New York: Doubleday, 1970), 152–81.

14. Family types are discussed in Lawrence Stone, "Family History in the 1980s: Past Achievements and Future Trends," *Journal of Interdisciplinary History* 22 (Summer 1981): 51–87. Descriptions of the single-parent family are found in, "Playing Both Mother and Father," *Newsweek* (15 July 1985): 42–43; and "The Single Parent: Family Albums," *Newsweek* (15 July 1985): 44–50. The blended family is described in Barbara Kantrowitz and Pat Wingert, "Step by Step," *Newsweek*, special edition on "The 21st Century Family" (Winter/Spring 1990): 24–27, 30, 34; and gay, lesbian, and skip-generation families in Jean Seligmann, "Variations on a Theme," *Newsweek*, special edition on "The 21st Century Family" (Winter/Spring 1990): 38–40, 44, 46.

Index

Abortion, 25, 68

Abuse, spouse, 61–62

Adoptions, 56

Adultery, 63–64; Spanish law, 44

Affection: demonstrations, 22; public display of, 21

African Americans: autonomy issue, 4; Cherokees, 83; Chickasaws, 95; courtship, 9–10; divorce, 94, 98, 115, 120; family ridiculed, 62; interracial unions banned, 92; romantic love, 51; sex ratios, 77; sexual exploitation, 66; stresses, 66; unpaid female labor, 135; women teachers, 138. *See also* Free blacks; Slavery

Alaska, 80, 82, 91, 98, 151

Alcoholism, 60–61

Alimony, 140

Anglos: attitudes casual, 115; birth control, 68; children, 56; diverse courtship rituals, 21; divorce, 115–16; as dominant culture, 19, 66; family size, 56; intermarriage, 78, 79, 84–85; justice system, 94–95; marriage to Native Americans, 77; marry people of color, 13; men resist intermarriage, 91; national origins, 88; religious commitments, 56–57; view of marriage, 45–46; view of Spanish-speaking women, 80; wedding ceremonies, 47–48

Annulments, 93–94, 132. *See also* Divorce, Legal separation

Antimiscegenation laws, 13, 92–93; Asians, 17, 19; Spanish heritage peoples, 19; struck down, 95

Apache Indians, 63, 88

Arizona: cohabitation, 90; gender roles, 54; Hispanic family, 67; intermarriage banned, 92; Mormons, 58

Asian-heritage peoples: assimilation, 100; autonomy issue, 4; courting, 10–11, 17–18; domestic labor, 67; intermarriage banned, 92; intermarriage resisted, 86–87; intramarriage, 58; romantic love, 11. *See also* Chinese people; Japanese American; Korean people; Punjabi people; Sikh people

Assimilation model, 99–100

Automobiles, 25

Autonomy, increasing, 4

Avoidance, concept of, 89

B

Banns of marriage, 27, 29

Betrothals, 27

Bigamy, 127–28

Birth control, 24–25, 68

197